Praise!

This is the third edition of the first 'Praise!' book. Corrections have been made and the layout improved. This collection of hymns is humbly and prayerfully offered as an encouragement to aid prayer and worship, and in support of the revival we so urgently need.

Some hymns have been written by established writers, such as I.D. Sankey, W.J. Sparrow-Simpson, Fanny Crosby, Horatius Bonar, George Herbert, Charles Wesley, Timothy Dudley-Smith and Isaac Watts, while others are by new writers and some who are living in glory with the Lord. With the exception of a very few, all the hymns have been set to new tunes - written by Harry Hicks - to give them new life and a fresh hearing. The music has been written to reflect the words while being easily and quickly learnt and sung by congregations, although some may be more suitable for solos and personal reflection.

The accompanying words only book is also available, either via Amazon or from the composer at
"Clifftop,"
30 Seaview Road,
Mundesley,
Norfolk.
NR11 8DH UK.

Email: harry.hicks147@icloud.com

Norfolk, England, 2019.

The second book – entitled 'Praise 2' - of over 400 hymns is also available.

1   A mighty fortress

Martin Luther

A migh-ty fort-ress is our God, a sword and shield vic-torious; he breaks the cruel op-pressor's rod and wins sal-va-tion glor-ious. The old sa-tan-ic foe, has sworn to work us woe! With craft and dread-ful might he arms him-self to fight. On earth he has no e-qual.

2. No strength of ours can match his might!
  We would be lost, rejected.
  But now a champion comes to fight,
  whom God himself elected.
  You ask who this may be?
  The Lord of hosts is he!
  Christ Jesus, mighty Lord,
  God's only Son, adored.
  He holds the field victorious.

3. Though hordes of devils fill the land
  all threat'ning to devour us,
  we tremble not, unmoved we stand;
  they cannot overpow'r us.
  Let this world's tyrant rage;
  in battle we'll engage!
  His might is doomed to fail;
  God's judgment must prevail!
  One little word subdues him.

4. God's word forever shall abide,
  no thanks to foes, who fear it;
  for God himself fights by our side
  with weapons of the Spirit.
  Were they to take our house,
  goods, honour, child, or spouse,
  though life be wrenched away,
  they cannot win the day.
  The Kingdom's ours forever.

2　A special day

Brenda Gallant

A special day,_____ a special day_____ When God came down with men to stay._____ He came to save_____ us all from sin,_____ The hu-man heart to en-ter in. Spe-cial day! Spe-cial day!__When God came down with men to stay.

2. He came a Babe in manger laid,
The One whose hands the world had made,
He bore our sicknesses and woe,
And tasted every earthly throe.
Special day! Special day!
When God came down with men to stay.

3. A special day! A special day!
When Jesus bore our sins away!
They nailed Him to a cruel tree,
He suffered there for you and me.
Special day! Special day!
When Jesus bore our sins away.

4. He rose again, and left the grave,
This sinless Saviour came to save,
He died for you to set you free,
That you with Him might ever be.
Special day! Special day!
When Jesus bore our sins away.

5. A special day, a special day,
When Christ returns with great array,
The trump shall sound, the dead arise
To meet the Saviour in the skies.
Special day! Special day!
When Christ returns with great array.

6. Will you be ready for that day?
Receive the Saviour while you may,
He waits to pardon all your sin,
Your willing heart to enter in.
Special day! Special day!
Receive the Saviour while you may.

3   A wonderful Saviour

F.J.Crosby

A won-der-ful Sav-iour is Je-sus my Lord, A won-der-ful sav-iour to me___ He hi-deth my soul in the cleft of the rock Where ri-vers of pleasure I see.___ He

Chorus

hi-deth my soul in the cleft of the rock, That sha-dows a dry-thir-sty land;___ He

hi-deth my life in the depths of His Love, And co-vers me there with His hand.___

2. A wonderful Saviour is Jesus my Lord,
   He taketh my burden away;
   He holdeth me up and I shall not be moved;
   He giveth me strength as my day.
   He hideth my soul in the cleft of the rock,
   That shadows a dry, thirsty land;
   He hideth my life in the depths of His Love,
   And covers me there with His hand.

3. With numberless blessings each moment He crowns,
   And, filled with His goodness divine,
   I sing in my rapture, "O glory to God
   For such a Redeemer as mine!"
   He hideth my soul....

4. When, clothed in His brightness, transported I rise
   To meet Him in clouds of the sky,
   His perfect salvation, His wonderful love,
   I'll shout with the millions on high.
   He hideth my soul.....

4   Above me

H.F.Lyte (1793-1847)

A - bove me hangs the silent sky; A - round me rolls the sea; The crew is all at rest, and I Am, Lord, a - lone with Thee. Go where I may, from all re - mote, Thou, Lord, art ev - er near; No se - cret thought, but Thou canst note; No word, but Thou canst hear.

2. When all around are sunk to sleep,
   Thy presence here I find;
To me Thou walkest o'er the deep,
   Or speakest in the wind.
In winds, and waves, and starry sky;
   I see Thee present here;
And, looking at myself, I cry,
   Can I still be Thy care?

3. I think of days and dangers past,
   When I have found Thee nigh;
And wonder how Thy love can last
   To one so vile as I.
I think of terrors near at hand,
   Of judgment yet to come;
When I before Thy face must stand
   And hear my final doom.

4. The sense of all I've been and done
   Would fill me with despair;
But to my Saviour's cross I run,
   And find a refuge there.
I know He has the power to aid,
   I know He has the will:
And He who once for sinners bled,
   Can rescue sinners still.

5. Lord, arm my soul with faith in Thee,
   And fill my heart with love,
My path from sin and danger free,
   And guide me safe above.
And while the waves around me beat,
   Lord, often thus descend,
And grant me here communion sweet
   With Thee, the sinner's friend.

Music © 2016 Harry Hicks

5 Alas! and did my Saviour bleed

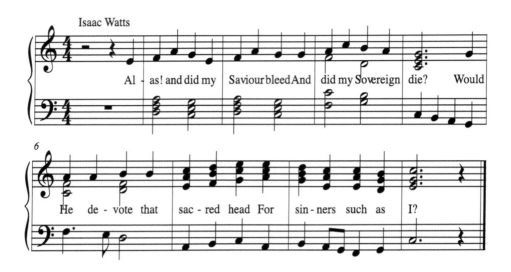

Isaac Watts

Al - as! and did my Saviour bleed And did my Sovereign die? Would

He de - vote that sac - red head For sin - ners such as I?

2. Thy body slain, sweet Jesus, Thine- And bathed in its own blood-
While the firm mark of wrath divine, His Soul in anguish stood.

3. Was it for crimes that I had done He groaned upon the tree?
Amazing pity! grace unknown! And love beyond degree!

4. Well might the sun in darkness hide And shut his glories in,
When Christ, the mighty Maker died, For man the creature's sin.

5. Thus might I hide my blushing face While His dear cross appears,
Dissolve my heart in thankfulness, And melt my eyes to tears.

6. But drops of grief can ne'er repay The debt of love I owe:
Here, Lord, I give my self away 'Tis all that I can do.

6   All day long

7 All for Jesus

Rev. W.J. Sparrow-Simpson

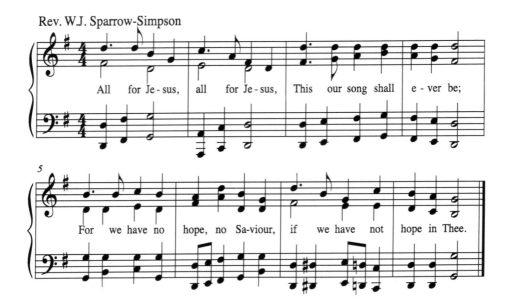

All for Je-sus, all for Je-sus, This our song shall e - ver be;

For we have no hope, no Sa-viour, if we have not hope in Thee.

2. All for Jesus- Thou wilt give us
Strength to serve Thee, hour by hour,
None can move us from the presence,
While we trust Thy love and power.

3. All for Jesus- at thine altar
Thou wilt give us sweet content;
There, dear Lord, we shall receive Thee
In the solemn sacrament.

4. All for Jesus - Thou hast loved us;
All for Jesus - Thou hast died;
All for Jesus - Thou art with us;
All for Jesus crucified.

5. All for Jesus - all for Jesus -
This the church's song must be;
Till, at last, her sons are gathered
One in love and one in Thee.

8 All glory to Jesus

A. Wittenmeyer

All glo-ry to Je-sus be giv'n, that life and sal-va-tion are free; And all may be washed and for-giv'n, and Je-sus can save ev-en me. Yes, Je-sus is migh-ty to save, and all his sal-va-tion may know On His Spi-rit I lean, and his blood makes me clean for his blood can wash whit-er than snow.

2. From darkness and sin and despair, out into the light of His love,
He's brought me and made me an heir to kingdoms and mansions above.
Yes Jesus is mighty to save, and all His salvation may know
On His Spirit I lean, and His blood makes me clean,
For His blood can wash whiter than snow.

3. The rapturous height of His love! The measureless depth of His grace!
My soul all His fullness would prove, and live in His loving embrace.
Yes Jesus is mighty to save, and all His salvation may know
On His Spirit I lean, and His blood makes me clean,
For His blood can wash whiter than snow.

4. In Him all my wants are supplied, His love makes my heaven below;
And freely His blood is applied, His blood that makes whiter than snow.
Yes Jesus is mighty to save, and all His salvation may know
On His Spirit I lean, and His blood makes me clean,
For His blood can wash whiter than snow....

All our lives

Brenda Gallant

All our lives are like a jour-ney
On a vast and chang-ing sea,
There are ma-ny dan-gers lurk-ing,
Ha - zar-dous to you and me.
Waves that seek to o-ver - whelm us,
Cur - rents strong to suck us down;
How we need a chart and com-pass,
That we may not sink and drown.

2. God the powerful Creator,
Made us for His own delight,
He, Himself, has made provision
So that we may sail aright.
Christ the Lord has gone before us,
Faced the storms of life alone;
If we take Him as our Saviour,
He will lead us safely on.

3. He has giv'n us chart and compass,
Light to guide us on our way,
If we read His word, the Bible
We will never want to stray.
There is comfort in our sorrow,
Guidance for our wandering feet,
Shelter when we face temptation
When the storms of life we meet.

4. Open then His word and read it,
Pray that through it He will speak,
If you need this free salvation,
You will find it when you seek.
Then, together you will journey
On towards the harbour light,
Which itself is but the entrance
To the heavenly mansions bright.

10   All the way

Fanny J. Crosby

All the way my Sav-iour leads me; what have I to ask be-side? Can I doubt His ten-der mer - cy, Who through life has been my guide? Heav'n-ly grace, di - vin-est com-fort, her by faith in Him I dwell! For I know what - e'er be - fall me, Je - sus do - eth all things well.

2. All the way my Saviour leads me,
cheers each winding path I tread,
gives me grace for every trial,
feeds me with the living bread.
Though my weary steps may falter,
and my soul a-thirst may be,
gushing from the rock before me,
Lo! a spring of joy I see.

3. All the way my Saviour leads me,
O the fulness of his love!
Perfect rest to me is promised
in my Father's house above.
When my spirit, clothed, immortal,
wings its flight to realms of day,
this, my song through endless ages:
Jesus led me all the way!

11   Allelulia! Sing to Jesus

2. Alleluia! Not as orphans
Are we left in sorrow now;
Alleluia! He is near us,
Faith believes, nor questions how,
Though the clouds from sight recieves Him
When the forty days were o'er,
Shall our hearts forget His promise,
"I am with you evermore"?

3. Alleluia! Bread of heaven,
Thou on earth, our food, our stay;
Alleluia, here the sinful
Flee to Thee from day to day.
Intercessor, Friend of sinners,
Earth's Redeemer, plead for me,
Where the songs of all the sinless
Sweep across the crystal sea.

4. Alleluia! sing to Jesus!
His the sceptre, His the throne.
Alleluia! His the triumph,
His the victory alone.
Hark, the songs of mighty Zion
Thunder like a mighty flood:
Jesus, out of ev'ry nation,
Hath redeemed us by His blood.

12   And is this life

Isaac Watts

And is this life prolonged to me are days and seasons giv'n? O let me then prepare to be A fitter heir of heav'n.

2. In vain these moments shall not pass,
These golden hours be gone:
Lord, I accept thine offered grace,
I bow before thy throne.

3. Now cleanse my soul from ev'ry sin,
By my Redeemer's blood:
Now let my flesh and soul begin
The honours of my God.

4. Let me no more my soul beguile
With sin's deceitful toys:
Let cheerful hope increasing still
Approach to heav'nly joys.

5. My thankful lips shall proud proclaim
The wonders of thy praise,
And spread the savour of the Name
Where'er I spend my days.

6. On earth let my example shine,
And when I leave this state,
May heav'n receive this soul of mine
To bliss supremely great.

Music © 2012 Harry Hicks

13 And must this body die?

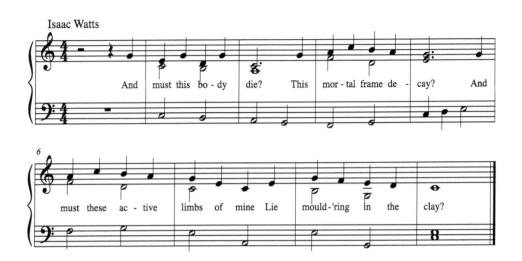

Isaac Watts

And must this bo-dy die? This mor-tal frame de - cay? And

must these ac - tive limbs of mine Lie mould-'ring in the clay?

2. Corruption, earth and worms,
Shall but refine this flesh,
Till my triumphant spirit comes
To put it on afresh.

3. God my Redeemer lives,
And often from the skies
Looks down, and watches all my dust,
Till he shall bid it rise.

4. Arrayed in glorious grace
Shall these vile bodies shine,
And every shape and every face
Look heav'nly and divine.

5. These lively hopes we owe
To Jesus' dying love;
We would adore his grace below,
And sing his power above.

6. Dear Lord, accept the praise
Of these our humble songs,
Till tunes of nobler sound we raise
With our immortal tongues.

14   Angels holy

J.S. Blackie

An-gels ho - ly, High and low - ly, Sing the prais - es of the Lord!

Earth and sky, all liv-ing na - ture, Man, the stamp of Thy Cre - a - tor,

Praise ye, praise ye, God the Lord! Praise ye, praise ye God the Lord!

2. Sun and moon bright, Night and noon light,
Starry temples azure-floored;
Cloud and rain, and wild wind's madness,
Sons of God that shout for gladness,
Praise ye, praise ye God the Lord!
Praise ye, praise ye God the Lord!

3. Ocean hoary, Tell His glory,
Cliffs, where tumbling seas have roared!
Pulse of waters, blithely beating,
Wave advancing, wave retreating,
Praise ye, praise ye God the Lord!
Praise ye, praise ye God the Lord!

4. Rock and high land, wood and island,
Crag, where eagle's pride hath soared;
Mighty mountains, purple-breasted,
peaks, cloud-cleaving, snowy-crested,
Praise ye, praise ye God the Lord!
Praise ye, praise ye God the Lord!

5. Rolling river, Praise Him ever,
From the mountains deep vein poured;
Silver fountain, clearly gushing,
Troubled torrent, madly rushing,
Praise ye, praise ye God the Lord!
Praise ye, praise ye God the Lord!

6. Praise Him ever, Bounteous Giver,
Praise Him, Father, Friend and Lord!
Each glad soul its free course winging,
Each glad voice its free song singing,
Praise ye, praise ye God the Lord!
Praise ye, praise ye God the Lord!

Music © 2016 Harry Hicks

15 Angels sang in celebration

Alan Luff

An-gels sang in ce - le - bra-tion, sang a new age come to birth, he - ral-ding a new cre - a - tion, pro - mi - sing God's peace on earth. Still we ache to hear their sing-ing, long to know their word ful-filled as an-oth-er year is turn-ing with a hope not to be stilled.

2. Mary sang of liberation,
God at work among the poor,
come heal the world's frustration,
love insistent at the door.
Longing for a new beginning,
myriad Marys sound her song;
round the world, while bells are ringing,
God is still at war with wrong.

3. Simeon sang to end his story,
sang of nations deep in night
soon to see both Israel's glory
and a whole world filled with light.
As we turn a page of history,
full of wonders, joy and pain,
we too pray to see God's victory
and the day when Christ will reign.

16 Approach, my soul

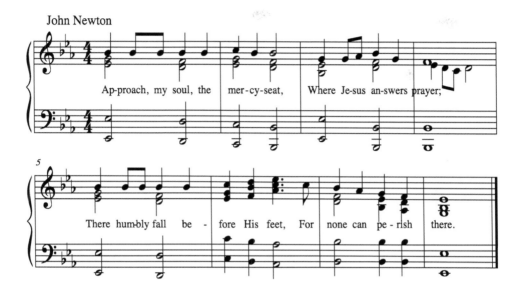

John Newton

Ap-proach, my soul, the mer-cy-seat, Where Je-sus an-swers prayer;

There humbly fall be - fore His feet, For none can pe - rish there.

2. Thy promise is my only plea;
With this I venture nigh;
Thou callest burdened souls to Thee
And such, O Lord, am I.

3. Bowed down beneath a load of sin,
By Satan sorely pressed,
By wars without, and fears within,
I come to Thee for rest.

4. Be Thou my Shield and Hiding-place,
That, sheltered near Thy side,
I may my fierce accuser face,
And tell him Thou hast died.

5. Oh, wondrous love! to bleed and die,
To bear the cross and shame,
That guilty sinners, such as I,
Might plead Thy gracious name!

17   Arise my soul

Isaac Watts

A - rise my soul, my joy - ful powers, And tri - umph in my God,

A - wake, my voice, and loud pro-claim His glo-rious grace - a - bound.

2. He raised me from the depths of sin,
The gates of gaping hell,
And fixed my standing more secure
Than 'twas before the fall.

3. The arms of everlasting love
Beneath my soul he placed,
And on the rock of ages set
My slippery footsteps fast.

4. The city of my blessed abode
Is walled around with grace
Salvation for a bulwark stands
To shield the sacred place.

5. Satan may vent his sharpest spite,
And all his legions roar,
Almighty mercy guards my life,
And bounds his raging power.

6. Arise, my soul, awake, my voice,
And tunes of pleasure sing,
Loud hallelujahs shall address
My Saviour and my King.

18 Arm, soldiers of the Lord

Stopford A. Brooke

after C. Steggall

Arm, sol - diers of the Lord! The fight __ is set with __ wrong - Take shield and breast-plate, helm and sword And sing __ your bat - tle song

2. Stand fast for Love, your Lord;
   Faith be your mighty shield;
And let the Spirit's burning sword
   Flash foremost in the field.

3. Truth be your girdle strong;
   And hope your helmet shine,
Whene'er the battle seemeth long
   And wearied hearts repine.

4. With news of gospel peace
   Let your swift feet be shod;
Your breastplate be the righteousness
   That keeps the soul for God.

5. And for the weary day,
   And for the slothful arm,
For wounds, distress, defeat, dismay,
   Take prayer, the heavenly charm.

6. "From strength to strength" your cry,
   Your battlefield the world;
Strike home, and press where Christ on high
   His banner hath unfurled.

19　As the light upon the river

Christopher Idle

As the light up-on the ri-ver at the ris-ing of the sun, shine, O
Lord, up-on our ci-ty; here on earth, your will be done: here we
meet in glad thanks-gi-ving, wor-ship, praise and prayer we bring, grief for
sin and joy for mer-cy, all for you, O Christ our King.

2. Crucified and risen Saviour,
God incarnate, First and Last,
yours the city of the future,
yours the pilgrims of the past!
Lord, revive your weary people!
Let your voice again be heard;
rid your church of all excuses
for our deafness to your word.

3. From our failure and our blindness,
bound by debts we cannot pay,
God of Jubilee, release us -
O renew us all, we pray!
In a world exhausted, restless,
still oppressing and oppressed,
Lord of Sabbath, bring us freedom,
resurrection, life and rest.

4. Strengthen us to love our neighbours -
welcome strangers at our door,
find the lost and reach the lonely
so that they shall weep no more:
in our homes, our crowded journeys,
work of leisure, calm or noise,
come to satisfy our longings,
Christ, the joy of all our joys!

5. As the rain upon our garden,
as the water from the spring,
pour on us your Holy Spirit,
gifts to use and songs to sing:
as the light upon the river
at the rising of the sun,
shine, O Lord, upon our city -
as in heav'n, your will be done.

20   As you travel

Brenda Gallant

As you tra-vel o'er life's sea, Who will your com-pan-ion be?

8ves in the bass

As you push to-ward the shore, Who's the hand up-on the oar?

Do not jour-ney on your own, Batt'-ling through the waves a-lone,

Take the Sav-iour as your guide, 'Til you reach the o-ther side.

2. When the storms of life abound,
Let your faith in Christ be found,
He will then your anchor be,
Save you from the angry sea.
You may trust Him with your all,
He will never let you fall,
You are safe with Him aboard,
Loving Saviour, Friend and Lord.

3. Be your voyage long or short,
Take great comfort from this thought;
He has promised to be near,
Giving comfort, joy and cheer.
So invite Him to your bark
Do not journey in the dark,
He will chart the troubled sea,
And your pilot ever be.

4. Praise Him for His wondrous love,
And those mansions up above,
He has promised to prepare,
He will guide you safely there.
Trust Him now, invite Him in,
He will deal with all your sin,
Come and live within your heart,
And His own sweet peace impart.

21　At Christmas time

Colin Ferguson

At Christ-mas time the church bells ring and Christ-ian folk their

car-ols sing a-round a crib and Christ-mas tree, for Christ is born for you and me.

So let us cel-e-brate his birth and praise him, Lord of all the earth.

2. The Christmas tree is evergreen; God's love will be forever seen.
Above the branches shines a star. For this brought wise men from afar;
A treetop memory of light In Bethlehem's once holy night.

3. See paper angels on the tree swing to the ancient melody
that once was sung to shepherd men upon the hills of Bethlehem.
Sing peace, goodwill to one and all, And hear their echo in this hall.

4. Beneath the tree our offerings lie for those in need and poverty;
no frankincense, not myrrh nor gold, no lambs out of a shepherd's fold,
but gifts that make a baby smile and joys to entertain the child.

5. Now decorate the tree with joy for Mary gave birth to a boy,
and Christmas will forever be a time for hope and harmony.
So light the lights, chase dark away, Let us rejoice this Christmas day.

Music © 2013 Harry Hicks
Words © Colin Ferguson

22   Author of faith

Charles Wesley

Au-thor of faith, e - ter-nal Word, Whose spi-rit breathes the ac-tive flame,

Faith, like its fi - nish - er and Lord, To - day as yes - ter - day the same.

2. To thee our humble hearts aspire,
And ask the gift unspeakable;
Increase in us the kindled fire,
In us the work of faith fulfil.

3. By faith we know thee strong to save
(Save us, O present Saviour thou!)
Whate'er we hope, by faith we have,
Future and past subsisting now.

4. To him that in thy name believes
Eternal life with thee is given;
Into himself he all receives -
Pardon, and holiness, and heaven.

5. The things unknown to feeble sense,
Unseen by reason's glimmering ray,
With strong commanding evidence
Their heavenly origin display.

6. Faith lends its realising light,
The clouds disperse, the shadows fly;
Th'Invisible appears in sight,
And God is seen by mortal eye.

23 Awake, my heart

Isacc Watts

A-wake, my heart, a - rise, my tongue, Pre - pare a tune - ful voice,

In God the life of all my joys, A loud I will re - joice.

2. 'tis he adorned my naked soul,
And made salvation mine,
Upon a poor polluted worm
He makes his graces shine.

3. And lest the shadow of a spot
Should on my soul be found
He took the robe the Saviour wrought,
And cast it all around.

4. How far the heav'nly robe exceeds
What earthly princes wear!
These ornaments, how bright they shine,
How white the arments are!

5. The Spirit wrought my faith and love,
And hope, and every grace;
But Jesus spent his life to work
The robe of righteousness.

6. Strangely, my soul, thou art arrayed
By the great sacred Three:
In sweetest harmony of praise
Let all thy powers agree.

24   At thy feet

W. Bright 1824-1901

At thy feet O Christ, - we lay Thine own gift of this new day;

Doubt of what it holds in store Makes us crave thine aid the more;

Lest it prove a time of loss, Mark, it, Saviour, with thy cross.

2. If it flow on calm and bright,
Be thyself our chief delight;
If it bring unknown distress,
Good is all that thou canst bless;
Only, while its hours begin,
Pray we, keep them clear from sin.

3. Fain would we thy word embrace,
Live each moment on thy grace,
All our selves to thee consign,
Fold up all thy wills in thine,
Think, and speak, and do, and be
Simply that which pleases thee.

4. Hear us, Lord and that right soon;
Hear, and grant the choicest boon
That thy love can e'er impart,
Loyal singleness of heart;
So shall this and all our days,
Christ our God, show forth thy praise.

25   Be present, Spirit of the Lord

Timothy Dudley-Smith

Be pre-sent, Spi-rit of the Lord, let sounds of earth be dumb; the Father's love __ be shed a-broad, the dew of bless __ ing on us poured, O si - lent Spi - rit, come!

2. In power unseen upon us rest,
   your gracious gifts impart:
a mind renewed, a spirit blessed,
a life where Christ is manifest,
   an understanding heart.

3. Love's sovereign work of grace fulfil,
   our souls to Christ incline,
intent to do the Father's will
and stand by faith before him still
   in righteousness divine.

4. O Spirit come, and with us stay;
   make every heart your home.
So work in us that we who pray
may walk with Christ in wisdom's way:
   O Holy Spirit, come!

26   **Beautiful Saviour**

Words written by German Jesuits as 'Schoenster Herr Jesu' in the 17th Century,
and published in the Muenster Gesangbuch in 1677,
and translated into English by Joseph August Seiss in 1873.

Beau-ti-ful Sav - iour, King of cre-a - tion,

Son — of God and Son — of Man! Tru-ly I'd love Thee, tru-ly I'd

serve Thee, Light of my soul;, my joy, — my crown.

2. Fair are the meadows, fair are the woodlands,
Robed in the flowers of blooming spring;
Jesus is fairer, Jesus is purer
He makes our sorrowing spirit sing.

3. Fair is the sunshine, fair is the moonlight,
Bright the sparkling stars on high;
Jesus shines brighter, Jesus shines purer
Than all the angels in the sky.

4. Beautiful Saviour, Lord of the nations,
Son of God and Son of Man!
Glory and honour, praise, adoration
Now and forevermore be thine!

Music © 2012 Harry Hicks

27   Behold the glories of the Lamb

Rev 5: 6-12

Isaac Watts

Be - hold the glo - ries of the Lamb a - midst his Fath-er's throne! Pre -

pare new ho - nours for his name, and songs be - fore un - known.

2. Let elders worship at his feet,
   the church adore around,
   With vials full of odours sweet,
   and harps of sweeter sound.

3. Those are the prayers of the saints,
   and these these hymns they raise:
   Jesus is kind to our complaints,
   He loves to hear our praise.

4. Eternal Father, who shall look
   into thy secret will?
   Who but the Son shall take that book
   and open every seal?

5. He shall fulfill thy great decrees,
   the Son deserves it well;
   Lo, in his hand the sovereign keys
   of heav'n, and death, and hell!

6. Now to the Lamb that once was slain
   be endless blessings paid;
   Salvation, glory, joy, remain
   for ever on thy head.

7. Thou hast redeemed our souls with blood,
   hast set the pris'ners free,
   Hast made us kings and priests to God
   and we shall reign with thee.

8. The words of nature and of grace
   are put beneath thy power;
   Then shorten these delaying days
   and bring the promised hour.

28   Behold the Saviour

S. Wesley Sen.

Be - hold the Sav - iour of man - kind Nailed to a shame-ful

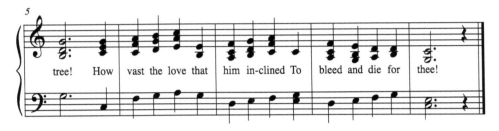

tree! How vast the love that him in-clined To bleed and die for thee!

2. Hark, how he groans! while nature shakes,
And earth's strong pillars bend;
The temple's veil in sunder breaks;
The solid marbles rend.

3. 'Tis done! the precious ransom's paid;
"Receive my soul," he cries;
See where he bows his sacred head!
He bows his head, and dies!

4. But soon he'll break death's envious chain,
And in full glory shine;
O Lamb of God! was ever pain,
Was ever love like thine?

29   Beneath the cross of Jesus

E.C.Clephane

Be— neath the cross of Je - sus I fain would take my stand, The sha - dow of a migh - ty rock, With - in a wear - y land; A home with-in the wil - der-ness, A rest up-on the way. From the burn - ing of the noon - tide heat, And the bur - den of — the day.

2. O safe and happy shelter!
A refuge tried and sweet!
O trysting-place where heaven's love
And heaven's justice meet!
As to the holy Patriarch
That wondrous dream was given,
So seems my Saviour's cross to me,
A ladder up to heaven.

3. There lies, beneath it's shadow,
But on the farther side,
The darkness of an awful grave
That gapes both deep and wide:
And there between us stands the cross,
Two arms outstretched to save;
Like a watchman set to guard the way
From that eternal grave.

4. Upon that cross of Jesus
Mine eyes at times I see
The very dying of the One
Who suffered there for me;
And from my smitten heart, with tears,
Two wonders I confess -
The wonders of His glorious love,
And my own unworthyness.

5. I take, O cross, thy shadow,
For my abiding place;
I ask no other sunshine than
The sunshine of His face;
Content to let the world go by,
To know no gain nor loss -
My sinful self my only shame,
My glory all the cross.

30   Beyond all mortal praise

Timothy Dudley-Smith

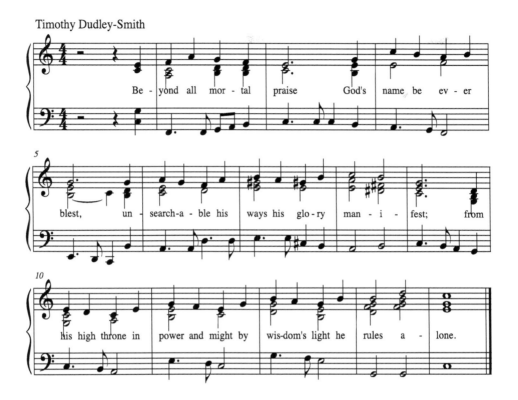

Be - yond all mor - tal praise God's name be ev - er blest, un - search-a - ble his ways his glo - ry man - i - fest; from his high throne in power and might by wis-dom's light he rules a - lone.

2. When times are in his hand   to whom all flesh is grass,
while as their Maker planned   the changing seasons pass.
He orders all: before his eyes
earth's empires rise,   her kingdoms fall.

3. He gives to humankind,   dividing as he will,
all powers of heart and mind,   of spirit, strength and skill:
nor dark nor night   but must lay bare
its secrets, where   he dwells in light.

4. To God the only Lord,   our father's God, be praise;
his holy name adored   through everlasting days.
His mercies trace   in answered prayer,
in love and care,   and gifts of grace.

31 Birth brings a promise

Marjorie Dobson

Birth brings a pro-mise of new life a-wak-ing, dawn-ing of hope through a child's op-en eyes.

Un-char-ted fu-ture is there for the ma-king, chal-lenge and change in a ba-by's first cries.

2. Every new life changes those who are around it,
   making demands of commitment and care,
   calling for love to enfold and surround it,
   reshaping patterns by claiming a share.

3. Jesus the new-born crossed time's moving stages,
   changing their course by the act of his birth,
   translating God from the mystery of ages,
   rooting our faith by his presence on earth.

4. Wonder and worship were waiting to greet him,
   love and devotion were his to command,
   life was transformed for the ones sent to meet him,
   touching their God in a child's outstretched hand.

5. Birth gives new promise of new life awaking,
   Jesus the new-born calls us to birth.
   All that he promised is ours for the taking
   when our commitments bring God down to earth.

Music © 2014 Harry hicks
Words © 1996 Stainer & Bell Ltd.

32   Bless the Lord, creation sings

Timothy Dudley-Smith

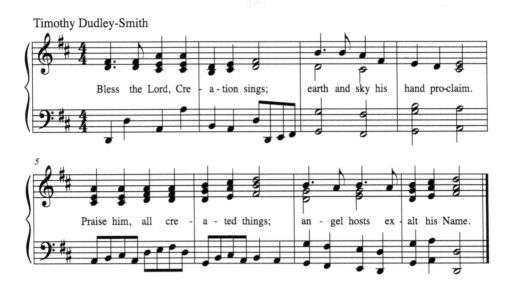

Bless the Lord, Cre - a - tion sings; earth and sky his hand pro-claim.

Praise him, all cre - a - ted things; an - gel hosts ex - alt his Name.

2. Bless the Lord! To heaven's throne   songs of endless glory rise;
   in the clouds his praise be shown,   sun and moon and starry skies.

3. Bless the Lord with ice and snow,   bitter cold and scorching blaze,
   floods and all the winds that blow,   frosty nights and sunlit days.

4. Bless the Lord in mist and cloud,   lightnings shine to mark his way;
   thunders speak his name aloud,   wind and storm his word obey.

5. Bless the Lord who brings to birth   life renewed by sun and rain;
   flowing rivers, fruitful earth,   bird and beast on hill and plain.

6. Bless the Lord! From earth and sky,   ocean depths and furthest shore,
   all things living bear on high   songs of praise for evermore.

7. Bless the Lord! His Name be blessed,   worshipped, honoured, loved, adored,
   and with holy hearts confessed,   saints and servants of the Lord.

8. Bless the Lord! The Father, Son,   and the Holy Spirit praise;
   high exalt the Three in One,   God of everlasting days!

33 Bless the Lord

Jonathan Meyrick

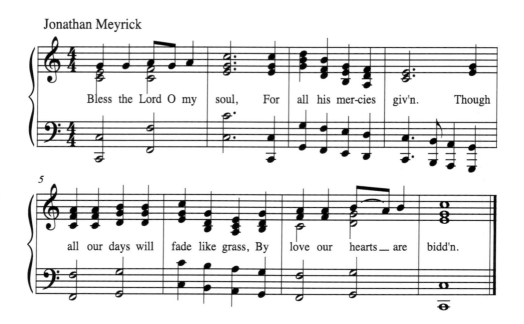

Bless the Lord O my soul, For all his mer-cies giv'n. Though
all our days will fade like grass, By love our hearts — are bidd'n.

2. Bless the Lord O my soul;
Though his life here has passed,
Integrity, kindness of heart -
Like faith, hope, love - will last.

3. Bless the Lord, O my soul;
Though hearts by grief are torn,
Help us, dear Lord, to trust in you;
New hope, new strength, is born.

4. Bless the Lord, O my soul,
As he goes through the dark,
On wings of love to God's own heart,
To Heaven, our life's true mark.

5. Bless the Lord, O my soul;
New Heav'ns, new earths, laid bare,
As springs of living water flow -
Ris'n life for all to share.

6. Bless the Lord, O my soul;
For in the fiercest fight,
Jesus reveals new model ways,
And gives eternal life.

34 Blessed are the humble
(The Beatitudes)

Isaac Watts

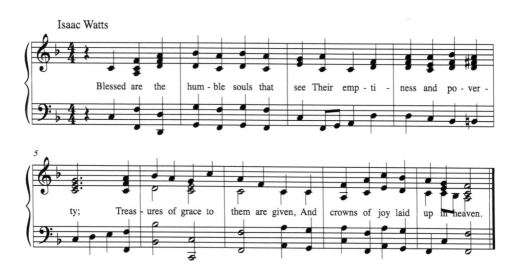

Blessed are the hum-ble souls that see Their emp-ti-ness and po-ver-ty; Treas-ures of grace to them are given, And crowns of joy laid up in heaven.

2. Blessed are the men of broken heart,
who mourn for sin and inward smart;
The blood of Christ divinely flows,
A healing balm for all their woes.

3. Blessed are the meek, who stand afar
From rage and passion, noise and war;
God will secure their happy state,
And plead their cause against the great.

4. Blessed are the souls that thirst for grace,
Hunger and long for righteousness,
They shall be well supplied and fed,
With living streams and living bread.

5. Blessed are the men whose feelings move
And melt with sympathy and love;
From Christ the Lord they shall obtain
Like sympathy and love again.

6. Blessed are the pure, whose hearts are clean
From the defiling powers of sin,
With endless pleasure they shall see
A God of spotless purity.

7. Blessed are the men of peaceful life
Who quench the coals of growing strife,
They shall be called the heirs of bliss,
The sons of God, the God of Peace.

8. Blessed are the suff'rers who partake
Of pain and shame for Jesus' sake;
Their souls shall triumph in the Lord,
Glory and joy are their reward.

Music © 2013 Harry Hicks

35 Blessed be

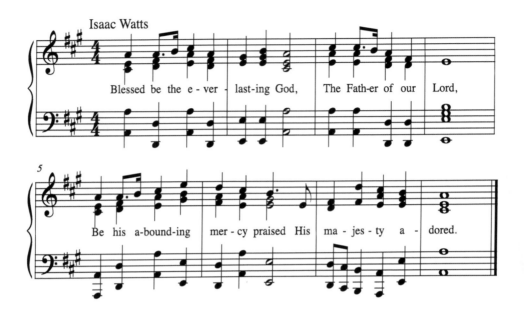

Isaac Watts

Blessed be the e-ver-last-ing God, The Fath-er of our Lord,

Be his a-bound-ing mer-cy praised His ma-jes-ty a-dored.

2. When from the dead he raised his Son,
And called him to the sky,
He gave our souls a lively hope
That they should never die.

3. What though our inbred sins require
Our flesh to see the dust!
Yet as the Lord our Saviour rose,
So all his followers must.

4. There's an inheritance divine
Reserved against that day,
'tis uncorrupted, undefiled,
And cannot waste away.

5. Saints by the power of God are kept
Till the salvation come;
We walk by faith as strangers here
Till Christ shall call us home.

36   Bright is the path

James Rowe

Bright is the path that I - tread to-day, Blue is the sky a-
bove, For I am walk-ing the heav'n-ly way Prais-ing my Sav-iour's
love. Sweet is the song - that my spi-rit sings,
Leav-ing my drea-ry past; I am a child of the King of kings;
Je - sus is mine at last, Je - sus is mine at last!

2. Sin and its pleasures their charm have lost, I have been cleansed within;
Never again shall my soul be tossed Out on the waves of sin.
Jesus has answered my heart's deep plea, From me by burden cast;
I am as glad as a soul can be, Jesus is mine at last, Jesus is mine at last!

3. Nothing can cause me to part from Him, Till I have ceased to roam;
Whether through sunshine or shadows dim, Jesus will lead me home.
Closely I'll cling to Him all the way, Fearing no stormy blast,
Singing right up to the land of day, Jesus is mine at last, Jesus is mine at last!

Music © 2009 Harry Hicks

37   Bright King of Glory

Bright King of Glo - ry, dread-ful God! Our spi-rits bow be - fore thy seat,

To thee we lift an hum-ble thought, And wor-ship at thine aw-ful feet.

2. Thy power hath formed, thy wisdom sways
   All nature with a sovereign word;
And the bright world of stars obeys
   The will of their superior Lord.

3. Mercy and truth unite in one,
   And smiling sit at thy right hand;
Eternal justice guards thy throne,
And vengeance waits thy dread command.

4. A thousand seraphs strong and bright
   Stand round the glorious Deity;
But who amongst the sons of light
   Pretends comparison with thee?

5. Yet there is one in human frame,
   Jesus, arrayed in flesh and blood,
Thinks it no robbery to claim
   A full equality with God.

6. Their glory shines with equal beams;
   Their essence is for ever one,
Though they are known by different names
   the Father God, and God the Son.

7. Then let the name of Christ our King
   With equal honours be adored;
His praise let every angel sing,
   And all the nations own their Lord.

38　Builder of the starry frame

Albert Bayly

Build - er of the star - ry frame, in your han-di-work re - joic - ing,

wor - ship we your glor-ious Name, hear - ti - ly your prais-es voic - ing.

2. For your creatures you have planned
taste of your divine enjoyment;
we, in arts of mind or hand
share your spirit's high employment.

3. Craftsmen, writer, artist, sage,
serve your purpose and your pleasure;
singer's voice and poet's page
echo your melodious measure.

4. Yet a joy more precious still
we, whom you created, owe you,
when our heart obeys your will
we may truly come to know you.

5. When your grace forms Christ in man,
crowning thus your whole creation,
we, in your redeptive plane,
share the joy of your salvation.

6. Heartily we then rejoice,
music to your glory making,
grateful soul and thankful voice
in one joyous song awaking.

Music © 2012 Harry Hicks
Words: 'Builder of the starry frame' by Albert Bayly (1901-84) © 1988 Oxford University Press.
Reproduced by permission. All rights reserved.

39　By angel's word

Jonathan Meyrick

By an-gel's word and heav'n-ly gift, Through Ma-ry's faith and joy-ful trust, Lord

Je - sus you were born; Your fa - ther's love takes root on earth,

Good - will to all, new hope of peace; Gift to a world___ for - lorn.

2. You gave us news so good to hear;
God's kingdom comes and mercy reigns -
Forgiveness conquers all.
See, shepherd climbs the steep cliffside;
See, father waits with breaking heart
For us to hear his call.

3. We seek to love as she did then;
With tears she bathed and kissed your feet,
Herself new-washed from sin.
We seek to follow like your frineds,
To offer peace and wolf-stalked sheep
And bring your harvest in.

4. We cry for mercy, eyes cast down;
We know we stand by love alone,
The love which bids us rise,
You bind our wounds when left to die,
Foe now made friend through tender care
You hear persistent cries.

5. We see love bleed on cruel cross;
We hear you plead forgiveness still
as carelessly they kill,
Show paradise to frightened thief,
Bring comfort to the ones who weep,
And trust your father's will.

6. But now dawn breaks as women wait,
joy conq'ring fear, they find new hope;
see resurrection light.
We walk as trav'llers on the road
Who find their Lord in broken bread,
Now clothed with power from high.

A general hymn for St.Lukestide, reflecting some distinctive themes of his gospel.
Written for the choirs of Exeter Diocese and the Devon branch of the RSCM,
to the tune 'Cornwall' by S.S.Wesley.

40　Called to be saints

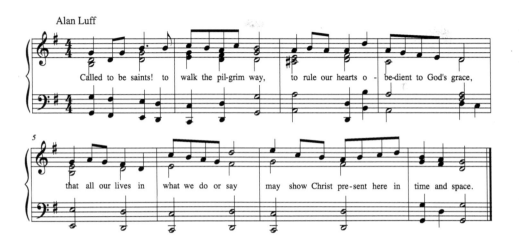

Alan Luff

Called to be saints! to walk the pil-grim way, to rule our hearts o - be-dient to God's grace, that all our lives in what we do or say may show Christ pre-sent here in time and space.

2. Called to be saints! to blossom and bear fruit;
to sow the seeds of penitence and prayer;
that in our lives Christ's beauty may take root
and come to flower in service and in care.

3. Called to be saints! to build upon the rock,
the one foundation that is Christ alone,
one with the fellow-workers of Christ's flock,
together built into one corner stone.

4. Called to be saints! to reach in love toward
the weak, the poor, victims of war and greed;
that workers may receive their due reward,
the poor be fed and the oppressed be freed.

5. Called to be saints! to find our hidden Lord
where conflict grows and sufferings increase,
to learn to speak the reconciling word
which frees the love of Christ to work for peace.

6. The saints are one! the faithful in their day
unite with us to keep our spirits strong,
while we who seek the will of God today
may hope to sing with the eternal song.

41   Chill of the nightfall

Timothy Dudley-Smith

Chill of the night-fall, lamps in the win-dows, let-ting their light fall clear on the snow;

bit-ter De-cem - ber bids us re-mem - ber Christ in the sta - ble long, long a - go.

2. Silence of midnight,
   voices of angels
   singing to bid night
   yield to the dawn;
   darkness is ended,
   sinners befriended,
   where in the stable
   Jesus was born.

3. Splendour of starlight
   high on the hillside,
   faint is the far light
   burning below;
   kneeling before Him
   shepherds adore him,
   Christ in the stable
   long, long ago.

4. Glory of daybreak!
   Sorrows and shadows,
   suddenly they break
   forth into morn;
   Sing out and tell now
   All shall be well now,
   for in the stable,
   Jesus is born!

42   Christ be my leader

Timothy Dudley-Smith

1. Christ be my leader as night as by day;
Safe through the darkness for he is the way.
Gladly I follow, my future his care,
Darkness is daylight when Jesus is there.

2. Christ be my teacher in age as in youth,
Drifting or doubting, for he is the truth.
Grant me to trust him; though shifting as sand,
Doubt cannot daunt me; in Jesus I stand.

3. Christ be my Saviour in calm as in strife;
Death cannot hold me, for he is the life.
Nor darkness nor doubting nor sin and its stain
Can touch my salvation: with Jesus I reign.

43 Christ calls us as disciples

Graham Adams

Christ calls us as dis-ci-ples to tread un-known ter-rain,
em-bark on new ad-ven-tures and change our-selves a-gain.
'Let's go a-cross the wa-ter, on to the o-ther side,'
and if a storm should greet us, may peace and faith a-bide.

2. By faith we're called to follow
   though like a mustard seed
   we know our hope is fragile
   and yearns to be set free:
   but we are called in weakness
   as waves crash all around,
   God knowing our potential:
   may peace and faith abound!

3. By faith we must remember
   we've not passed here before;
   this way eludes our mapping;
   we're safer on the shore:
   but we are called to follow
   God's promises ahead
   which break the flowing torrents:
   in hope we too shall tread!

4. Christ calls us as disciples
   to do what we do not know,
   to where the Spirit prompts us;
   that mustard seeds might grow!
   Let's go across the waters,
   beyond what we can see,
   that as your promise shapes us,
   new worlds shall dare to be!

44 Christ high-ascended

Christ high-as-cen-ded, now in glo-ry seat-ed, Throned and ex-al-ted, vic-to-ry com-ple-ted,

Death's dread dom-in-ion fi-nal-ly de-feat-ed, we are his wit-nes-ses.

2. Christ from the Father ev'ry pow'r possessing,
who on his chosen lifted hands in blessing,
sends forth his servants, still in faith confessing,
we are his witnesses.

3. Christ, who in dying won for us salvation,
lives now the first-born of the new creation;
to win disciples out of ev'ry nation,
we are his witnesses.

4. Christ in his splendour, all dominion gaining,
Christ with his people evermore remaining,
Christ to all ages gloriously reigning,
we are his witnesses.

5. As at his parting, joy shall banish grieving,
faith in his presence strengthens our believing;
filled with his Spirit, love and pow'r receiving,
we are his witnesses.

Music © 209 Harry Hicks
Words: 'Christ high-ascended' by Timothy Dudley-Smith (b. 1926) © Timothy Dudley-Smith
in Europe and Africa. © Hope Publishing Company in the United States of America and the rest of the world.
Reproduced by permission of Oxford University Press. All rights reserved.

45   Christ is coming

Brenda Gallant

Christ is co-ming, Ha-le-lu-jah! Christ is co-ming back a-gain,

He is co-ming as He pro-mised, He will take His po-wer and reign.

Are you rea-dy for His Ad-vent, Will He find you watch-ing here,

Are you washed and cleansed and wait-ing, In His glo-ry thus to share.

2. Christ is coming, Hallelujah,
Christ is coming back again,
Every eye will then behold Him,
Every voice take up the strain,
Those who set at nought and scorned Him,
Those who cursed His precious Name,
They will bow the knee before Him,
Overwhelmed in guilt and shame.

3. Christ is coming, Hallelujah,
Christ is coming back again.
Will you welcome His appearing,
Will you join the glad refrain?
Even so, oh come, Lord Jesus,
Come and claim your chosen bride,
Come and take us up to glory,
There forever to abide.

46 Christ is our light!

Leith Fisher

Christ is our light! the bright and morn-ing star cov'-ring
with rad-iance all from near and far. Christ be our light, shine
on, shine on, we pray in - to our hearts, in - to our world to - day.

2. Christ is our love! baptized that we may know
the love of God among us, swooping low.
Christ be our love, bring us to turn our face
and see you in the light of heaven's embrace.

3. Christ is our joy! transforming wedding guest!
Through water turned to wine the feast was blessed.
Christ be our joy; your glory let us see,
as your disciples did in Galilee.

Words © Leith Fisher
Music © 2013 Harry Hicks

47   Christ is risen

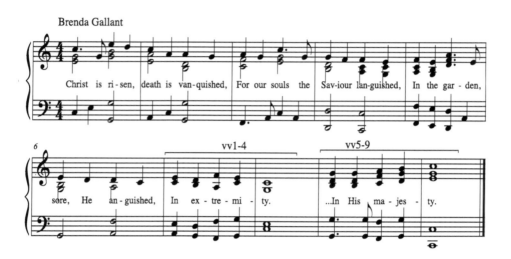

Brenda Gallant

Christ is ri-sen, death is van-quished, For our souls the Sav-iour lan-guished, In the gar-den,

sore, He an-guished, In ex-tre-mi-ty.   ...In His ma-jes-ty.

vv1-4   vv5-9

2. Christ is risen, how He suffered
As his sinless self He proffered,
All He had to God He offered,
In humility.

3. Christ is risen, sin's grip broken,
It is finished, He has spoken,
Shed His blood, that blessed token
Of eternity.

4. Christ is risen, tomb is bare now,
For His body is not there now,
This good news is here to share now,
With integrity.

5. Christ is risen, task completed,
Satan's tactics all defeated,
Now in heaven Christ is seated
In His majesty.

6. Christ is risen, Jubilation!
He has purchased our salvation,
Let us praise Him with elation
And in ecstasy.

7. Christ is risen, now He's pleading,
With the father interceding,
All His vanquished foes He's leading
In His victory.

8. Christ is risen, He's returning,
Evil forces overturning,
He'll 'catch up' all those who're yearning
In expectancy.

9. Let us join our hearts in praising,
All our voices gladly raising,
Songs and hymns of joy thus phrasing,
In glad psalmody.

48   Christ is the only answer

Brenda Gallant

Christ is the on-ly an-swer To ev'-ry hu-man need,
The au-thor of sal - va-tion, A long ac-com-plished deed.
His name to sin-ners gi - ven Brings ac-cess to God's throne,
An en-trance in - to hea - ven For those who are His own.

2. No other name is given
Whereby we must be saved,
No other side was riven
For sinners so depraved.
This name it gives protection,
Brings with it victory,
His glorious resurrection
Is hope for you and me.

3. Our God has spoken to us
Through Christ who is the Word,
A living demonstration
That hard hearts might be stirred.
He gives us an example,
In suffering and in love,
That we may be well fitted
To dwell with Him above.

4. And so this loving Saviour
Can give us grace to show
That henceforth our behaviour
Reveals the One we know.
Then He, Himself will bless us,
And be our great reward,
This Christ, who is the Answer;
Our ever living Lord.

Music © 2013 Harry Hicks
Words © 1986 Brenda Gallant

49   Christ is the world's true light

G.W. Briggs

Christ is the world's true Light, Its Cap-tain of Sal - va - tion,
The Day-star shin - ing bright To ev-'ry man and na - tion;
New life, new hope a - wakes, Where - 'er men own His sway:
Free - dom her bon - dage breaks And night is turned to day.

2. In Christ all races meet,
Their ancient feuds forgetting,
The whole round world complete,
From sunrise to its setting:
When Christ is throned as Lord,
Men shall forsake the sword,
To ploughshare beat the sword,
To pruning-hook the spear.

3. One Lord, in one great name
Unite us all who own Thee;
Cast out our pride and shame
That hinder to enthrone Thee;
The world has waited long,
Has travelled long in pain;
To heal its ancient wrong,
Come, Prince of Peace, and reign.

Music © 2018 Harry Hicks

50   Christ the Lord

M. Weisse tr. Catherine Winkworth

Christ the Lord is ris-en a-gain, Christ has bro-ken ev'-ry chain.

Hark, an-ge-lic voi-ces cry, sing-ing ev-er-more on high:

Al - le-lu - ia, Al - le-lu - ia, Al - le - lu - ia!

2. He who gave for us his life,
who for us endured the strife,
is our pascal Lamb today;
we too sing for joy and say:
Alleluia, alleluia, alleluia.

3. He who bore all pain and loss
comfortless upon the Cross,
lives in glory now on high,
pleads for us, and hears our cry:
Alleluia, alleluia, alleluia.

4. Ho whose path no records tell,
who descended into hell,
who the strong man armed hath bound,
now in highest heav'n is crowned.
Alleluia, alleluia, alleluia.

5. He who slumbered in the grave
is exalted now to save;
now through Christendom it rings
that the Lamb is King of kings.
Alleluia, alleluia, alleluia.

6. Now he bids us tell abroad
how the lost may be restored,
how the penitent forgiven,
how we too may enter heaven.
Alleluia, alleluia, alleluia.

7. Thou, our pascal Lamb indeed,
Christ, thy ransomed people feed;
take our sins and guilt away:
let us sing by night and day:
Alleluia, alleluia, alleluia.

51 Christ the Lord is risen today!

Fanny J. Crosby

Christ the Lord is risen to-day! He is risen in-deed! He cap-tive led cap-tiv-i-ty, He robbed the grave of vic-to-ry, He broke the bars of death.

Chorus

Al - le-lu - ia! Al - le-lu - ia! Al - le lu - ia

1st time A - men!

2nd time Al - le-lu - ia - A - men.

2. Christ the Lord is risen today!
He is risen indeed!
Let every mourning soul rejoice,
All sing with one united voice;
The Saviour rose today.
Alleluia! Alleluia! Alleluia! Amen!
Alleluia! Alleluia! Alleluia! Amen!

3. Christ the Lord is risen today!
He is risen indeed!
The great and glorious work is done;
Free grace to all through Christ the Son;
Hosanna to His Name!
Alleluia! Alleluia! Alleluia! Amen!
Alleluia! Alleluia! Alleluia! Amen!

4. Christ the Lord is risen today!
He is risen indeed!
Let all that fill the earth and sea
Break forth in tuneful melody;
And swell the mighty song.
Alleluia! Alleluia! Alleluia! Amen!
Alleluia! Alleluia! Alleluia! Amen!

Music © 2016 Harry Hicks

52　Christ's pastures

Isaac Watts

Thou whom my soul ad - mires a - bove, all - earth - ly joy, and earth - ly - love, Tell me dear shep - herd, let me - know, - Where - doth thy sweet - est pas - ture grow?

2. Where is the shadow of that rock
That from the son defends his flock?
Fain would I feed among thy sheep,
Among them rest, among them sleep.

3. Why should thy bride appear like one
That turns aside to paths unknown?
My constant feet would never rove,
Would never seek another love.

4. The footsteps of thy flock I see;
Thy sweetest pastures here they be;
A wondrous feast thy love prepares,
Bought with thy wounds, and groans, and tears.

5. His dearest flesh he makes my food,
And bids me drink his richest blood;
Here to these hills my soul will come,
Till my beloved leads me home.

53   Christian people everywhere

Timothy L. Woods

Christ - ian peop-ple ev -'ry-where: Ce - le-brate the world we share!

All cre-a - tion sig - ni-fies God at work be - fore our eyes;

All cre-a - tion will be free: God de-sires our li - ber - ty:

Sparks of hope in us ig -nite: Help us bear a Gos - pel light!

2. Ev'ry grain of sand on earth
Tells a story, has its worth;
Glory found in everything -
Panda bears and wasps that sting,
Crescent moons and chuckling streams,
Bold inventions, pleasant dreams:
Sparks of hope in us ignite:
Help us bear a gospel light!

3. Heavy rain and sullen sky
Make us groan and wonder why
Global temperatures mayrise -
conflicts rage, the planet dies -
Streets and homes awash with mud,
Will there be another flood?
Sparks of hope in us ignite:
Help us bear a gospel light!

4. Teach us Lord to live with care,
Celebrate the world we share!
And we'll turn to you again,
Lord of sun and wind and rain -
away with apathy and fear,
let's proclaim the kingdom here!
Sparks of hope in us ignite:
Help us bear a gospel light!

54 Christians! Join in celebration

Janet H. Wootton

Christ-ians! Join in ce-le-bra-tion, see the hope in ev-ery face,
Catch a glimpse of new cre-a-tion e-ven here in time and space:
child-ren thrive in peace, un-daun-ted, work re-ceives its fair re-ward,
homes are built and crops are plant-ed, can we see this world re-stored?

2. People join in celebration
where the truth of God is heard
spoken out in confrontation
with the powers that hold the world,
tearing through the web of lying,
naming debt, disease and war,
through the bravest, prophesying:
'Death and pain could be no more!'

3. Christians! Join in celebration,
Sweeping far beyond our schemes.
Dare to hear God's invitation
in a hundred human dreams.
'Break your chainlinks with corruption,
struggle free from guilt and fear,
join the surge of hope's eruption,
God's great carnival is here!'

4. People! Join in celebration,
fan the flame from place to place,
form a vivid constellation
starring all the human race.
Let God's image blaze unhindered,
glorious in diversity.
If our crazed abuse were ended,
then creation might be free.

55   Come and see where Jesus lay

Timothy Dudley-Smith

Come and see where Je - sus lay. cold with in the si lent cave.
Go and tell that Je - sus reigns! Sin and death are o - ver-thrown.

See, the stone is rolled a - way void and ten - ant - less the grave:
Dead to sin and all its pains, live to make his glo - ries known.

Clothes to shroud the form and head still their ab - sent Lord dis - play;
Raised in tri - umph as he said, he who all the world sus - tains,

Christ is ri - sen from the dead! Come and see where Je - sus lay.
Christ is ri - sen from the dead! Go and tell that Je - sus reigns!

56   Come let us join a joyful tune

Isaac Watts

Come let us join a joy - ful tune To our ex - al - ted Lord, Ye saints on high a - round his throne, And we a-round his board. While once up-on this low-er ground Wea-ry and faint ye stood, What dear re-fresh - ments here - ye found From this im-mor - tal food!

2. The tree of life that near the throne
   In heaven's high garden grows,
   Laden with grace, bends gently down
   Its ever-smiling boughs.
   Hovering among the leaves there stands
   The sweet celestial Dove,
   And Jesus on the branches hangs
   The banner of his love.

3. 'tis a young heaven of strange delight
   While in his shade we sit;
   His fruit is pleasing to the sight,
   And to the taste as sweet.
   Now life is spread through dying hearts,
   And cheers the drooping mind;
   Vigour and joy and juice imparts
   Without a sting behind.

4. Now let the flaming weapon stand
   And guard all Eden's trees;
   There's ne'er a plant in all that land
   That bears such fruits as these.
   Infinite grace our souls adore,
   Whose wondrous hand has made
   This living branch of sovereign power
   To raise and heal the dead.

57 Come with gladness

Brenda Gallant

Come with gladness and rejoice, Lift up your heart and soul and voice;

Unto us a child is born, He the garb of flesh has worn.

Come to the earth from realms of light, Pierced the gloom of nature's night.

2. Come with worship, come with awe,
Kneel before Him and adore.
See within that tiny child,
God and man are reconciled.
He, entwined in swaddling bands,
Holds the whole world in His hands.

3. Come with wonder as you view,
All that God has done for you.
How He stooped with wondrous grace,
And confined to time and space.
God within a human frame,
As a little baby came.

4. Come with understanding heart,
Knowing you can share a part,
On this happy Christmas day,
Homage at the manger pay.
See your God in weakness lie,
Tiny baby, born to die.

5. Come with wide enlightened eyes,
Hear the message from the skies,
Unto you is born this day
One to take your sins away.
This the Saviour, Christ the Lord,
Only true and living word.

6. Come with grief and anguish sore,
See a little babe no more,
Rather view Him lifted high,
Hanging on a cross to die.
This the reason for His birth,
Why He came from heav'n to earth.

7. Come with thankfulness and praise,
Lift your heart in joyful lays,
He who died now lives again,
King of kings for aye to reign.
Give to Him your life, your all,
At His feet in worship fall.

8. Come with expectation too,
For His promise will come true,
He will rend the clouds aside,
Claim His cleansed and waiting bride.
Work and watch and praise and pray,
'Till you see Him on that day.

Music © 2013 Harry Hicks
Words © 1992 Brenda Gallant

58 Come, all harmonious tongues

Isaac Watts

Come - all har-mon-ious tongues, Your nob-ler mu-sic bring, 'tis
Christ __ the ev - ver last-ing God, And Christ - the - man we sing.

2. Tell how he took our flesh
To take away our guilt,
Sing the dear drops of sacred blood
That hellish monsters spilt.

3. Alas, the cruel spear
Went deep into his side,
And the rich flood of purple gore
Their murderous weapons dyed.

4. The waves of swelling grief
Did o'er his bosom roll,
And mountains of almighty wrath
Lay heavy on his soul.

5. Down to the shades of death
He bowed his awful head,
Yet he arose to live and reign
When death itself is dead.

6. No more the bloody spear,
The cross and nails no more;
For hell itself shakes at his name,
And all the heav'ns adore.

7. There the Redeemer sits
High on the Father's throne;
The Father lays his vengeance by,
And smiles upon his Son.

8. There his full glories shine
With uncreated rays,
And bless his saints' and angels' eyes
To everlasting days.

Music © 2013 Harry Hicks

59   Come, gracious Spirit

Simon Browne (1680- 1732)

Come, gra-cious Spi-rit, heav'n-ly Dove, with light___ and com___ fort from a - bove; come, be our Guar - dian, be our Guide, o'er ev' - ry thought and step pre - side.

2. The light of truth to us display,
and make us know and choose your way;
plant holy fear in every heart,
that we from God may ne'er depart.

3. Lead us to Christ, the living Way,
nor let us from his pastures stray;
lead us to holiness, the road
that we must take to dwell with God.

4. Lead us to heav'n, that we may share
fullness of joy for ever there;
lead us to God, our final rest,
to be with him for ever blest.

60 Come, happy souls

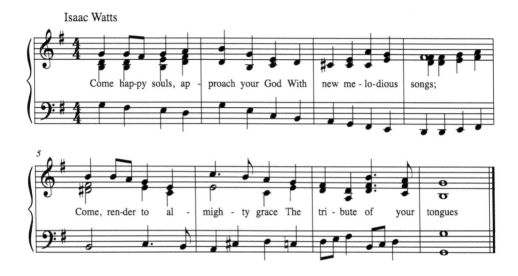

Isaac Watts

Come hap-py souls, ap - proach your God With new me - lo-dious songs;

Come, ren-der to al - migh - ty grace The tri - bute of your tongues

2. So strange, so boundless was the love
That pitied dying men,
The Father sent his equal Son
To give them life again.

3. Thy hands, dear Jesus, were not armed
With a revenging rod,
No hard comission to perform
The vengeance of a God.

4. But all was mercy, all was mild,
And wrath forsook the throne,
When Christ on the kind errand came,
And brought salvation down.

5. Here, sinners, you may heal your wounds,
And wipe your sorrows dry;
Trust in the mighty Saviour's Name,
And you shall never die.

6. See, dearest Lord, our willing souls
Accept thine offered grace;
We bless the great Redeemer's love,
And give the Father praise.

61   Come, Holy Ghost, in love

Richard ll of France Tr. R. Palmer

Come, Ho-ly Ghost in love, Shed on us from a-bove Thine own bright ray: Di-vine-ly good Thou art, Thy sac-red gifts im-part To glad-den each sad heart; O come to-day.

2. Come tenderest Friend and best,
Our most delightful Guest,
With soothing power;
Rest which the weary know,
Shade in the noon-tide glow,
Peace when deep griefs o'erflow;
Cheer us this hour!

3. Come, Light serene and still,
Our inmost bosoms fill;
Dwell in each breast:
We know no dawn but Thine;
Send forth thy beams divine,
On our dark souls to shine,
And make us blest.

4. Exalt our low desires,
Extinguish passion's fires,
Heal every wound:
Our stubborn spirits bend,
Our icy coldness end,
Our devious steps attend,
While heavenward bound!

5. Come, all the faithful bless!
Let all who Christ confess
His praise employ;
Give virtue's rich reward,
Victorious death accord,
And with our glorious Lord
Eternal joy!

62   Come, Holy Ghost

C. Wesley

Come, Ho - ly Ghost, all quick' - ning fire! Come, and my hal - lowed heart in - spire,

sprinkl-ed with the a - ton - ing blood; Now to my soul thy self re - veal;

Thy migh-ty work - ing let me feel, And know that I am born of God.

2. Thy witness with my spirits bear,
   That God, my God, inhabits there.
   Thou with the father, and the Son,
   Eternal light's co-equal beam;
   Be Christ in me, and I in him,
   Till perfect we are made in one.

3. When wilt thou my whole heart subdue;
   Come, Lord, and form my soul anew,
   Emptied of pride, and wrath, and hell,
   Less than the least of all thy store
   Of mercies, I myself abhor;
   All, all my vileness may I feel.

4. Humble, and teachable, and mild,
   O may I, as a little child,
   My lowly Master's steps pursure!
   Be anger to my soul unknown;
   Hate, envy, jealousy, be gone;
   In love create thou all things new.

5. Let earth no more my heart divide;
   With Christ may I be crucified,
   To thee with my whole soul aspire;
   Dead to the world and all its toys,
   Its idle pomp, and fading joys,
   Be thou alone my one desire!

6. Be thou my joy, be thou my dread;
   In battle cover thou my head;
   Nor earth, nor hell I then shall fear;
   I then shall turn my steady face -
   Want, pain defy - enjoy disgrace -
   Glory in dissolution near.

7. My will be swallowed up in thee;
   Light in thy light still may I see,
   Beholding thee with open face;
   Called the full power of faith to prove,
   Let all my hallowed heart be love,
   And all my spotless life be praise.

8. Come, Holy Ghost, all quickning fire!
   Come, my consecrated heart inspire,
   Sprinkled with the atoning blood;
   Still to my soul thyself reveal;
   Thy mighty working may I feel,
   And know that I am one with God.

64 Come, holy Spirit

Isaac Watts

Come, ho-ly Spi-rit, heav'n-ly Dove, With all thy quick'n-ing powers,

Kin-dle a flame of sa-cred love, In these cold hearts of ours.

2. Look, how we grovel here below,
   Fond of these trifling toys;
   Our souls can neither fly nor go
   To reach eternal joys.

3. In vain we tune our formal songs,
   In vain we strive to rise;
   Hosannas languish on our tongues,
   And our devotion dies.

4. Dear Lord! and shall we ever lie
   At this poor dying rate?
   Our love so faint, so cold to thee,
   And thine to us so great?

5. Come holy Spirit, heavenly Dove,
   With all thy quickening powers;
   Come shed abroad a Saviour's love,
   And that shall kindle ours.

63 Come, Holy Spirit, come

Michael Forster

Come, Ho-ly Spi-rit, come! In-flame our souls-with love, trans-
for-ming ev'-ry heart and home with wis-dom from a-bove. O-
let us not-des-pise the hum-ble path Christ trod, but-
choose, to shame-the world-ly wise, the fool-ish-ness___ of God.

2. All-knowing Spirit, prove the poverty of pride, by knowledge of the father's love in Jesus crucified.
And grant us faith to know the glory of that sign, And in our very lives to show the marks of love divine.

3. Come with the gift to heal the wounds of guilt and fear, and to oppression's face reveal the kingdom drawing near.
Where chaos longs to reign, descend, O Holy Dove, and free us all to work again the miracles of love.

4. Spirit of truth, arise; inspire the prophet's voice: expose to scorn the tyrant's lies, and bid the poor rejoice.
O Spirit, clear our sight, all prejudice remove, And help us to discern the right, and covet only love.

5. Give us the tongues to speak, in ev'ry time and place, to rich and poor, to strong and weak, the words of love and grace.
Enable us to hear the words that others bring, Interpreting with open ear the special song they sing.

6. Come Holy Spirit, dance within our hearts today, our earthbound spirits to entrance, our mortal fears allay.
And teach us to desire, all other things above, that self-consuming holy fire, the perfect gift of love!

Based on 1 Cor 12, 4-11

65　Come, let us lift our joyful eyes

Isaac Watts

Come, let - us - lift our | joy - ful eyes | Up to the courts a - | bove,

And smile - to - see our | Fa - ther there | Up - on a throne - of | love.

2. Once 'twas a seat of dreadful wrath,
  And shot devouring flame;
  Our God appeared consuming fire,
  And vengeance was his name.

3. Rich were the drops of Jesus' blood,
  That calmed his frowning face,
  That sprinkled o'er the burning throne,
  And turned the wrath to grace.

4. Now may we bow before his feet,
  And venture near the Lord;
  No fiery cherub guards his seat,
  Now double-flaming sword.

5. The peaceful gates of heavenly bliss
  Are opened by the Son.
  High let us raise our notes of praise,
  And reach th'Almighty throne.

6. To thee ten thousand thanks we bring,
  Great Advocate on high;
  And glory to th'eternal King
  That lays his fury by.

66 Come, sound his praise abroad

Isaac Watts

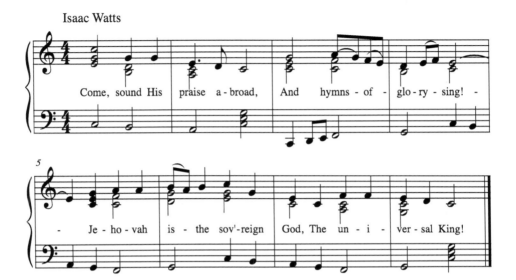

Come, sound His praise a-broad, And hymns of glory sing! -

- Je-ho-vah is the sov'-reign God, The un-i-ver-sal King!

2. He formed the deeps unknown;
He gave the seas their bound:
The wat'ry worlds are all His own,
And all the solid ground.

3. Come, worship at His throne,
Come, bow before the Lord:
We are His work, and not our own,
He formed us by His word.

4. Today attend his voice,
Nor dare provoke His rod;
Come. like the people of His choice,
And own your gracious God.

67 Come, Thou Almighty King

Anon., 1757

Come, Thou Al - migh - ty King, Help us Thy name to sing,
Help us to praise; Fa - ther all glo - ri - ous,
O'er all vic - to - ri - ous, An - cient of days

2. Jesus, our Lord, arise,
   Scatter our enemies,
   And make them fall;
   Let Thine Almighty aid,
   Our sure defence be made,
   Our souls on Thee be stayed;
   Lord, hear our call.

3. Come, Thou Incarnate Word,
   Gird on thy mighty sword;
   Our prayer attend,
   Come, and Thy people bless,
   And give Thy word success;
   Spirit of holiness,
   On us descend.

4. Come, holy Comforter,
   Thy sacred witness bear,
   In this glad hour;
   Thou, Who Almighty art,
   Now rule in every heart,
   And ne'er from us depart,
   Spirit of power!

5. To the great One in Three
   Eternal praises be,
   Hence, evermore!
   His sovereign majesty
   May we in glory see,
   And in eternity,
   Love and adore.

68   Come, Thou Saviour

Martin Luther

Come, Thou Sav-iour of our race, Choic-est Gift of heav'n-ly grace!

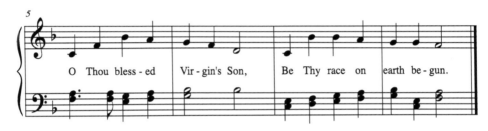

O Thou bless - ed Vir - gin's Son, Be Thy race on earth be - gun.

2. Not of mortal blood or birth,
He descends from heaven to earth:
By the Holy Ghost conceived,
Truly man to be believed.

3. Wondrous birth! O wondrous Child
Of the virgin, undefiled!
Though by all the world disowned,
Still to be in heav'n enthroned.

4. From the Father forth He came,
And returneth to the same;
Captive leading death and hell,
High the song of triumph swell.

5. Equal to the Father now,
Though to dust Thou once didst bow;
Boundless shall Thy kingdom be;
When shall we its glories see?

6. Brightly doth Thy manger shine!
glorious is its light divine:
Let not sin o'ercloud this light,
Ever be our faith thus bright.

69   Comfort all your people, Lord

Gwyneth M. Francis-Williams

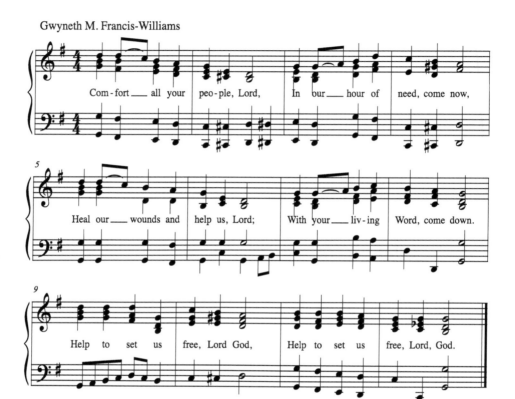

Com-fort __ all your peo-ple, Lord, In our __ hour of need, come now,

Heal our __ wounds and help us, Lord; With your __ liv-ing Word, come down.

Help to set us free, Lord God, Help to set us free, Lord, God.

2. Lift us with your Spirit, Lord,
Open up our hearts, come now,
Teach us to be patient, Lord,
Guide us with your Light, come down.
Help to set us free, Lord God,
Help to set us free, Lord God.

3. Comfort all your people, Lord,
In our hour of need, come now,
Let us be a witness, Lord,
To your heavenly grace, come down.
Help to set us free, Lord God,
Help to set us free, Lord God.

Creation

Brenda Gallant

Cre - a - tion, oh__ won-der-ful sto - ry, How God formed the earth and the sea,

Re - veal - ing His po-wer and glo - ry Through crea-ture and flow - er and tree.

2. From darkness creating the night light,
   Ruled over by moon and the stars,
   The sun set to measure the daylight,
   And planets, like Jupiter, Mars.

3. The seas with abundance of fishes
   Were ordered to stay in their place,
   According to the divine wishes,
   And all-seeing, His infinite grace.

4. The plants, herbs and seeds were all growing,
   And each was inherently good,
   For God, with his foresight and knowing,
   Was planning for mankind his food.

5. The birds of the air with their singing,
   The creeping things after their kind,
   Yet now in their order were bringing
   The fellowship God wished to find.

6. So God formed a man from the earth's dust,
   And gave him a garden to tend,
   One who was perfect, sinless and just,
   A being to treat as a friend.

7. Thus Adam appeared in perfection,
   And Eve, and a helpmate was giv'n,
   But, because of sin and rejection,
   The fellowship bond has been riv'n.

Redemption

Brenda Gallant

Re - demp-tion, oh won-der-ful - sto - ry, 'Tis ours to de-clare to you all, How

God in His po-wer and__ glo - ry Has res - cued man-kind from the fall.

2. By sending His Son as our Saviour
   The fellowship can be restored,
   He forgives our sinful behaviour,
   As promised in His Holy Word.

3. Christ took all our sins and our sorrows,
   As He hung there upon the cross,
   Now we can have hopeful tomorrows,
   And fear neither judgement or loss.

4. By rising from death in the garden,
   He promises we can be free,
   A personal faith brings us pardon,
   For He has said "Come unto Me."

5. At this harvest time celebration
   Praise the Lord for all He has done,
   And there will be great jubilation,
   If you turn in faith to His Son.

6. Creation shows forth all God's glory,
   Perfection in all He has made,
   Creation and Redemption's story,
   Have for us God's great love displayed.

Music © 2013 Harry Hicks
Words © 2013 Brenda Gallant

71 Cross of Jesus

F.W. Faber

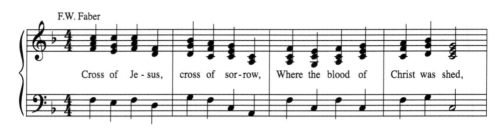

Cross of Je - sus, cross of sor-row, Where the blood of Christ was shed,

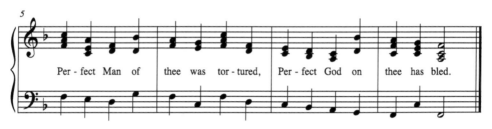

Per - fect Man of thee was tor - tured, Per - fect God on thee has bled.

2. Here the King of all the ages
Throned in light ere worlds could be
Robed in mortal flesh, is dying,
Crucified by sin for me.

3. Up in heaven, sublimest glory
Circled round Him from the first;
But the earth finds none to serve Him,
None to quench His raging thirst.

4. Who shall fathom that descending,
From the rainbow-circled throne,
Down to earth's most base profaning,
Dying desolate, alone.

5. From the "Holy, Holy, Holy,
We adore Thee, O Most High,"
Down to earth's blaspheming voices
And the shout of "Crucify."

6. Cross of Jesus, cross of sorrow,
Where the blood of Christ was shed,
Perfect Man on Thee was tortured,
Perfect God on thee has bled.

72 Crown Him!

Rev. Thomas Kelly

Look, ye saints, the sight is glo-rious; see the Man of Sor-rows now.

From the fight re-turn vic-tor-ious; ev'-ry knee to Him shall bow!

Chorus

Crown Him! Crown Him! An-gels, crown Him! Crown the Sav-iour "King of kings!"

Crown Him! Crown Him! An-gels, crown Him! Crown the Sav-iour King of kings!

2. Crown the Saviour! Angels, crown Him! Rich the trophies Jesus brings;
In the seat of pow'r enthrone Him while the vault of heaven rings.
Crown Him! Crown him! Angels, crown Him!
Crown the Saviour "King of kings!"
Crown Him! Crown him! Angels, crown Him!
Crown the Saviour "King of kings!"

3. Sinners in derision crowned Him, mocking thus the Saviour's claim;
Saints and angels crowd around Him, own His title, praise his name.
Crown Him!.......

4. Hark the bursts of acclamation! Hark those loud triumphant chords!
Jesus takes the highest station, oh what joy the sight affords!
Crown Him!.......

73   Day by day

Day by day, dear Lord, of thee three things I pray: To see thee more clear-ly, Love thee more dear-ly to-fol-low, to-fol-low, to-fol-low thee, to-fol-low thee more-near-ly day-by day.

Alternative words:

Day by day dear Lord, of thee three things I pray:
To trust thee more fully Leave things more holy,
To lean, to lean on, To lean on thee, To lean on thee
Securely day by day.

Music © 2009 Harry Hicks

74 Dear Christians

Martin Luther

Dear Christ-ians, one and all, re-joice, With ex-ul-ta-tion spring-ing, And
with u-ni-ted heart and voice And ho-ly rap-ture sing-ing, Pro-claim the won-ders
God has done, How His right arm the vict'-ry won. What price our ran-som cost Him!

2. Fast bound in Satan's chains I lay;
Death brooded darkly o'er me.
Sin was my torment night and day;
In sin my mother bore me.
But daily deeper still I fell;
My life became a living hell,
So firmly sin possessed me.

3. My own good works all came to naught,
No grace or merit gaining;
Free will against God's judgment fought,
Dead to all good remaining.
My fears increased till sheer despair
Left only death to be my share;
The pangs of hell I suffered.

4. But God had seen my wretched state
Before the world's foundation,
And mindful of His mercies great,
He planned for my salvation.
He turned to me a father's heart;
He did not choose the easy part
But gave His dearest treasure.

5. God said to His beloved Son:
"It's time to have compassion.
Then go, bright jewel of My crown,
And bring to all salvation.
From sin and sorrow set them free;
Slay bitter death for them that they
May live with You forever."

6. The Son obeyed His Father's will,
Was born of virgin mother;
And God's good pleasure to fulfill,
He came to be my brother.
His royal pow'r disguised He bore;
A servant's form, like mine, He wore
To lead the devil captive.

7. To me He said: "Stay close to Me,
I am your rock and castle.
Your ransom I Myself will be;
For you I strive and wrestle.
For I am yours, and you are Mine,
And where I am you may remain;
The foe shall not divide us.

8. "Though he will shed My precious blood,
Me of My life bereaving,
All this I suffer for your good;
Be steadfast and believing.
Life will from death the vict'ry win;
My innocence shall bear your sin,
And you are blest forever.

9. "Now to My Father I depart,
From earth to heav'n ascending,
And, heav'nly wisdom to impart,
The Holy Spirit sending;
In trouble He will comfort you
And teach you always to be true
And into truth shall guide you.

10. "What I on earth have done and taught,
Guide all your life and teaching;
So shall the kingdom's work be wrought
And honored in your preaching.
But watch lest foes with base alloy
The heav'nly treasure should destroy;
This final word I leave you."

75 Dear Jesus, ever at my side

F. W. Faber

Dear Je - sus, ev - er at my side, How lov - ing Thou must be___ To leave Thy home in Heav'n, to guide A lit - tle child like me.

2. Thy beautiful, Thy shining face,
   I see not, though so near,
The sweetness of thy soft, low voice
   I am too deaf to hear.

3. I cannot feel Thee touch my hand,
   With pressure light and mild,
To check with me, as my mother does
   Her erring little child.

4. But I have felt Thee in my thoughts,
   Fighting with sin for me,
And when my heart loves God, I know
   The sweetness comes from thee.

5. And when, dear Saviour, I kneel down,
   Morning and night to prayer,
Something there is within my heart
   That tells me Thou art there.

6. Yes, when I pray Thou prayest, too,
   Thy prayer is all for me,
But when I sleep, Thou sleepest not,
   But watchest patiently.

76   Depth of mercy

C. Wesley

Depth of mer-cy! can there be Mer-cy still re-served for me?

Can my God His wrath for-bear? Me, the chief of sin-ners. spare?

2. I have long withstood His grace,
Long provoked Him to His face,
Would not hearken to His calls,
Grieved him by a thousand falls.

3. Whence to me this waste of love?
Ask my Advocate above!
See the cause in Jesus' face,
Now before the Throne of grace.

4. Kindled His relentings are;
Me He now delights to spare;
Cries, 'How shall I give thee up?'
Lets the lifted thunder drop.

5. There for me the Saviour stands;
Shows His wounds, and spreads His hands!
God is love! I know, I feel;
Jesus weeps and loves me still!

6. Jesus, answer from above:
Is not all Thy nature love?
With Thou not the wrong forget?
Suffer me to kiss Thy feet?

7. If I rightly read Thy heart,
If Thou all compassion art,
Bow Thine ear, in mercy bow!
Pardon and accept me now.

8. Pity from Thine eyes let fall;
By a look my soul recall;
Now the stone to flesh convert,
Cast a look and break my heart.

9. Now incline me to repent;
Let me now my fall lament;
Now my foul revolt deplore;
Weep, believe, and sin no more.

77 Descend from heaven, immortal Dove

Isacc Watts

De-scend from heaven, im - mor-tal Dove, Stoop down and take us on thy wings,

And mount and bear us far — a - bove The reach of these in - fer-ior things.

2. Beyond, beyond this lower sky,
Up where eternal ages roll,
Where solid pleasure never die,
And fruits immortal fest the soul.

3. O for a sight, a pleasing sight
Of our almighty Father's throne!
There sits our Saviour crowned with light
Clothed in a body like our own.

4. Adoring saints around him stand,
And thrones, and powers before him fall;
And God shines gracious through the man,
And sheds sweet glories on them all.

5. A what amazing joys they feel
While to their golden harps they sing,
And sit on every heavenly hill,
And spread the triumphs of their King!

6. When shall the day, dear Lord, appear,
That I shall mount to dwell above,
And stand and bow amongst them there,
And view thy face, and sing, and love!

78   Do I believe

Do I be - lieve what Je - sus saith, And think the gos - pel true?

Lord, make me bold to own my faith, and prac-tise vir - tue too.

2. Suppress my shame, subdue my fear,
Arm me with heav'nly zeal,
That I may make thy pow'r appear,
And works of praise fulfill.

3. If men should see my virtue shine,
And spread my name abroad,
Thine is the pow'er, the praise is thine,
My Saviour and my God.

4. Thus when the saints in glory meet,
Their lips proclaim thy grace;
They cast their honours at thy feet,
And own their borrowed rays.

79   Emmanuel, the true expression

Brenda Gallant

Em - man - u - el, the true ex-pres-sion of a heav'n-ly Fath - er's love. In our hearts a deep im-pres-sion: His own pre-sence thus to prove. God with us, O won-drous sto - ry, stoop-ing low to earth He came; From the heights of heav'n - ly glo - ry to the depths of earth-ly shame.

2. Emmanuel - oh can you grasp it?
'tis a wonder rich and rare,
To your heart then firmly clasp it,
This great truth beyond compare.
God himself, so high and holy,
In a manger bed to lie,
Came as babe, so weak and lowly,
then, as man, to bleed and die.

3. Emmanuel - it is the reason
for this time of joy and mirth,
And to us the Christmas season
Is to celebrate the birth.
Of the One who loves us dearly
Even though we're marred by sin,
He came down to show us clearly
That our love he fain would win.

4. Emmanuel - embrace the glory
Of his wondrous love to man.
As you hear again his story,
Praise Him for redemption's plan.
Give your heart, your life an off'ring
With thanksgiving glad and true,
To the One who now is proff'ring
Everlasting life to you.

5. Emmanuel - he came to save us
By his earthly life and death.
But he'll come again to raise us,
This is what the scripture saith;
He will come again in glory,
In the twinkling of an eye,
To complete the gospel story
That will never, never die.

80 Enthroned is Jesus now

En-throned is Je-sus now__ up-on his heav'n-ly seat;__ The king-ly crown is on his brow, the saints are at his feet.

Chorus

There__ with the glo-ri-fied, safe__ by our Sav-iour's side, we__ shall be sat-tis-fied, by and by! There__ with the glo-ri-fied, safe__ by the Sav-iour's side, we__ shall be sa-tis-fied, by and by!

2. In shining white they stand,
   A great and countless throng;
   Palmy sceptre in each hand,
   On ev'ry lip a song.
   There with the glorified, safe by our Saviour's side,
   We shall be glorified, by and by,
   There with the glorified, safe by our Saviour's side,
   We shall be glorified, by and by!

3. They sing the Lamb of God,
   Once slain for each of them;
   The Lamb through whose atoning blood
   Each wears his diadem.
   There with the glorified, safe by our Saviour's side,
   We shall be glorified, by and by,
   There with the glorified, safe by our Saviour's side,
   We shall be glorified, by and by!

4. Thy grace, O Holy Ghost,
   Thy blessed help supply,
   That we may join the radiant host,
   Triumphant in the sky!
   There with the glorified, safe by our Saviour's side,
   We shall be glorified, by and by,
   There with the glorified, safe by our Saviour's side,
   We shall be glorified, by and by!

81   Eye has not seen, nor ear has heard

Timothy Dudley-Smith

Eye has not seen, nor ear has heard, nor can the mind con-ceive what God has pledged with-in his word for those he bids believe.

2. The secret things of God above
   To faith by wisdom shown,
   The sacred mysteries of love,
   His Spirit now makes known.

3. Such love fulfilled its holiest part
   when Christ was crucified:
   the flower of love's eternal heart,
   the Lord of Glory died.

4. He died to do the Father's will,
   He rose by love's design,
   He ever lives, immortal still,
   the Prince of life divine.

5. His immemorial purpose done,
   what blessings yet unfold!
   Shall he who gave his only Son
   Another gift withhold?

6. All things are ours! Our life restored
   is one with Christ above:
   and ours, for ever with the Lord,
   the hidden depths of love.

82   Faith looks to Jesus

Geo. Goodman

Faith looks to Je - sus cru - ci - fied and ri - sen from the dead.

Faith rests up-on his pro - mi - ses, be - lie - ving - all He said.

Faith makes con-fes - sion of His Name, hold forth His faith - ful Word.

Faith takes her cross and fol - lows Him, her Sav - iour and her Lord.

2. Faith sees beyond this passing world, with open vision keen.
Faith all endures as seeing Him, beloved, but yet unseen.
Faith suffers with her Lord below to reign with Him above.
Faith ever seeks to walk in light and ever works by love.

3. Faith loves to be obedient, for she hears her Master's voice.
Faith walks in separation, and a pilgrim is by choice.
Faith hastens to His coming - oh, the rapture and the bliss!
Faith knows she will be like Him when she sees Him as He is.

4. O grant us, Lord, like precious faith, with them that went before,
That we may keep our garments white until the conflict's o'er;
Nor lose our crown, nor faint until the race is fully run,
When we at last shall see Thy face and hear Thee say, "Well done!"

Music © 2015 Harry Hicks

83   Father, let me dedicate

L. Tuttiett

Fath-er let me de-di-cate All this year to Thee, In what-ev-er world-ly state Thou wilt have me be: Not from sor-row, pain, or care, Free-dom dare I claim; This a-lone shall be my prayer, "Glo-ri-fy Thy Name."

2. Can a child presume to choose
Where or how to live?
Can a Father's love refuse
All the best to give?
More Thou givest every day
Than the best can claim,
Nor witholdest aught that may
Glorify Thy Name.

3. If in mercy Thou wilt spare
Joys that yet are mine;
If on life, serene and fair,
Brighter rays may shine:
Let my glad heart, while it sings,
Thee in all proclaim,
And, whate'er the future brings
"Glorify Thy Name."

4. If Thou callest to the cross,
And its shadow come,
Turning all my gain to loss,
Shrouding heart and home;
Let me think how Thy dear Son
To His glory came,
And in deepest woe pray on,
"Glorify Thy Name."

84   Fear not the future

Fear not the fu-ture, it is in God's hands, Go where he bids you, fol-low His com-mands Strength will be giv-en what - ev-er life de-mands; Go forth, go forth, go forth.

2. God's way is perfect, make it your delight,
For you are precious in His holy sight,
Follow His leading, walking in His light,
Go forth, go forth, go forth.

3. Lean on His promise, take it to your heart,
He will be with you now you've made a start,
Just trust Him fully, He will do His part,
Believe, believe, believe.

4. Go then with blessings ringing in your ears,
His promises alleviate your fears,
Take with you love and our continuing prayers,
Goodbye, goodbye, goodbye.

85   Fear not! God is thy shield

E.G.Taylor.

Fear not! God is thy shield, and He thy great re - ward; His
might has won the field:____ thy strength is in the Lord. Fear
not! 'tis God's own voice that speaks to thee this word: lift
up your head, re - joice____ in Je - sus Christ thy Lord!

2. Fear not! for God has heard   the cry of thy distress;
The water of His word   thy fainting soul shall bless.
Fear not! 'tis God's own voice   that speaks to thee this word;
Lift up you head, rejoice   in Jesus Christ thy Lord!

3. Fear not! be not dismayed!   He evermore will be
With thee, to give His aid,   and He with strengthen thee.
Fear not! 'tis God's own voice   that speaks to thee this word;
Lift up you head, rejoice   in Jesus Christ thy Lord!

4. Fear not! ye little flock;   your Saviour soon will come,
The glory to unlock   and bring you to His home!
Fear not! 'tis God's own voice   that speaks to thee this word;
Lift up you head, rejoice   in Jesus Christ thy Lord!

Music © 2012 Harry Hicks

86   Finished

Brenda Gallant

vv1-8

"Fin-ished," thought Ju-das, "The deed has been done, I have be-trayed Him, God's dear-ly loved Son. Fin-ished in-deed, the price I've been paid, But, is it Him, or my-self I've be-trayed?"

vv9-11

"Fin-ished," said Je-sus, "Now go forth and tell All the dis-ci-ples, and Pe-ter as well." Fin-ished in-deed, the price has been paid. All the world's sin on the Lamb has been laid.

2. "Finished," wept Peter,
"My Lord I've denied,
Now He will shortly
Be crucified.
Finished indeed,
My poor heart is broken,
He is denied by words I have spoken."

3. Finished, feared the ten,
And all ran away,
They loved Him dearly,
But just could not stay.
Finished indeed, their hopes were all gone,
Hadn't He really been God's only Son?

4. "Finished," said Pilate,
And called for a bowl,
"I'll now wash my hands
And cleanse my own soul;.
Finished indeed, now take him away,
You crucify Him, and have your own way."

5. "Finished," mused soldiers,
And packed up their gear,
But who is that Man
Suspended up there?
Finished indeed, His ministry o'er,
No-one to grieve but the sick and the poor.

6. "Finished," mourned Mary,
And stood 'neath the cross,
Her heart was broken,
By such a great loss.
Finished indeed, her spirit was torn,
Although 'twas for this her Son had been born.

7. "Finished," cried Jesus,
"My work is complete,
The law's just demands
My death will now meet.
Finished indeed, my work is all done,
My dying ensures the victory won."

8. "Finished," sobbed Mary,
"The sepulcre's bare,
Where have they laid Him,
Oh, tell me please, where?"
Finished indeed, no more in the tomb,
His voice is speaking to banish your gloom.

(V9 in music)

10. Finished, yes finished
the work has been done.
Praise him forever,
God's well beloved Son.
Finished indeed, salvation is free,
So lovingly wrought, for you and for me.

11. Finished oh praise Him,
The blood has been shed,
Give thanks to the one
With the thorn-scarred head.
Finished indeed, yet only begun,
Let all the world praise and honour the Son.

87   Firm as the earth

Isaac Watts

Firm as the earth thy gos-pel stands, My Lord, my hope, my trust; If

I am found in Je - sus' hands, My soul can-not be lost.

2. His honour is engaged to save
The meanest of his sheep,
All that his heavenly Father gave
His hands securely keep.

3. Nor death, nor hell shall e'er remove
His favourites from his breast;
In the dear bosom of his love
They must for ever rest.

88 For Mary

J.R.Peacey

For Ma-ry, Mo-ther of our Lord, God's ho-ly name be praised, who first the Son of God a-dored, as on her child she gazed.

2. Brave, holy Virgin, she believed,
    though hard the task assigned,
and by the Holy Ghost conceived
    the Saviour of mankind.

3. The busy world had got no space
    or time for God on earth;
a cattle manger was the place
    where Mary gave him birth.

4. She gave her body as God's shrine,
    her heart to piercing pain;
she knew the cost of love divine,
    when Jesus Christ was slain.

5. Dear Mary, from your lowliness
    and home in Galilee
there comes a joy and holiness
    to every family.

6. Hail, Mary, you are full of grace,
    above all women blest;
and blest your Son, whom your embrace
    in birth and death confessed.

89 For those disciples

Brenda Gallant

For those di-sci-ples long a - go, Death seemed the bit - ter end,

For they in wear - i - ness and woe Had lost their dear-est friend.

2. They had not understood His word
That he would rise again,
And when that dreadful deed occurred
It left them numb with pain.

3. But God in His Almightiness,
Did vindicate His Son,
And from the darkness of distress
Revealed a vict'ry won.

4. When Mary, blinded by her tears
And bowed with sorrow low
Gave voice to her consuming fears,
The Lord she did not know.

5. But He, in triumph, spoke her name,
Her sorrow quickly fled,
She went to spread abroad His fame:
Christ risen from the dead!

6. "I go a-fishing," Peter said,
And others joined him too.
Their lives were empty, purpose dead,
They knew not what to do.

7. But Jesus stood upon the shore,
Inviting them to dine,
Then, soothing Peter's heart so sore,
Revealed His great design.

8. A recommission he received,
And then the Spirit's dower,
Now all who have in Christ believed,
Can know that selfsame power.

90   From the night of ages waking

Timothy Dudley-Smith

From the night of a - ges wa-king mor - ning comes with heart and mind,

day of grace in splen-dour break-ing, mists and shad-ows fall be-hind;

in the sha-dows of his glo - ry Christ the Light of life has shined.

2. Christ in light immortal dwelling,
Word by whom the worlds were made;
Light of lights, our dark dispelling,
Lord of lords in light arrayed.
In the brightness of his glory
See the Father's love displayed.

3. Risen Lord in radiance splendid,
Christ has conquered Satan's sway;
Sin and shame and sorrow ended,
Powers of darkness flee away;
In the brightness of his glory
Walk as children of the day.

4. Light to lighten every nation,
Shining forth from shore to shore,
Christ who won the world's salvation
Now let all the earth adore;
In the brightness of his glory
Light of life for evermore.

Music © 2012 Harry Hicks   Words: 'From the night of ages waking' by Timothy Dudley-Smith (b. 1926)
© Timothy Dudley-Smith in Europe and Africa. © Hope Publishing Company in the United States of America
and the rest of the world. Reproduced by permission of Oxford University Press. All rights reserved.

91   From thee, my God

Isaac Watts

From thee, my God, my joys shall rise, and run e - ter - nal rounds, Be - yond the lim - its of the skies and all cre - a - ted bounds

2. The holy triumphs of my soul
Shall death itself out-brave,
Leave dull mortality behind,
And fly beyond the grave.

3. There, where my blessed Jesus reigns
In heaven's unmeasured space,
I'll spend a long eternity
In pleasure and in praise.

4. Millions of years my wondering eyes
Shall o'er the beauties rove,
And endless ages I'll adore
The glories of thy love.

5. Sweet Jesus, every smile of thine
Shall fresh endearments bring,
And thousand tastes of new delight
From all thy graces spring.

6. Haste, my beloved, fetch my soul
Up to thy blessed abode,
Fly, for my spirit longs to see
My Saviour and my God.

Music © 2013 Harry Hicks

92 Full of Glory (longer version)

Frederick W. Faber

Full of glo-ry, full of won-ders, full of glo-ry, full of won-ders, Ma-jes-ty Di-vine, Ma-jes-ty Di-vine, Ma-jes-ty Di-vine, Ma-jes-ty Di - vine, Ma-jes-ty Di-vine.

'Mid Thine ev - er - last-ing thun-ders How Thy light-nings shine! Shore-less O-cean! Who shall sound Thee? Thine own'e - ter - ni - ty is round Thee, Ma - jes - ty Div - vine, Ma - jes - ty Di - vine.

2. Timeless, spaceless, single, lonely,
Timeless, spaceless, single, lonely,
Yet sublimely Three, Yet sublimely Three,
Yet sublimely Three, Yet sublimely Three,
Yet sublimely Three.
Thou art grandly, always, only
God in Unity!
Lone in grandeur, lone in glory,
Who shall tell thy wonderous story,
Awful Trinity, Awful Trinity?

3.Splendours upon splendours beaming
Splendours upon splendours beaming
Change and intertwine! Change and intertwine!
Change and intertwine! Change and intertwine!
Change and intertwine!
Glories over glories streaming
All translucent shine!
Blessings, praises, adorations
Greet Thee from the trembling nations
Majesty Divine, Majesty Divine!

Music © 2016 Harry Hicks

93   Full of Glory (shorter version)

Frederick William Faber

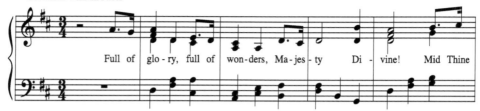

Full of glo-ry, full of won-ders, Ma-jes-ty Di - vine! Mid Thine

ev - er-last-ing thin-ders How Thy light-nings shine!___ Shore-less O-cean, who shall

sound Thee? Thine.own e - ter-ni - ty is round Thee, Ma - jes-ty-Di - vine!

2. Timeless, spaceless, single, lonely,
   Yet sublimely Three,
Thou art grandly, always, only
   God in Unity!
Lone in grandeur, lone in glory,
Who shall tell Thy wondrous story,
   Awful Trinity?

3. Speechlessly, without beginning,
   Sun that never rose!
Vast, adorable, and winning,
   Day that hath no close!
Bliss from Thine own glory tasting,
Everliving, everlasting,
   Life that ever grows!

4. Thine own Self for ever filling
   With self-kindled flame,
In Thyself Thou art distilling
   Unctions without name!
Without worshipping of creatures
Without veiling of Thy features,
   God always the same!

5. 'Mid Thine uncreated morning,
   Like a trembling star
I behold creation's dawning
   Glimmering from afar;
Nothing giving, nothing taking,
Nothing changing, nothing breaking,
   Waiting at time's bar!

6. I with life and love diurnal
   See myself in Thee,
All embalmed in love eternal,
   Floating in Thy sea:
'Mid Thine uncreated whiteness
I behold Thy glory's brightness
   Feed itself on me.

7. Splendours upon splendours beaming
   Change and intertwine;
Glories over glories streaming
   All translucent shine!
Blessings, praises adorations
Greet Thee from the trembling nations
   Majesty Divine!

94 Fully trusting

J.C.Morgan

All my doubts I give to Je - sus! I've his grac - ious pro-mise heard: I "shall
ne - ver be con - found-ed:" I am trust - ing in that word.

Chorus

I am trust-ing, ful-ly trust-ing, sweet-ly
trust - ing in His word, I am trust - ing, ful-ly trust-ing, sweet-ly trust - ing in His word.

2. All my sins I lay on Jesus! He doth wash me in His blood:
He will keep me pure and holy, He will bring me home to God.
I am trusting, fully trusting, Sweetly trusting in His word,
I am trusting, fully trusting, Sweetly trusting in His word.

3. All my fears I give to Jesus! Rests my weary soul on Him;
Though my way be hid in darkness, Never can His light grow dim.
I am trusting, fully trusting, Sweetly trusting in His word,
I am trusting, fully trusting, Sweetly trusting in His word.

4. All my joys I give to Jesus! He is all I want of bliss:
He of all the worlds is master, He has all I need in this.
I am trusting, fully trusting, Sweetly trusting in His word,
I am trusting, fully trusting, Sweetly trusting in His word.

5. All I am I give to Jesus! All my body all my soul,
All I have, and all I hope for, While eternal ages roll.
I am trusting, fully trusting, Sweetly trusting in His word,
I am trusting, fully trusting, Sweetly trusting in His word.

95   Give us the wings

Isaac Watts

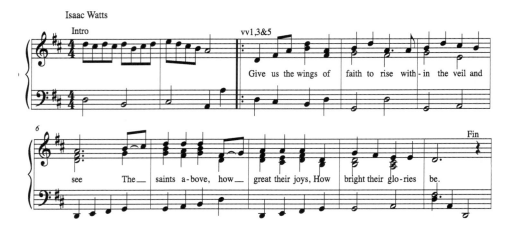

Give us the wings of faith to rise with-in the veil and
see The__ saints a-bove, how__ great their joys, How bright their glo-ries be.

Once they were mourn-ing here be-low,__ Their couch was wet with tears, They wrestled hard, as__

we do now With sins and doubts and fears. Twiddly bit after vv2&4

1. Give us the wings of faith to rise   within the veil and see
The saints above, how great their joys,   How bright their glories be.

2. Once they were mourning here below,   Their couch was wet with tears,
They wrestled hard, as we do now   With sins and doubts and fears.

3. We ask them whence their vict'ry came,   they with united breath
ascribe the conquest to the Lamb,   Their triumph to His death.

4. They marked the footsteps that He trod,   His zeal inspired their breast,
And foll'wing their incarnate God,   They reached their promised rest.

5. Our glorious leader claims our praise   For His own pattern giv'n,
While the great cloud of witnesses   Show the same path to heav'n.

96　Gloria, gloria

Barbara Rusbridge

2. Jesus, blessed Lamb of God,
to you our voice we raise.
You take away our sins, O Lord,
Receive our song of praise! Sing:
Gloria, Gloria in excelsis, in excelsis.
Gloria, Gloria in excelsis Deo.

3. Holy Lord in highest heaven,
how our hearts rejoice
in God the Father, Son and Spirit,
so with loudest voice sing:
Gloria, Gloria in excelsis, in excelsis.
Gloria, Gloria in excelsis Deo.

97 Glorious Saviour

C. Wesley

Glor-ious Sav-iour of my soul, I lift it up to thee;
Thou hast made the sin-ner whole, Hast set the cap-tive free! Thou my debt of
death hast paid; Thou hast raised me from my fall; Thou hast full a-
tone-ment made; My Sav-iour died for all.

2. What could my Redeemer move
To leave his Father's breast?
Pity drew him from above,
And would not let him rest;
Swift to succour sinking man,
Sinking into endless woe,
Jesus to our rescue ran,
And God appeared below.

3. God, in this dark vale of tears,
A man of grief was seen;
Here for three and thirty years
He dwelt with sinful men.
Did they know the Deity?
Did they own him, who he was?
See the Friend of Sinners, see!
He hangs on yonder cross!

4. Yet thy wrath I cannot fear,
Thou gentle, bleeding Lamb!
By thy judgement I am clear,
Healed by thy stripes I am;
Thou for me a curse was made,
That I might in thee blest;
Thou hast my full ransom paid,
And in thy wounds I rest.

Music © 2016 Harry Hicks

98   Glory be to God on high (1st tune)

Charles Wesley

Glo-ry be to God on high, God in whom we live and die,
God, who guides us by his love, Takes us to his throne a-bove!
An-gels that sur-round his throne Sing the won-ders he hath done,
Shout, while we on earth re-ply, Glo-ry be to God on high!

2. God of everlasting grace,
Worthy thou of endless praise,
Thou hast all thy blessings shed
On the living and the dead:
Thou wast here their sure defence,
Thou hast borne their spirits hence,
Worthy thou of endless praise,
God of everlasting grace.

3. Thanks be all ascribed to thee,
Blessing, power and majesty.
Thee, by whose almighty name
They their latest fear o'ercame;
Thou the victory hast won,
Saved them by thy grace alone,
Caught them up thy face to see,
Thanks be all ascribed to thee!

4. Happy in thy glorious love,
We shall from the vale remove,
Glad partakers of our hope,
We shall soon be taken up;
Meet again our heavenly friends,
Blest with bliss that never ends,
Joined to all thy hosts above,
Happy in thy glorious love!

98   Glory be to God on high (2nd tune)

Charles Wesley

Glo ry be to God on high, God in whom we live and die,
God, who guides us by his love, Takes us to his throne a bove!
An gels that sur round his throne Sing the won ders he has done,
Shout, while we on earth re ply, Glo ry be to God on high!

2. God of everlasting grace,
Worthy thou of endless praise,
Thou hast all thy blessings shed
On the living and the dead:
Thou wast here their sure defence,
Thou hast borne their spirits hence,
Worthy thou of endless praise,
God of everlasting grace.

3. Thanks be all ascribed to thee,
Blessing, power and majesty.
Thee, by whose almighty name
They their latest fear o'ercame;
Thou the victory hast won,
Saved them by thy grace alone,
Caught them up thy face to see,
Thanks be all ascribed to thee!

4. Happy in thy glorious love,
We shall from the vale remove,
Glad partakers of our hope,
We shall soon be taken up;
Meet again our heavenly friends,
Blest with bliss that never ends,
Joined to all thy hosts above,
Happy in thy glorious love!

Music © 2015 Harry Hicks

99   Glory be to God on high

C. Wesley

Glo-ry be to God on high, God whose glo-ry fills the sky;

Peace on earth to man for-giv'n Man, the well - be - loved of heav'n

2. Sovereign Father, Heavenly King!
Thee we now presume to sing:
Glad, thine attributes confess,
Glorious all, and numberless.

3. Hail, by all thy works adored,
Hail, the everlasting Lord!
Thee with thankful hearts we prove
God of power, and God of love.

4. Christ our Lord and God we own,
Christ, the Father's only Son,
Lamb of God, for sinners slain,
Saviour of offending man.

5. Bow thine ear, in mercy bow,
Hear, the world's atonement, Thou!
Jesus, in thy name we pray,
Take, O take our sins away!

6. Powerful Advocate with God,
Justify is by thy blood;
Bow thine ear, in mercy bow,
Hear, the world's Atonement, Thou!

7. Hear, for thou, O Christ, alone
Art with thy great Father, one;
One the Holy Ghost with thee;
One supreme, eternal Three.

100 Glory be to Jesus

Isaac Watts

Glo - ry _ be to Je - sus, Who - in - bit - ter - pains

Poured - for - me the life blood From His sa - cred veins.

2. Grace and life eternal
In that blood I find;
Blest be His compassion,
Infinitely kind!

3. Blest through endless ages
Be the precious stream,
Which from endless torments
Did the world redeem.

4. Abel's blood for vengeance
Pleaded to the skies;
But the blood of Jesus
For our pardon cries.

5. Oft as earth exulting
Wafts its praise on high,
Angel-hosts rejoicing
Make their glad reply.

6. Lift ye then your voices;
Swell the mighty flood;
Louder still and louder
Praise the precious blood.

101 Glory in highest heaven

Charles Wesley

Glo - ry in high - est hea - ven to our ex - al - ted Sa -
viour, who left be-hind for all man-kind these to-kens of his fa - vour: his
bleed - ing love and mer - cy, his all - re - dee - ming pas - sion; who
here dis - plays, and gives the grace which gives us our sal - va - tion.

2. Louder than gathered waters,
or bursting peals of thunder,
we lift our voice
and speak our joys,
and shout our loving wonder.
Shout, all our elder brethren,
while we record the story
of him that came
and suffered shame,
to carry us to glory.

3. Angels in fixed amazement
around our altars hover,
with eager gaze
adore the grace
or our eternal Lover:
himself and all his fulness
who gives to the believer;
and by this bread
whoe'er are fed
shall live with God for ever.

Music © 2015 Harry Hicks

102   Glory, glory everlasting

T. Kelly

Glo - ry, glo ry e - ver - last - ing Be to Him who bore the cross,

Who re - deemed our souls by tast - ing Death, the death de - served by us!

Spread His glo - ry, spread His glo - ry Who re - deemed His peo - ple thus.

Spread His glo - ry, spread His glo - ry Who re - deemed His peo - ple thus.

2. His is love, 'tis love unbounded,
   Withour measure, without end;
   Human thought is here confounded,
   'Tis too great to comprehend.
   Praise the Saviour, praise the Saviour,
   Magnify the sinner's Friend.
   Praise the Saviour, praise the Saviour,
   Magnify the sinner's Friend.

3. While we hear the wondrous story
   Of the Saviour's cross and shame,
   Sing we "Everlasting glory
   Be to God and to the Lamb."
   Hallelujah! Hallelujah!
   Give ye glory to His Name.
   Hallelujah! Hallelujah!
   Give ye glory to His Name.

103   Go forth

C. J. Meyrick

"Go forth, make peo-ple mine; Bap-tise them in my name; that fueled with power of love di-vine, their hearts may flame." The Christ sings out! Dis-ci-ples all, we hear his call: "Pro-claim my love."

2. "Go forth - all people need
My Father's tender care,
It shows in ev'ry loving deed
that's done on earth."
As Christ sings out -
disciples all, we hear his call:
"Live out my love."

3. "Bring hope - the world's lost sight:
its path has gone astray,
In cold dark caves of fear bring light
to show the way."
So Christ sings out!
Disciples all, we hear his call:
"Ignite my love."

4. "Go forth - let people feel
round them my arms of love;
forgive and bless, embrace and heal -
the marks of God."
Still Christ sings out!
Disciples all, we hear his call:
"Become my love."

Originally written to the tune 'Darwall's 148th.'

Words © 2004 C. J. Meyrick
Music © 2016 Harry Hicks

104 Go into all the world

Albert Bayly

'Go in-to all the world': clear was the Mas-ter's call;
send-ing his men to give good news of God to all. Then
forth they went to preach his Word; land af - ter land their ti-dings heard.

2. Age after age the Lord
summoned his Church anew;
age after age his realm
greater and wider grew:
till now a myriad tongues confess
his glory, and his Kingdom bless.

3. Rings out his call today,
rousing his Church again;
sends her to tell the world
he comes to save and reign:
man's crowded life he shall control,
and with his Spirit fill the whole.

4. Christ shall mankind unite,
love his design fulfil,
science his truth declare,
power shall obey his will,
his might to save, his right to claim
this great world's life we now proclaim.

Music © 2012 Harry Hicks   Words: 'Go into all the world' by Albert Bayly (1901-84)
© 1988 Oxford University Press. Reproduced by permission. All rights reserved.

105   God be with you

God be with you till we meet a-gain! By His coun-sels guide, up-hold you,
with his sheep se-cure-ly fold you, God be with you till we meet a-gain! Till we

Chorus

meet! (Till we meet!) Till we meet! (Till we meet!) Till we meet at Je-sus' feet! Till we
meet! (Till we meet!) Till we meet! (Till we meet!) God be with you till we meet a-gain!

2. God be with you till we meet again!
'Neath His wings securely hide you,
Daily manna still provide you:
God be with you till we meet again!
Till we meet! Till we meet!
Till we meet at Jesus' feet!
Till we meet! Till we meet!
God be with you till we meet again!

3. God be with you till we meet again!
When life's perils thick confound you,
Put His loving arms around you;
God be with you till we meet again!
Till we meet! Till we meet!
Till we meet at Jesus' feet!
Till we meet! Till we meet!
God be with you till we meet again!

4. God be with you till we meet again!
Keep love's banner floating o'er you,
Smite death's threatening wave before you;
God be with you till we meet again!
Till we meet! Till we meet!
Till we meet at Jesus' feet!
Till we meet! Till we meet!
God be with you till we meet again!

106   God in his wisdom

Timothy Dudley-Smith

God in his wis dom, for our learn ing gave his in spired and
ho ly word: prom ise of Christ, for our dis cern ing,
by which our souls are moved and stirred, find ing our hearts with
in us burn ing when, as of old, his voice is heard.

2. Symbol and story, song and saying,
life-bearing truths for heart and mind,
God in his sovereign grace displaying
  Tenderest care for humankind.
Jesus our Lord this love portraying,
open our eyes to seek and find.

3. Come then with prayer and contemplation,
see how in Scripture Christ is known;
wonder anew at such salvation
here in these sacred pages shown;
lift every heart in adoration,
children of God by grace alone!

107　God loved the world

Brenda Gallant

God loved the world but sore-ly grieved, That men his love __ had spurned, Their
hearts by __ sin had been de-ceived, To their __ own ways __ they turned.

2. The Son of God came down to earth,
   He left His throne above,
   He came to give us second birth,
   And show His Father's love.

3. He came to seek and save the lost,
   To give them inward peace,
   But oh, with what an awful cost,
   He paid for their release!

4. This heavenly peace is free to all
   Who on His name believe.
   Oh, have you heard the Saviour's call?
   Will you His peace receive?

5. He'll give you joy from day to day,
   His presence you will know,
   No matter what may come your way,
   The Lord will see you through.

6. No fear in life, no fear in death,
   With Christ your dearest friend,
   For He who grants you daily breath,
   Is with you to the end.

7. Then praise Him for His love and grace,
   Rest sweetly in His care,
   Until, one day, you see His face,
   Eternity to share.

108   God of the seas

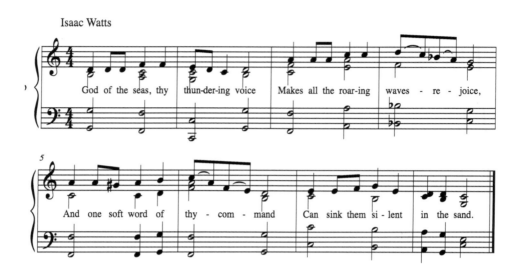

Isaac Watts

God of the seas, thy thun-der-ing voice Makes all the roar-ing waves - re - joice,

And one soft word of thy - com - mand Can sink them si - lent in the sand.

2. If but a Moses wave thy rod,
the sea divides, and owns its God;
The stormy floods their Maker knew,
And let his chosen armies through.

3. The scaly flocks amidst the sea,
To thee, their Lord, a tribute pay;
The meanest fish that swims the flood
Leaps up, and means a praise to God.

4. The larger monsters of the deep,
On thy command attendance keep,
By thy permission sport and play,
And cleave along their foaming way.

5. If God his voice of tempest rears,
Leviathan lies still and fears,
Anon he lifts his nostril high,
And spouts the ocean to the sky.

6. How is thy glorious power adored,
Amidst those watery nations, Lord!
Yet the bold men that trace the seas,
Bold men, refuse their master's praise.

7. What scenes of miracle they see,
And never turn a song to thee!
While on the flood they safely ride,
They curse the hand that smooths the tide.

8. Anon they plunge in watery graves,
And some drink death among the waves;
Yet the surviving crews blaspheme,
Nor own the God that rescued them.

9. O for some signal of thine hand!
Shake all the seas, Lord, shake the land,
Great Judge, descend, lest men deny
That there's a God that rules the sky.

109   God of the star-fields

Albert Bayly

God of the star-fields, sown with light's splen-dour; thy Word a -

far wields in - fi - nite sway. Yet in a sta - ble,

born of a vir-gin, in-fant in man-ger, thy great-ness lay.

2. Seraphs before him
cried 'Holy, holy';
swift to adore him,
serving his will,
now in a manger,
cradled with cattle,
only poor shepherds
worship him still.

3. But now, behold them!
Magi come riding,
wisdom has told them
here they will find
King of the nations,
Lord of all creatures,
ruler and Saviour,
hope of mankind.

4. Hell's might defying,
see him go fearless
to his cross, dying,
love's sacrifice.
then to his rising,
sin and death conquered,
for our redeption
costliest price.

5. Praise and devotion
bring him, O peoples!
Sky, earth and ocean
Hail him as Lord.
For above all names,
His, the most worthy,
By all creation
Shall be adored.

110 God shows His love

Brenda Gallant

God shows His love and glory In ev'ry thing we see, The oft re-pea-ted sto-ry In ev'ry flower and tree. The gran-deur of the moun-tains, The splen-dour of the lake, The spark-ling wa-ter foun-tains Re-veal Him for our sake.

2. God shows himself unwilling
That even one be lost,
The whole creation filling
And with His seal embossed.
Thus He revealed the mystery
Of creatorial power,
And spoke, throughout all history
Until this very hour.

3. But God again, has spoken
Through His beloved Son,
That those whom sin has broken
From Satan's power be won.
This perfect revelation
Is ours to recognise,
Accept the free salvation
And press toward the skies.

4. Oh, have you heard Him speaking
Through Jesus Christ, the Lord,
For He is ever seeking
Those who will heed His word.
He gives the invitation;
"Come unto me, and rest."
Through trial and tribulation,
In Him you will be blest.

Music © 2013 Harry Hicks
Words © 2013 Brenda Gallant

111 God speaks to us today

Colin Ferguson

God speaks to us to-day___ in all of his cre-

a - tion, the breath-less beau-ty of his word the good-ness in the

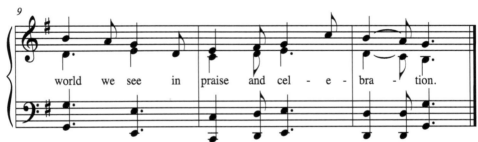

world we see in praise and cel - e - bra - tion.

2. God speaks to us today
in history and tradition.
The faith and hope our parents knew,
the ways of life they thought were true,
their dreams meet our ambition.

3. God speaks to us today
in daily conversation
with loving family and friends,
in fellowship with all he sends
we find our stimulation.

4. God speaks to us today
in our imagination;
deep in our hearts his quiet voice
speaks out and makes our souls rejoice
with holy inspiration.

5. God speaks to us today;
love has no apprehension,
however bright or bleak the day,
we travel on God's living way,
In eager expectation.

112 God who didst so dearly buy

C. Wesley

God who didst so dear-ly buy These wretch-ed souls of ours,
Help us Thee to glor-i-fy With all our ran-somed powers; Ours
they are not, ___ Lord, but thine; O let the ves-sels of Thy grace, Body, soul, and spi-rit join ___ In our Re-dee-mer's praise!

2. True and faithful witness, thee,
O Jesus, we recieve;
Fulness of the Deity,
In all they people live!
First-begotten from the dead,
Call forth thy living witnesses;
King of saints, thine empire spread
O'er all the ransomed race.

3. Grace, the fountain of all good,
ye happy saints, receive,
With the streams of peace o'erflowed,
With all that God can give;
He who is, and was, in peace
And grace, and plenitude of power,
Comes, your favoured souls to bless,
And never leave you more.

4. Let the Spirit before his throne,
Mysterious One and seven,
In his various gifts sent down,
Be to the churches given;
Let the pure seraphic joy
From Jesus Christ, the Just, descend;
Holiness without alloy,
And bliss that ne'er shall end.

113   God will take care of you

Frances R. Havergal

2. God will take care of you all through the night,
   Holding thy hand, He so tenderly keeps;
   Darkness to Him is the same as the light;
   He never slumbers and He never sleeps
    Under His care, Under His care,
   Safely I'm dwelling while under His care.

3. God will take care of you all through the year,
   Crowning each day with his kindness and love,
   Sending you blessings and shielding from fear,
   Leading you on to that bright home above.
    Under His care, Under His care,
   Safely I'm dwelling while under His care.

Music © 2016 Harry Hicks

114 God who made the earth

Sarah B. Rhodes

God, who made the earth,_____ The air, the sky, the sea, Who

gave the light its birth,_____ Car - eth for me.

2. God, who made the grass,
The flower, the fruit, the tree,
The day and night to pass,
Careth for me.

3. God, who made the sun,
The moon, the stars, is he
Who when life's clouds come on,
Careth for me.

4. God, who sent His Son
To die on Calvary,
He, if I lean on Him,
Will care for me.

5. When in heaven's bright land,
I all His loved ones see,
I'll sing with that blest band:
God cared for me.

115　God's promise

Brenda Gallant

God's pro-mise now has been ful-filled, His Son in flesh ap - pears, The One whose com - ing was fore-told Down through the pass-ing years.

2. He came to bruise the serpent's head,
To triumph over sin,
To bridge the gap twixt man and God,
And let the sinner in.

3. The angels plainly gave the news
"To you this day is born,"
But sadly some reject the love
So freely giv'n and shown.

4. "No room" was heard, when, long ago
God needed place to stay,
An outcast in a stable bare,
Rejected, in the hay.

5. But there were those who saw the light,
And eager to obey,
They went with haste and found the child,
And worshipped where he lay.

6. They left the stable full of joy
To spread the news abroad,
Their lives were changed because they knew
Christ, their incarnate Lord.

7. Beyond the cradle looms the cross,
It's message plain for all,
Atonement for mankind was planned
Before man's dreadful fall.

8. His birth, His life, His death were all
To save us from our sin,
Look unto Him and be ye saved;
Invite the Saviour in!

9. Without Him life is lived in vain,
He came to be the Way,
His second Advent soon will come,
Be ready for that day!

116   God's Spirit

Brenda Gallant

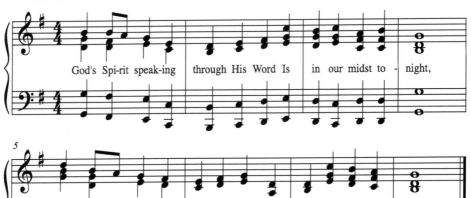

God's Spi-rit speak-ing through His Word Is in our midst to - night,

And when His voice is tru - ly heard Dark - ness and sin take flight.

2. He speaks because he loves you so,
    And craves you for His own,
Such love that made His heart o'erflow
    To make a cross His throne.

3. The Spirit takes the things of Christ
    And makes them real to you,
He shows you that His death sufficed,
    There's nothing more to do.

4. "If you have ears, then let them hear,"
    Our Lord said long ago,
His message sounds forever clear
    That you His peace might know.

5. Will you then heed His loving voice,
    Confess your sin and woe,
Wholeheartedly make Him your choice
    As to His cross you go.

6. Then onward into life anew,
    His Spirit in your heart,
Say "Lord, what Thou wilt have me do,
    And give me grace to start."

117   Grant me, Lord, Serenity

David Mowbray

Grant me, — Lord, Se - ren - i - ty, in - ward peace, tran - qui - li - ty to ac - cept the troubl-ing range of the - things I can-not change.

2. Grant me courage, Lord, to do
all the tasks you wish me to do:
courage to defy the strong,
to put right each glaring wrong.

3. Grant me wisdom to discern,
at each puzzling twist and turn,
when to halt, when to advance,
how to judge the difference.

4. Grand me powers beyond my own
which in Jesus Christ you've shown.
Life in all its fullness then
shall be mine, thank God. Amen.

Music © 2013 Harry Hicks
Words © David Mowbray

118   Great God, how infinite art thou!

Isaac Watts

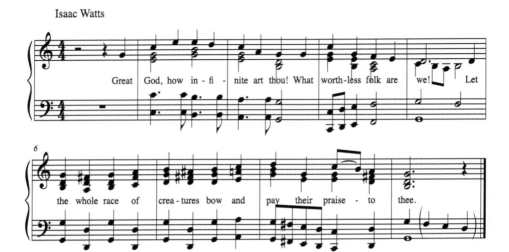

Great God, how in-fi-nite art thou! What worth-less folk are we! Let
the whole race of crea-tures bow and pay their praise - to thee.

2. Thy throne eternal ages stood,
Ere seas and stars were made;
Thou art the ever-living God
Were all the nations dead.

3. Nature and time quite naked lie
To thine immense survey,
From the formation of the sky
To the great burning day.

4. Eternity with all its years
Stands present in thy view;
To thee there's nothing old appears,
Great God, there's nothing new.

5. Our lives through various scenes are drawn,
and vexed with trifling cares;
While thine eternal thought moves on
Thine undisturbed affairs.

6. Great God, how infinite art thou!
What worthless worms are we!
Let the whole race of creatures bow
And pay their praise to thee.

Music © 2013 Harry Hicks

119 Hail, Father, Son and Holy Ghost

Charles Wesley

Hail, Fa-ther, Son, and | Ho - ly Ghost, | One God in Per-sons Three;

Of thee we make our | joy - ful boast, | Our songs we make - of thee.

2. Thou neither canst be felt or seen;
   Thou art a spirit pure;
Thou from eternity hast been,
   And always shalt endure.

3. Present alike in every place,
   Thy Godhead we adore;
Beyond the bounds of time and space
Thou dwell'st for evermore.

4. In wisdom infinite thou art,
   Thine eye doth all things see,
And every thought of every heart
   Is fully known to thee.

5. Whate'er thou wilt in earth below
   Thou dost in heaven above;
But chiefly we rejoice to know
   Th'Almighty God of love.

6. Mercy, with love, and endless grace
   O'er all thy works doth reign;
But mostly thou delight'st to bless
   Thy favourite creature, man.

7. Wherefore let every creature give
   To thee the praise designed;
But chiefly, Lord, the thanks receive,
   The hearts of all mankind.

120   Hallelujah, He is risen!

Hal - le - lu - jah, He is ris - en! Je - sus has gone up on high!

Burst the bars of death a - sund - er; Ang - els shout and men re - ply:

Chorus

He is ri - sen, He is ri - sen, liv - ing now, no more to die,

He is ri - sen, he is ri - sen, jus - ti - fied in him are we.

2. Hallelujah, He is risen! Our exalted head to be!
Sends the witness of the Spirit, that our advocate is He:
He is risen, He is risen, living now, no more to die,
He is risen, He is risen, justified in Him are we.

3. Hallelujah, He is risen! Death for aye has lost his sting,
Christ, Himself the resurrection, from the grave his own will bring:
He is risen, He is risen, living Lord and coming King,
He is risen, He is risen, living Lord and coming King.

Music © 2008 Harry Hicks.

121 Happy the heart

Isaac Watts

Hap-py the heart where — gra-ces - reign, Where___ love in - spires the - breast;

Love is the bright - est - of the - train, and streng-thens all - the rest

2. Knowledge, alas! 'tis all in vain,
And all in vain our fear,
Our stubborn sins will fight and reign
If love be absent there.

3. 'tis love that makes our cheerful feet
In swift obendience move,
The devils know and tremble too,
But Satan cannot love.

4. This is the grace that lives and sings
When faith and hope shall cease,
'tis this shall strike our joyful strings
In the sweet realms of bliss.

5. Before we quite forsake our clay,
Or leave this dark abode,
The wings of love bear us away
To see our smiling God.

Music © 2014 Harry Hicks

122 Hark! The voice of love and mercy

J. Evans

Hark! the voice of love and mer - cy Sound a - loud from Cal - va - ry;

See! it rends the rocks a - sun - der, Shakes the earth and veils the sky.

"It is fin - ished" "It is fin - ished!" Hear the dy - ing Sav - iour cry!

2. "It is finished!" oh what pleasure
Do the wondrous words afford!
Heavenly blessing without measure
Flow to us from Christ the Lord.
"It is finished!"
"It is finished!"
Saints the dying words record.

3. Finished all the types and shadows
Of the ceremonial law;
Finished all that God has promised;
Death and hell no more shall awe.
"It is finished!"
"It is finished!"
Saints from hence your comfort draw.

4. Tune your harps anew, ye seraphs;
Join to sing the pleasing theme;
All on earth and all in heaven,
Join to praise Immanuel's Name.
Hallelujah!
Hallelujah!
Glory to the bleeding Lamb!

123 Hark! what mean these holy voices

J. Cawood

Hark! what mean these ho - ly voi - ces, Sweet-ly sound-ing through the skies?

Lo! th'an-gel - ic host re - joi - ces, Heav'n-ly hal - le - lu - jahs rise.

Lis - ten to the won-drous sto - ry, Which they chant in hymns of joy!

Glo - ry in the high - est, glo - ry; Glo - ry be to God most high!

2. Peace on earth, goodwill from heaven,
Reaching far as man is found -
Souls redeemed, and sins forgiven;
Loud our golden harps shall sound.
Christ is born, the great Annointed;
Heaven and earth His praises sing;
Glad recieve your God appointed
For your Prophet, Priest and King.

3. Hasten, mortals, to adore Him;
Learn His name and taste His joy;
Till in heaven ye sing before Him,
Glory be to God Most High!
Let us learn the wondrous story
Of our great Redeemer's birth;
Spread the brightness of His glory,
Till it cover all the earth.

124 Have you love in your heart

Brenda Gallant

Have you love in your heart That will ne-ver de-part, No mat-ter how tes-ted and tried, Is the Lord all in all, Have you heard His love call, "For you, help-less sin-ner I died." He gave His love Sa-tan's fet-ters to move, And now He is liv-ing His re-demp-tion to prove.

2. Have you joy in your heart
That will never depart
No matter what sorrows sweep o'er,
Only His joy will stay
When your sky seems all grey
And earth's trifles attract you no more.
He is your joy
And your life will employ
To show forth His praises
And the tempter destroy.

3. Have you peace in your heart
That will never depart
No matter what trials may come,
Is the Lord in control
And is heaven your goal,
That blessed, eternal, bright home.
He is your peace,
He can give you release,
His arm will support you,
And His love never cease.

125   He gave his life

Christopher Porteous

He gave his life in self-less love, for sinners once he came; He had no stain of sin himself but bore our sin and shame: He took the cup of pain and death, His blood was freely shed; We see his body on the cross, we share the living bread.

2. He did not come to call the good but sinners to repent;
it was the lame, the deaf, the blind for whom his life was spent:
to heal the sick, to find the lost - it was for such he came,
and round his table all may come to praise his Holy Name.

3. They heard him call his father's name - then 'Finished!' was his cry;
like them we have forsaken him and left him there to die:
the sins that crucified him then are sins his blood has cured;
the love that bound him to a cross our freedom has ensured.

4. His body broken once for us is glorious now above;
the cup of blessing we receive, A sharing of his love:
As in his presence we partake, His dying we proclaim
Until the hour of majesty When Jesus comes again.

126   He is risen, he is risen

Mrs. C.F.Alexander

He is ri sen, he is ri sen: tell it with a joy ful voice;

He has burst his three days' pri son, let the whole wide earth re joice.

Death is con quered, man is free, Christ has won the vic to ry.

2. Come, ye sad and fearful-hearted,
with glad smile and radiant brow;
Lent's long shadows have departed,
all his woes are over now,
and that passion that he bore:
Sin and pain can vex no more.

3. Come, with high and holy hymning,
chant our Lord's triumphant day;
not one darksome cloud is dimming
yonder glorious morning ray,
breaking o'er the purple East,
brighter far our Easter feast.

127 He lay in a manger

Brenda Gallant

He lay in a man ger,____ 'Twas gi ven to Him,____ That
poor lit tle stran ger, In sta ble so dim.____ In great con de scen sion That
One from on high____ Should leave His great man sion, And come here to die.

2. That baby so tender,
So humble and meek,
Left heaven's sheer splendour,
Our lost souls to seek.
The manger that held Him,
And gave Him repose,
He exchanged for a cross,
Nailed there by His foes.

3. Now ris'n and victorious,
And seated on high,
Our Saviour all glorious,
Desires to draw nigh,
But not as a stranger,
Unloved and unknown,
Your heart, not a manger,
Should be His blest throne.

Music © 2013 Harry Hicks
Words © 2013 Brenda Gallant

128   He will take care of you

Frances R. Havergal

He will take care of you, He will take care of you, He will take care of you
All through the day. Je-sus is near you to keep you from ill,
Je-sus is with you, and watch-ing you still. He will take care of you,
He will take care of you, He will take care of you All through the day.

2. He will take care of you (x3)
All through the night.
Jesus, the Shepherd, His faithful one keeps,
He never slumbers, and He never sleeps.
He will take care of you (x3)
All through the night.

3. He will take care of you (x3)
All through the years.
Crowning each day with His kindness and love,
Leading you on to the bright home above.
He will take care of you (x3)
All through the years.

4. He will take care of you (x3)
All through your life.
Nothing can alter His love for His own,
He will not leave you one moment alone.
He will take care of you (x3)
All through your life.

129   Healer of the sick

Francis Leftley

Healer of the sick, Lord Jesus Son of God; Lord how we long for you: walk here among us. *Chorus* Bind up our broken lives, comfort our broken hearts, Banish our hidden fears - Lord, come with power. Bring new light to the blind, bring peace to troubled minds, Hold us now in your arms, set us free now.

2. Bearer of our pain, Lord Jesus, Lamb of God; Lord, we cry to you: Walk here among us.
Bind up our broken lives, comfort our broken hearts,
Banish our hidden fears, Lord, come with power.
Bring new light to the blind, bring peace to troubled minds,
Hold us now in your arms, set us free now.

3. Calmer of our fears, Lord Jesus, Prince of Peace; Lord how we yearn for you: Walk here among us.
Bind up our broken lives,...........

4. Saviour of the world, Lord Jesus, mighty God; Lord how we sing to you: Walk here among us.
Bind up our broken lives,...........

Music © 2010 Harry Hicks

130 Hear how the bells of Christmas play

Timothy Dudley-Smith

2. Let all the waiting earth rejoice, lift every heart and every voice. O praise him! Allelulia!
Sing now the song to angels given, Glory to God in highest heaven! O praise him! Allelulia!

3. As through the silence of the skies shepherds in wonder heard arise, O praise him! Allelulia!
So may we hear again with them Songs in the night at Bethlehem, O praise him! Allelulia!

4. All nature sang at Jesus' birth Hail the Creator come to earth! O praise him! Allelulia!
Sun, moon and shining stars above, Tell out the story of his love, O praise him! Allelulia!

5. Hear how the bells of Christmas play! Well may they ring and joy and say, O praise him! Allelulia!
Come now to worship and adore, Christ is our peace for evermore, O praise him! Allelulia!

131   Heavenly Father

C.J.Meyrick

Hea-ven-ly Fa-ther, now tune our re - joic-ing, lif-ting our hearts by the dawn of your love; Like John's proud fa - ther, hope joy-ful-ly voi-cing, our tongues are loosed to the praise of your name.

2. Jesus baptised, saw the Spirit alighting,
heavenly sonship confirmed by God's call -
called to embody his heart of self-giving;
we sing with joy to the praise of his name.

3. Spirit, released by the Lord's resurrection,
kindling new fire in the lives of the saints;
guiding, directing and freshly expressing
God's love for all; we give praise to your name.

4. Trinity, Holy, in service unite us,
by grace held safe in the love that sets free;
washed clean and healed of the sins that would blight us,
people of faith; we give praise to your name.

Written for Rochester Cathedral and the Dedication of the Baptismal Fresco
on June 24th 2004, to the tune 'Broadwalk,' by Robert Ashfield.

132 Hence from my soul

Isaac Watts

Hence from my soul, sad thoughts, be gone, And leave me to my joys, My tongue shall tri - umph in my God, And make a joy - ful - noise, And make a joy - ful noise.

2. Darkness and doubts had veiled my mind,
   And drowned my head in tears,
   Till sovereign trace with shining rays
   Dispelled my gloomy tears,
   Dispelled my gloomy tears.

3. O what immortal joys I felt,
   And raptures all divine,
   When Jesus told me, I was his,
   And my Beloved mine,
   And my Beloved mine.

4. In vain the tempter frights my soul,
   And breaks my peace in vain,
   One glimpse, dear Saviour, of thy face,
   Revives my joys again,
   Revives my joys again.

133   Here at thy cross

Here at the cross, my dy - ing God, I lay my soul - be -
neath - thy love, Be-neath the drop - pings of - thy blood,
Je - sus, nor shall it - e'er re - move.

2. Not all that tyrants think or say,
   With rage and lightning in their eyes,
   Nor hell shall fright my heart away,
   Should hell with all its legions rise.

3. Should worlds conspire to drive me thence,
   Moveless and firm this heart should lie;
   Resolved (for that's my last defence)
   If I must perish, there to die.

4. But speak, my Lord, and calm my fear,
   Am I not safe beneath thy shade?
   Thy vengeance will not strike me here,
   Nor Satan dares my soul invade.

5. Yes, I'm secure beneath thy blood,
   And all my foes shall lose their aim,
   Hosanna to my dying God,
   And my best honours to his Name.

Music © 2013 Harry Hicks

134   High on a hill

Isaac Watts

High on a hill of dazzl'-ing light, The King of Glo-ry spreads his seat, And troops of an-gels stretched for flight, Stand wait-ing round his aw-ful feet.

2. "Go," saith the Lord, "my Gabriel go,
"Salute the virgin's fruitful womb,
"Make haste, ye cherubs, down below,
Sing and proclaim the Saviour come."

3. Here a bright squadron leaves the skies,
And thick around Elisha stands;
Anon a heavenly soldier flies,
And breaks the chains from Peter's hands.

4. Thy winged troops, O God of hosts,
Wait on thy wandering church below,
Here we are sailing to thy coasts,
Let angels be our convoy too.

5. Are they not all thy servants, Lord?
At thy command they go and come
With cheerful haste obey thy word,
And guard thy children to their home.

Music © 2014 Harry Hicks

135 Holy Father, in Thy mercy

Isabella S. Stevenson

Ho - ly Fa — ther in thy mer — cy Hear our anx-ious prayer, Keep our loved ones, now far dis - tant 'Neath thy care.

2. Jesus, Saviour, let Thy presence
Be their light and guide;
Keep, oh, keep them, in their weakness,
At Thy side.

3. When in sorrow, when in danger,
When in loneliness,
In Thy love look down and comfort
Their distress.

4. May the joy of Thy salvation
Be their strength and stay;
May they love and may they praise Thee
Day by day.

5. Holy Spirit, let Thy teaching
Sanctify their life;
Send Thy grace, that they may conquer
In the strife.

6. Father, Son, and Holy Spirit,
God the One in Three,
Bless them, guide them, save them, keep them
Near to Thee.

Music © 2015 Harry Hicks

136   Holy Jesus, by Thy Passion

W.J.Sparrow-Simpson

Ho - ly Je - sus, by The Pas-sion, By the woes which none can share,

Borne in more than king-ly fash-ion, By Thy love be - yond com-pare:

Cru - ci - fied, I turn to Thee, Son of Ma - ry, plead for me.

2. By the treachery and trial,
By the blows and sore distress,
By desertion and denial,
By Thine awful loneliness:
Crucified, I turn to Thee,
Son of Mary, plead for me.

3. By Thy look so sweet and lowly,
While they smote Thee on the face.
By Thy patience, clam and holy,
In the midst of keen disgrace:
Crucified, I turn to Thee,
Son of Mary, plead for me.

4. By the hour of condemnation,
By the blood which trickled down,
When for us and our salvation
Thou didst wear the robe and crown:
Crucified, I turn to Thee,
Son of Mary, plead for me.

5. By the path of sorrows dreary,
By the cross, Thy dreadful load,
By the pain, when, faint and weary,
Thou didst sink, upon the road:
Crucified, I turn to Thee,
Son of Mary, plead for me.

6. By the spirit which could render
Love for hate and good for ill,
By the mercy, sweet and tender,
Poured upon thy murderers still:
Crucified, I turn to Thee,
Son of Mary, plead for me.

137   Holy Spirit, hear us

C. Wesley

Holy Spirit hear us; Help us while we sing;____
Breathe in____ to____ the____ Music Of____ the____ praise we bring.

2. Holy Spirit, prompt us
When we kneel to pray;
Nearer come to teach us
What we ought to say.

3. Holy Spirit, shine Thou
On thy Book we read;
Gild its holy pages
With the light we need.

4. Holy Spirit, give us
Each a lowly mind;
Make us more like Jesus,
Gentle, pure and kind.

5. Holy Spirit, help us
Daily by Thy might,
What is wrong to conquer,
And to choose the right.

138 Holy Spirit, truth divine

Samuel Longfellow (1819-1892)

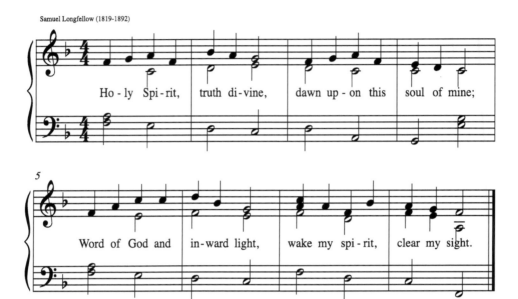

Ho-ly Spi-rit, truth di-vine, dawn up-on this soul of mine;

Word of God and in-ward light, wake my spi-rit, clear my sight.

2. Holy Spirit, love divine,
glow within this heart of mine;
kindle evry high desire,
perish self in your pure fire.

3. Holy Spirit, power divine,
fill and nerve this will of mine;
by you may I strongly live,
bravely bear, and nobly strive.

4. Holy Spirit, right divine,
King within my conscience reign;
be my law, and I shall be
firmly bounded, ever free.

5. Holy Spirit, peace divine,
still this restless soul of mine;
speak to calm this tossing sea,
stayed in your tranquility.

6. Holy Spirit, joy divine,
gladden now this heart of mine;
in the desert ways I sing,
'Spring, O well, for ever spring!'

139   Holy, holy, holy is the Lord!

F.J.Crosby

2. Praise him, praise him, shout aloud for joy! Watchmen of Zion, herald the story;
Sin and death his kingdom shall destroy, all the earth shall sing of his glory;
Praise him, ye angels, ye who behold him robed in his splendour, matchless divine!
Holy, holy, holy is the Lord, Let the hills be joyful before him!

3. King eternal, blessed be his name! So may his children gladly adore him;
When in heav'n we join the happy strain, when we cast our bright crowns before him;
There is his likeness joyful awaking, there we shall see him, there shall we sing!
Holy, holy, holy is the Lord, Let the hills be joyful before him!

140 Holy, holy, holy Lord

J. Montgomery

Holy, ho - ly, ho - ly___ Lord God of hosts! when heav'n and earth, Out of dark - ness, at Thy word, Is - sued in - to glor - ious birth, All Thy works be - fore Thee stood, And Thine eyes be - held them good: While they sang with sweet ac - cord, Ho - ly, ho - ly, ho - ly Lord!

2. Holy, holy, holy! Thee,
One Jehovah evermore,
Father, Son, and Spirit! we -
Dust and ashes - would adore:
Lightly by the world esteemed,
From that world by Thee redeemed,
Sing we here, with glad accord,
Holy, holy, holy Lord!

3. Holy, holy, holy! All
Heav'n's triumphant choir shall sing,
When the ransomed nations fall
At the footstool of their King:
Then shall saints and seraphim,
Hearts and voices, swell one hymn,
Round the throne, with full accord,
Holy, holy, holy Lord!

141   Home at last

I.D.Sankey

Home at last, thy la-bour done, safe and blest, the vic-t'ry won;

Jor-dan passed, from pain set free, An-gels now have wel-comed thee.

Refrain

Depth of mer - cy, oh, how sweet thus to rest at Je-sus' feet,

In yon world of light a-far, safe with-in the gates a-jar.

2. When dark waves were beating hard thy frail bark on Jordan's flood,
Thou didst sing so glad and free, "Yes, the gate's ajar *for me!*"
Depth of mercy, oh, how sweet, thus to rest at Jesus' feet,
In yon world of light afar, safe within *the gates ajar!*

3. One short day of joy below, such as pardoned sinners know;
Then away on wings of love to thy home prepared above.
Depth of mercy, ...

4. When earth's songs have all been sung, labour ended, trials done,
"We'll meet again," oh, happy word! and be "for ever with the Lord."
Depth of mercy, ...

Music © 2012 Harry Hicks

142 Hosanna to our conquering King

Isaac Watts

Ho-san-na to our con-quer-ing King! The prince of dark-ness flies,_____ His troops rush head - long - down to hell Like light-ning from - the skies.

2. There, bound in chains, the lions roar,
And fright the rescued sheep,
But heavy bars consign their power
And malice to the deep.

3. Hosanna to our conquering King,
All hail, incarnate love!
Ten thousand songs and glories wait
To crown thy head above.

4. Thy victories and thy deathless fame
Through the wide world shall run,
And everlasting ages sing
The triumphs thou hast won.

143   Hosanna to the living Lord

R. Heber

Ho san na to   the   liv ing Lord!   Ho san na to   th'In   car nate Word!

8ves in the bass

To Christ, Cre a tor,   Sav iour, King,   Let earth, let heaven 'Ho   san na' sing.

Refrain

Ho san na, Lord!   Ho san na, Lord!   Ho san na in the   high   est!

2. 'Hosanna Lord!' Thine angels cry,
'Hosanna Lord!' Thy saints reply;
Above, beneath us, all around,
The dead and living swell the sound.
Hosanna Lord! Hosanna Lord!
Hosanna in the highest!

3. O Saviour! with protecting care,
Return to this thy house of prayer;
Assembled in Thy sacred name,
Here we Thy parting promise claim.
Hosanna Lord! Hosanna Lord!
Hosanna in the highest!

4. But chief in every cleansed breast,
Eternal! bid thy Spirit rest;
And make our secret soul to be
A temple pure, and worthy Thee.
Hosanna Lord! Hosanna Lord!
Hosanna in the highest!

5. So, in the last and dreadful day,
When earth and heaven shall pass away,
Thy flock, redeemed from sinful stain,
Shall swell the sound of praise again.
Hosanna Lord! Hosanna Lord!
Hosanna in the highest!

144   Hosanna to the Prince of Light

Isaac Watts

Ho-san - na to the Prince of Light, That clothed him - self in clay,

8ves in the bass

En-tered the i - ron gates of death, And tore the bars a - way.

2. Death is no more the king of dread
    Since our Emmanuel rose,
    He took the tyrant's sting away,
    And spoiled our hellish foes.

3. See how the Conqueror mounts aloft,
    And to his Father flies,
    With scars of honour in his flesh,
    And triumph in his eyes.

4. There our exalted Saviour reigns,
    And scatters blessings down,
    Our Jesus fills the middle seat
    Of the celestial throne.

5. Raise your devotion, mortal tongues,
    To reach his blessed abode,
    Sweet be the accents of your songs
    To our Incarnate God.

6. Bright angels, strike your loudest strings,
    Your sweetest voices raise,
    Let heaven, and all created things,
    Sound our Emmanuel's praise.

Music © 2013 Harry Hicks

145   Hosanna to the royal Son

Isaac Watts

Ho - san-na to the ro - yal Son Of Da-vid's an-cient line,

His na-tures two, his per-son one, My-ster-ious and di vine.

2. The root of David here we find,
   And offspring is the same;
   Eternity and time are joined
   In our Emmanuel's name.

3. Bless'd he that comes to wretched men
   With peaceful news from heav'n;
   Hosannas of the highest strain
   To Christ the Lord be giv'n.

4. Let mortals ne'er refuse to take
   Th'hosanna on their tongues,
Lest rocks and stones should rise, and break
   Their silence into songs.

146   Hosanna, with a cheerful sound

Isaac Watts

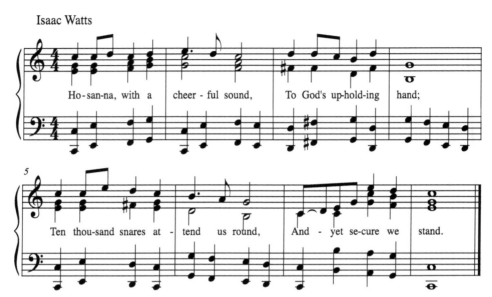

Ho-san-na, with a cheer-ful sound, To God's up-hold-ing hand;

Ten thou-sand snares at - tend us round, And - yet se-cure we stand.

2. That was a most amazing power
   That raised us with a word,
   And ev'ry day and ev'ry hour
   We lean upon the Lord.

3. The evening rests our weary head,
   And angels guard the room;
   We wake and we admire the bed
   That was not made our tomb.

4. The rising morning can't assure
   That we shall end the day,
   For death stands ready at the door
   To seize our lives away.

5. Our breath is forfeited by sin
   To God avenging law;
   We own thy grace, immortal King,
   In ev'ry gasp we draw.

6. God is our sun, whose daily light
   Our joy and safety brings:
   Our feeble flesh lies safe at night
   Beneath his shady wings.

Music © 2013 Harry Hicks

147 How can I

Kenneth J. Summers

How can I, Lord, ___ ex-press your love - with which you gave your all for me, - your arms out - stretched, ___ as high a- bove - you died for me ___ up-on a tree? ___

2. Lord, it is through the living poor,
   whose needs expose hypocrisy
   in us who give, yet close the door,
   and bar them from society?

3. Through costly ointment, touching needs,
   which went beyond what we can see,
   a woman gave you more than deeds
   could do, in off'ring gen'rously

4. all that she had for you, in love,
   in acts beyond our mortal sense,
   and, in so doing, linked above
   with heaven's perfume of incense.

5. For, in her love we also find
   that love in which we find a place
   in heav'n above, where, intertwined,
   your love and ours and filled with grace.

148 How fearsome and far

John Coutts

How fear some and far the un i verse runs! Who counts ev' ry star? Who num bers new suns? But Christ is the King of un think a ble space; so stand up and sing of his good ness and grace.

2. Strange secrets of life   new knowledge can tell.
Amazing the strife   Of microbe and cell!
Yet Christ is the friend   Of the tiniest flower.
Rejoice without end   In his goodness and power.

3. The last and the least   our Jesus calls best,
proclaiming the feast   his Father has blessed.
To ruin and shame him   They nail him up high,
But now we proclaim him   For daring to die.

4. That sorrow is past;   let wrong do its worst.
He'll reign at the last   Who ruled at the first -
The Lord of all years   That are coming to birth,
As laughter and tears   grow together on earth.

5. Then go, sister, go   and pray, brother, pray:
Let everyone know   the Christ of today.
His truth sets us free   (how this story rings true!).
He conquered for me   And he's calling for you.

149   How shall I sing that majesty

John Mason

How shall I sing that majesty which an-gels do ad-mire?

Let dust in dust and si-lence lie; sing, sing, ye heav-en-ly choir.

Thou-sands of thou-sands stand a-round thy throne, O God-most high;

Ten thou-sand times ten thou-sand sound thy praise; but who am I?

2. Thy brightness unto them appears, whilst I thy footsteps trace;
A sound of God comes to my ears, but they behold thy face.
They sing because thou art their sun; Lord, send a beam on me;
For where heaven is but once begun there allelulias be.

3. Enlighten with faith's light my heart, inflame it with love's fire;
Then shall I sing and bear a part with that celestial choir.
I shall, I fear, be dark and cold, with all my fire and light;
Yet when thou dost accept their gold, Lord, treasure up my mite.

4. How great a being, Lord, is thine, which doth all beings keep!
Thy knowledge is the only line to sound so vast a deep.
Thou art a sea without a shore, a sun without a sphere;
Thy time is now and evermore, thy place is ever near.

150 How shall we sing salvation's song?

Timothy Dudley-Smith

How shall we sing salvation's song when justice stands denied. when greed and tyranny and wrong prevail on ev'ry side? Shall silent fall our voice of praise, as on the willow hung the harps that told of happier days when songs of home were sung?

2. Yet still we sing as Moses sang beside the parted wave,
when Canaan's skies in triumph rang to God the strong to save.
We too in psalms like David sing, as David's faith we claim,
who sang as shepherd boy and king of God's eternal name.

3. And we have blessings more than they in Christ our risen Lord,
himself our Life and Truth and Way, his Spirit on us poured.
For ours the cross where Jesus died, the love that bore our sins;
to him, enthroned and glorified, salvation's song begun.

151 How strong thine arm

Isaac Watts

How strong thine arm is, migh-ty God, Who would not fear thy Name!

Je-sus, how sweet thy grac-es are! Who would not love the Lamb!

2. He has done more than Moses did,
Our Prophet and our King;
From bonds of hell he freed our souls,
And taught our lips to sing.

3. In Red-sea by Moses' hand
The' Egyptian host was drowned;
But His own blood hides all our sins,
And guilt no more is found.

4. When though the desert Israel went,
With manna they were fed;
Our Lord invites us to his flesh,
And calls it living bread.

5. Moses beheld the promised land,
Yet never reached the place;
But Christ shall bring his followers home
To see his Father's face.

6. Then shall our love and joy be full,
And feel a warmer flame;
And sweeter voices tune the song
Of Moses and the Lamb.

Music © 2012 Harry Hicks

152 How vast a fortune

Isaac Watts

How vast a for-tune we— pos-sess! How rich thy boun-ty, King of Grace! This world is ours, and worlds to come, Earth is our lodge, and heav'n— our home.

2. All things are ours, the gifts of God;
The purchase of a Saviour's blood:
While the good Spirit shews us how
To use and to improve them too.

3. If peace and plenty crown my days,
They help me, Lord, to speak thy praise!
If bread of sorrow be my food,
Those sorrows work my lasting good.

4. I would not change my blest estate
For all the world calls good or great:
And while my faith can keep her hold,
I envy not the sinner's gold.

5. Father, I wait thy daily will;
Thou shalt divide my portion still:
Grant me on earth what seems thee best,
Till death and heav'n reveal the rest.

153   How wondrous great

Isaac Watts

How - Won - drous great, - how glo - rious bright Must - our - Cre - a - tor be,____ Who - dwells - a midst the dazz' - ling light Of - vast - in - fi - ni - ty!____

2. Our soaring spirits upward rise
Toward the celestial throne,
Fain would we see the blessed Three,
And the Almighty One.

3. Our reason stretches all its wings,
And climbs above the skies;
But still how far beneath thy feet
Our grovelling reason lies!

4. Lord, here we bend our humble souls,
And awfully adore,
For the weak pinions of our mind
Can stretch a thought no more.

5. Thy glories infinitely rise
Above our labouring tongue;
In vain the highest seraph tries
To form an equal song.

6. In humble notes our faith adores
The great mysterious King,
While angels strain their nobler powers,
And sweep th'immortal string.

154   Hush my dear

Isaac Watts

Hush, my dear, lie still and slumber, Holy angels guard thy bed,
Heav'n-ly bless-ings with-out num-ber, Gent-ly fall-ing on thy head.
How much bet-ter thou'rt at-ten-ded Than the Son of God could be,
When from hea-ven he des-cen-ded, and be-came a child-like thee!

2. Soft and easy is thy cradle, Coarse and hard thy Saviour lay:
When His birthplace was a stable, And His softest bed was hay.
Oh, to tell the wondrous story, How His foes abused their King;
How they killed the Lord of glory, Makes me angry while I sing.

3. Hush, my child, I did not chide thee, Though my song may seem so hard;
'Tis thy mother sits beside thee, And her arms shall be thy guard.
May'st thou learn to know and fear Him, Love and serve Him all thy days;
Then to dwell forever near Him, Tell His love and sing His praise.

155   Hush you, my baby

Timothy Dudley-Smith

Hush you, my baby, the night wind is cold. The lambs on the hill-side are safe in the fold. Sleep with the star-light and wake with the morn, The Lord of all glo-ry A ba-by is born.

2. Hush you my baby, so soon to be grown,
watching by moonlight on mountains alone,
toiling and travelling so sleep while you can,
till the Lord of all glory is seen as a man.

3. Hush you, my baby, the years will not stay;
the cross on the hilltop the end of the way.
Dim in the darkness, In grief and in gloom,
the Lord of all glory Lies cold in the tomb.

4. Hush you, my baby, the Father on high
in power and dominion the darkness puts by.
Bright from the shadows, The seal and the stone,
The Lord of all glory Returns to his own.

5. Hush you, my baby, the sky turns to gold;
the lambs on the hillside are loose from the fold.
Fast fades the midnight And new springs the morn,
For the Lord of all glory A Saviour is born.

156   I adore Thee

(Alto solo?)

Rev. W.J.Sparrow-Simpson

I a-dore Thee! I a-dore Thee! Glor-ious ere the

world be-gan; Yet more won-der-ful Thou shi-nest, thou di-vine, yet

still di-vin-est in Thy dy-ing love for man.

2. I adore Thee, I adore Thee,
Thankful at Thy feet to be;
I have heard Thy accent thrilling,
Lo! I come, for Thou art willing
Me to pardon, even me.

3. I adore Thee, I adore Thee,
Born of woman yet divine,
Stained with sins I kneel before Thee,
Sweetest Jesus, I implore Thee,
Make me ever only Thine.

157 I came a wanderer

Julia Sterling

I came a wand-'rer, and a-lone, my way was dark as night;

I looked to Thee, O bless-ed one, and then I found the light.

Chorus

O Je-sus, Sav-iour, Lamb of God, how much I owe to Thee,

for all the won-ders of Thy grace, and all Thy love to me!

2. I came with all my doubts and fears, no hope but in Thy Word;
and while I gazed upon the blood, thy pard'ning voice I heard.
O Jesus, Saviour, Lamb of God, how much I owe to Thee,
For all the wonders of thy grace, and all thy love to me!

3. Oh, may the Spirit's power be felt in this poor heart of mine!
and make thy Word my lamp and light, my shield and strength divine.
O Jesus, Saviour,........

4. Oh, teach me Lord, thy voice to know amid the surging throng;
be Thou my hope, my life, my joy, my everlasting song.
O Jesus, Saviour, ...

Music © 2012 Harry Hicks

158   I come with joy

Brian A. Wren

I come with joy,— a child of God, For-
giv - en loved— and free,— The life of Je - sus
to re - call, in love laid down— for me.—

2. I come with Christians far and near
to find, as all are fed,
the new community of love
in Christ's communion bread.

3. As Christ breaks bread, and bids us share,
each proud division ends.
The love that made us, makes us one,
And strangers now are friends.

4. The Spirit of the risen Christ,
unseen, but ever near,
is in such friendship better known,
alive among us here.

5. Together met, together bound
by all that God has done,
we'll go with joy, to give the world
the love that makes us one.

159   I know He cares for me

Howard L. Brown

1. I've found it true, so ve - ry true, my Sav - iour cares for
2. I've come to know, as on I go, my Sav - iour cares for
3. My all I give, for Him I live, be - cause He cares for

me. His prom - ise holds, His love un - folds, I know He
me. Close by my side, what - 'ere be - tide, I know He
me. This pre - cious One, God's on - ly Son, 'Tis He who

cares for me.
cares for me.
cares for me.

Chorus

I know He cares for me, I

know He cares for me, His way is best, I've

proved by test and I know He cares for me.

160 I know I'll see Jesus some day

Avis. R. Christiansen

Sweet is the hope that is thrill-ing my soul: I know I'll see Je-sus some day! Then

what if the dark clouds of sin o'er me roll, I know I'll see Je-sus some day! I

Refrain

know I'll see Je-sus some day! I know I'll see Je-sus some day! What a

joy it will be When His face I shall see, I know I'll see Je-sus some day!

2. Though I must travel by faith, not my sight,
   I know I'll see Jesus some day!
   No evil can harm me, no foe can affright;
   I know I'll see Jesus some day!
   I know I'll see Jesus some day!
   What a joy it will be
   When His face I shall see,
   I know I'll see Jesus some day!

3. Darkness is gath'ring, but hope shines within,
   I know I'll see Jesus some day!
   What joy when He comes to wipe out ev'ry stain
   I know I'll see Jesus some day!
   I know I'll see Jesus some day!
   What a joy it will be
   When His face I shall see,
   I know I'll see Jesus some day!

Music © 2013 Harry Hicks

161   I know that my Redeemer lives

C. Wesley

I know that my Re- dee - mer lives, And ev - er prays for

me; A to-ken of His love he gives, A pledge of li - ber - ty

2. I find Him lifting up my head,
   He brings salvation near,
His presence makes me free indeed,
   And he will soon appear.

3. He wills that I should holy be,
   What can withstand His will?
The counsel of His grace in me
   He surely will fulfil.

4. Jesus, I hang upon Thy word;
   I steadfastly believe
Thou wilt return and claim me, Lord,
   And to Thyself receive.

5. Joyful in hope, my spirit soars
   To meet Thee from above,
Thy goodness thankfully adores;
   And sure I taste Thy love.

6. Thy love I soon expect to find,
   In all its depth and height;
To comprehend the Eternal Mind,
   And grasp the Infinite.

7. When God is mine, and I am his,
   Of paradise possessed,
I taste unutterable bliss,
   And everlasting rest.

161 I know that my Redeemer lives

C. Wesley

I know that my Re-dee-mer lives, And ev-er prays for
me; A to-ken of His love he gives, A pledge of li-ber-ty

2. I find Him lifting up my head,
He brings salvation near,
His presence makes me free indeed,
And he will soon appear.

3. He wills that I should holy be,
What can withstand His will?
The counsel of His grace in me
He surely will fulfil.

4. Jesus, I hang upon Thy word;
I steadfastly believe
Thou wilt return and claim me, Lord,
And to Thyself receive.

5. Joyful in hope, my spirit soars
To meet Thee from above,
Thy goodness thankfully adores;
And sure I taste Thy love.

6. Thy love I soon expect to find,
In all its depth and height;
To comprehend the Eternal Mind,
And grasp the Infinite.

7. When God is mine, and I am his,
Of paradise possessed,
I taste unutterable bliss,
And everlasting rest.

Music © 2016 Harry Hicks

162   I know that my Redeemer lives

S. Medley

2. He lives, triumphant from the grave;
   He lives, eternally to save;
   He lives, all-glorious in the sky;
   He lives, exalted there on high.

3. He lives, to bless me with His love,
   And still He pleads for me above;
   He lives to raise me from the grave,
   And me eternally to save.

4. He lives, my kind, wise, constant Friend;
   Who still will keep me to the end;
   He lives, and while he lives I'll sing,
   Jesus, my Prophet, Priest, and King.

5. He lives my mansion to prepare;
   And he will bring me safely there;
   He lives, all glory to His name!
   Jesus, unchangeably the same!

163   I lay my sins on Jesus

Horatius Bonar

I lay my sins on Je - sus, the spot - less Lamb of God; He bears them all and frees us from th'a - cur - sed load. I bring my guilt to Je - sus to wash my crim - son stains white in his blood most pre - cious till not a spot remains

2. I lay my wants on Jesus, all fullness dwells in Him:
He heals all my diseases, he doth my soul redeem.
I lay my griefs on Jesus, my burdens and my cares:
He from them all releases; he all my sorrows shares.

3. I rest my soul on Jesus, this weary soul of mine;
His right hand me embraces, I on his breast recline.
I love the name of Jesus, Emmanuel, Christ the Lord,
Like fragrance on the breezes, his Name abroad is poured.

4. I long to be like Jesus, meek, loving, lowly, mild;
I long to be like Jesus, the Father's heav'nly child.
I long to be with Jesus amid the heav'nly throng,
To sing with saints his praises, to learn the angels' song.

164   I lift my heart to Thee

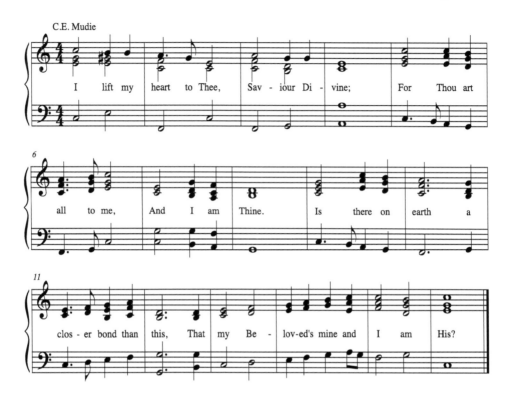

I lift my heart to Thee, Sav-iour Di - vine; For Thou art all to me, And I am Thine. Is there on earth a clos - er bond than this, That my Be - lov-ed's mine and I am His?

2. Thine am I by all ties;
But chiefly Thine,
That through Thy sacrifice
Thou, Lord, art mine.
By Thine own cords of love, so sweetly wound
Around me, I to Thee am closely bound.

3. To Thee, Thou dying Lamb,
I all things owe;
All that I have and am,
And all I know.
All that I have is no longer mine,
And I am not my own; Lord, I am Thine.

4. How can I, Lord, withhold
Life's brightest hour
From Thee; or gathered gold,
Or any power?
Why should I keep one precious thing from Thee,
When Thou hast given Thine own dear Self for me?

Music © 2016 Harry Hicks

165   I need Thee

Mrs. A.S. Hawks

I need Thee ev'ry hour, Most gra - - cious Lord; No ten - der voice like Thine Can peace af - ford.

Chorus

I need Thee, Oh I need Thee! Ev' - ry hour I need thee: Oh, bless me now, my Sav-iour! I come to Thee.

2. I need Thee ev'ry hour:
Stay Thou near by;
Temptations lose their power
When Thou art nigh.
I need Thee, Oh, I need Thee!
Ev'ry hour I need Thee:
Oh, bless me now my Saviour!
I come to Thee.

3. I need Thee every hour,
In joy or in pain;
Come quickly and abide,
Or life is vain.
I need Thee......

4. I need Thee every hour;
Teach me Thy will;
And Thy rich promises
In me fulfil.
I need Thee.....

5. I need Thee every hour,
Most Holy One;
Oh, make me Thine indeed,
Thou blessed Son!
I need Thee.....

166   I stand all amazed

C.H. Gabriel

I stand all a-mazed at the love Je-sus of-fers me, con-fused at the grace that so ful-ly he prof-fers me; I trem-ble to know that for me he was cru-ciu-fied, That for me, a sin - ner, He suf-fered, He bled, He died.

Chorus

O it is won-der-ful that He should care for me E-nough to die for me! O it is won-der-ful! O it is won-der-ful that he should care for me E-nough to die for me! Won - der-ful to me!

2. I marvel that he would descend from His throne above
To rescue a soul so rebellious and proud as mine;
That He should extend His great love unto such as me!
Sufficient to own, to redeem and to justify.
   O it is wonderful that He should care for me
   Enough to die for me!
   O it is wonderful,
   O it is wonderful that He should care for me,
   Enough to die for me!
   Wonderful to me!

3. I think of His hands, pierced and bleeding to pay the debt,
Such mercy, such love and devotion can I forget?
No, no! I will praise and adore at the mercy seat,
Until at the glorified throne I kneel at His feet.
   O it is wonderful that He should care for me
   Enough to die for me!
   O it is wonderful,
   O it is wonderful that He should care for me,
   Enough to die for me!
   Wonderful to me!

167   I stand amazed

G.H.Gabriel

I stand a-mazed at the love Je-sus of-ers me, Con-fused at the grace that so ful-ly He prof-fers me; I trem-ble to know that for me he was cru-ci-fied, that for me, a sin-ner, He suf-fered, He bled, He died. Oh, it is won-der-ful that He should care for me, e-nough to die for me! Oh, it is won-der-ful, won-der-ful to me!

2. I marvel that He should descend from His throne divine
To rescue a soul so rebellious and proud as mine;
That he should extend His great love unto such as I;
Sufficient to own, to redeem, and to justify.
Oh, it is wonderful that he should care for me,
Enough to die for me!
Oh, it is wonderful, wonderful to me!

3. I think of His hands pierced and bleeding to pay the debt!
Such mercy, such love and devotion can I forget?
No, no! I will praise and adore at the mercy-seat,
Until at the glorified throne I kneel at His feet.
Oh, it is wonderful........

168   I will sing of my Redeemer

P.P.Bliss

I will sing of my Re-deem-er, And His won-drous love to me;
On the cru-el cross He suff-ered, From the curse to set ___ me free.

Chorus

Sing, oh sing of my Re-deem-er! With His blood He pur-chased me!

On the cross He sealed my par-don, Paid the debt and set me free!

2. I will tell the wondrous story,
  How my lost estate to save,
In His boundless love and mercy,
  He the ransom freely gave.
Sing, oh sing of my Redeemer!
With his blood He purchased me!
On the cross He sealed my pardon,
Paid the debt and made me free.

3. I will praise my dear Redeemer,
  His triumphant power I'll tell;
  How the victory He giveth
  Over sin, and death, and hell.
  Sing, oh sing.........

4. I will sing of my Redeemer,
  And His heavenly love to me;
He from death to life hath brought me,
  Son of God, with Him to be.
  Sing, oh sing........

169   I will sing

Christopher Idle

I will sing the Lord's high triumph, ruling earth and sky and sea; God, my strength, my song, my glory, my salvation now is he. Through the waters, through the waters, God has brought us liberty, God has brought us liberty.

2. By the storm and by the mountain grace and judgement both are shown;
All who planned the people's ruin power divine has overthrown.
Nations tremble, nations tremble;
God has made his mercy known, God has made his mercy known.

3. Who is like the God of Israel, faithful, holy, throned above?
Stretching out the arm of anger, yet he guides us by his love.
To our homeland, to our homeland,
God will see us safely move, God will see us safely move.

4. Praise our God, who in the thunder led a nation through the sea;
Praise the One whose blood released us from our deeper slavery.
Alleluia, allelulia,
Christ is risen, we are free! Christ is risen, we are free!

170 I'm not ashamed

I'm not ashamed to name my Lord,
Or to defend his cause,
Maintain the honour of his word,
Maintain the honour of his word,
The glory of his cross.

2. Jesus, my God! I know his name,
His name is all I trust;
He will not put my soul to shame,
He will not put my soul to shame,
Nor let my hope be lost.

3. Firm as his throne his promise stands,
And he can well secure
What he entrusted to my hands
What he entrusted to my hands
Until that final hour.

4. Then he'll make known my guilty name
Before his Father's face,
And in the new Jerusalem,
And in the new Jerusalem
Appoint to me a place.

Music © 2008 Harry Hicks

171 If Christ were born in Burnley

Albert Bayly

If Christ were born in Burn-ley this Christ-mas night, this Christ-mas night; I know not if the moors would shine with heav'n-ly light, with heav'n-ly light. But this I know, my heart would glow, and all its in-ner rad-iance show, if Christ were born in Burn-ley.

2. If Christ were born in Burnley
this Christmas-tide,
this Christmas-tide;
I know not if with treasures rare
the wise would ride,
the wise would ride.
But I would bring
my offering,
to kneel and worship hastening;
if Christ were born in Burnley.

3. If Christ were born in Burnley
this Christmas-day,
this Christmas-day;
I know not if the busy throng
would bid him stay,
would bid him stay.
But he might rest
my heart's own guest,
of praise and glory worthiest;
if Christ were born in Burnley.

Feel free to substitute Burnley for your town.....

172   If I live for the Saviour

Gladys B. Muller

Chas. F. Weigle

If I | live for the | Sav-iour each | day, | And en - | dea-vour His | sweet will to | do, | In the

day of my | Lord | I shall | have my re - | ward, | For | He is so | faith-ful and | true. | - | - | If I

Chorus

live for Him | here, | He'll re - | mem-ber me | there, | I am | sure He will | ne - ver for - | get; | With

joy all com - | plete, | I shall | rest at His | feet, | In the | land where the | sun ne - ver | sets.

2. Let me labour for Jesus through life, Let me share His reproach all the way;
In the day that will come He will welcome me home, He'll remember me there in that day.
If I live for him here He'll remember me there, I am sure he will never forget;
With joy all complete, I shall rest at His feet, In the land where the sun never sets.

3. By His grace I'll endeavour each day To be faithful to Jesus my Lord;
I will work, I will pray, till I hear Jesus say, "Enter in and receive thy reward."
If I live for him here He'll remember me there, I am sure he will never forget;
With joy all complete, I shall rest at His feet, In the land where the sun never sets.

173 In death's strong grasp

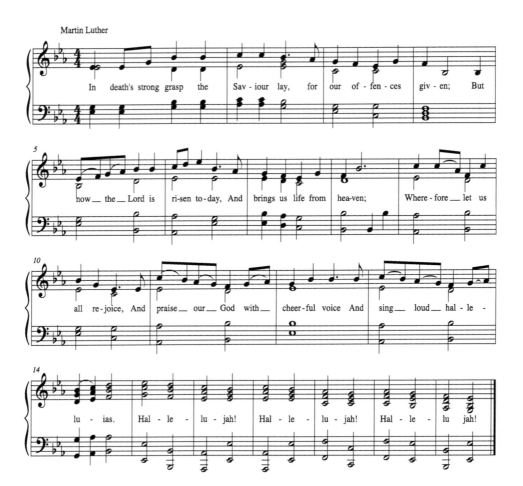

Martin Luther

In death's strong grasp the Sav-iour lay, for our of-fen-ces giv-en; But
now the Lord is ri-sen to-day, And brings us life from hea-ven; Where-fore let us
all re-joice, And praise our God with cheer-ful voice And sing loud hal-le-
lu-ias. Hal-le-lu-jah! Hal-le-lu-jah! Hal-le-lu jah!

2 No son of man could conquer death,
  Such mischief sin had wrought us;
For innocence dwelt not on earth,
  And therefore death had brought us
Into thralldom from of old,
  And ever grew more strong and bold,--
His shadow lay athwart us. Hallelujah!
Hallelujah! Hallelujah! Hallelujah!

3 But Jesus, God's eternal Son,
  Is come for our salvation,
The cause of death He has undone,
  And stopped its devastation;
Ruined all his right and claim,
  And left him nothing but the name,--
His sting is lost forever. Hallelujah!
Hallelujah! Hallelujah! Hallelujah!

4 It was a strange and dreadful strife,
  When life and death contended;
The victory remained with Life,
  The reign of death was ended;
Holy Scripture plainly saith,
  That death is swallowed up by death,
Made henceforth a derision. Hallelujah!
Hallelujah! Hallelujah! Hallelujah!

5 Here the true Paschal Lamb we see,
  Whom God so freely gave us;
He died on the accursed tree,
  So strong His love! to save us:
See! His blood doth mark our door,
  Faith points to it, death passes o'er,--
The murd'rer cannot harm us. Hallelujah!
Hallelujah! Hallelujah! Hallelujah!

6 So let us keep the festival,
  Whereto the Lord invites us;
Christ is Himself the joy of all,
  The sun which warms and lights us:
By His grace He doth impart
  Eternal sunshine to the heart;
The night of sin is ended. Hallelujah!
Hallelujah! Hallelujah! Hallelujah!

7 Then let us feast this Easter-day
  On the true Bread of heaven;
The Word of grade hath purged away
  The old and wicked leaven:
Christ alone our souls will feed,
  He is our meat and drink indeed;
Faith lives upon no other. Hallelujah!
Hallelujah! Hallelujah! Hallelujah!

Music © 2016 Harry Hicks

174   In faith we come

Jan Grimwood

In faith we come, with joy we praise, for on this day he has-been raised. From death to life, the scars he bears: our ri-sen Lord!

2. Yet in that room with doors locked tight
disciples waited in the night;
consumed by pain and guilt and grief.
All hope had gone.

3. This, in the stillness, Christ appeared,
and joy replaced their grief and fears.
'My peace I give to you', said he:
their risen Lord!

4. 'As I was sent, so I send you,
my kingdom's work you too must do.
Go with the Spirit filling you.'
He breathed on them.

5. And as we leave this place tonight,
we walk in resurrection light,
the darkness pierced that we may see
our risen Lord!

175   In stillness, God

Kenneth J. Summers

In still - ness, God, we hear - your voice, a - bove - the

noi - ses of - the world. Still our own hearts, that we - re -

joice and know you as - our on - ly Lord.

2. Be with us, Lord, in all our search
so we may serve you with our heart,
and so discover with your church
how we can always play our part.

3. Lord, in discovering we come
to realise afresh with you
the way in which you call us home
to live with you in all we do.

4. So, in this Lententide may we
walk with you on our pilgrimage
and so become what we can be
and thus receive your heritage.

176   In the beginning

Brenda Gallant

In the be-gin-ning was the Word, The Word was with our God.

By His own voice cre - a - tion stirred Where foot had ne - ver trod.

2. In Him was life, in Him was light,
The light for every man,
Because He knew the sinner's plight
He wrought salvation's plan.

3. He came unto His own, but they
Received Him not, we're told,
They turned their hearts from him away;
Remained outside the fold.

4. But those who did the Word receive,
The sons of God became,
This is for all who will believe
In that most precious name.

5. The Word made flesh, among us dwelt,
His glory to behold,
Then let that word our hard hearts melt,
As in the days of old.

6. His glory, full of truth and grace,
Is ours this Christmas time,
We see, reflected in Christ's face
The heights of love sublime.

7. This wondrous mystery we declare
To all who will take heed,
That in the fulness we may share,
And then be blessed indeed.

177 In the fullness

Brenda Gallant

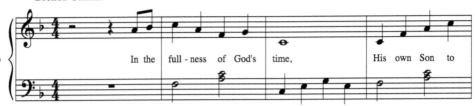

In the full-ness of God's time, His own Son to

earth came down, Glad-ly left the heav'n-ly clime, Laid a-side His King-ly crown,

Clothed Him with our hu-man frame, As an in-fant hum-bly came.

2. In a manger Jesus lay,
Turned aside by thoughtless man,
God with us had come to stay
In accordance with His plan.
Only shepherds knew His worth
When He came to this poor earth.

3. In the fullness of God's time
Wise men saw his natal star,
Travelled from their native clime,
Gathered to Him from afar.
Guided by God's heavenly light,
Faith gave way to wondrous sight.

4. As they knelt before the child
Deity had been revealed;
Holy infant meek and mild,
God in human flesh concealed.
Incense brought they to their King,
Gold and myrrh, an offering.

5. In the fullness of God's time
Jesus grew to be a man.
In this sin-marred earthly clime
Lived His sinless human span.
Then upon the cross He died,
For our sins was crucified.

6. Praise the Lord! This story's true!
Jesus lived and died for all!
Now He's risen and lives for you;
He will save you if you call.
Come to Him this advent, come,
For the Saviour King: make room!

178   In the hollow of His hand

O - soul, tossed on the bil-lows a - far from friend-ly land, Look
up to Him who holds thee in the hol - low of His hand. In the hol-low of His hand! In the
hol-low of His hand! Oh, how safe are all who trust Him, In the hol - low of his hand!

2. Though raging winds may drive thee a wreck upon the land,
Still cling to Him who holds thee   in the hollow of His hand.
In the hollow of His hand!   In the hollow of His hand!
Oh how safe are all who trust Him, in the hollow of His hand!

3. When strength is spent in toiling, and wearily you stand,
Then rest in Him who holds thee in the hollow of His hand.
In the hollow of His hand!   In the hollow of His hand!
Oh how safe are all who trust Him, in the hollow of His hand!

4. When by the swelling Jordan,   your feet in sinking sand,
Remember still He holds thee   in the hollow of His hand.
In the hollow of His hand!   In the hollow of His hand!
Oh how safe are all who trust Him, in the hollow of His hand!

5. And when at last we're gathered   with all the ransomed band,
We'll praise our God who holds thee   in the hollow of His hand.
In the hollow of His hand!   In the hollow of His hand!
Oh how safe are all who trust Him, in the hollow of His hand!

179   Is it well with thy soul?

Brenda Gallant

Is it well with thy soul? Is it well with thy soul? Can you say 'It is
well with my soul?' _____ Je-sus died on the tree, Pur-chased par-don for
thee, Can you say 'It is well with my soul'? Yes, it is well, I
know it is well, Pre-cious blood for my clean-sing, What a sto-ry to tell!

2. Is it well in thy life,
Is it well in thy life,
Are you living in His victory,
In the toil and the strife,
Is it well in thy life,
Is there peace and His sweet harmony?
Yes it is well,
I know it is well,
His power worketh in me,
All temptation to quell.

3. Is it well in thy home,
Is it well in thy home,
Is Christ in control over all?
Problems great, problems small,
Does he deal with them all,
Is it well, is it well in thy home?
Yes it is well,
I know it is well,
For Christ is my Captain,
And with me He doth dwell.

4. Now the Bible is true,
Has a message for you,
It calls you to faith in the Lord.
Do be sure you are right,
For a terrible plight
Awaits those who turn from the Word.
Will you believe?
And His promise receive,
Are you trusting in Jesus
Unto Him will you cleave?

180   It is well with my soul

Horatio G. Spafford

2. Though Satan should buffet, though trials should come, Let this blest assurance control,
That Christ has regarded my helpless estate, And has shed His own blood for my soul,
And has shed His own blood for my soul.

3. My sin, oh, the bliss of this glorious thought! My sin, not in part but the whole,
Is nailed to the cross, and I bear it no more, Praise the Lord, praise the Lord, O my soul,
Praise the Lord, Praise the Lord O my soul!

4. For me, be it Christ, be it Christ hence to live: If Jordan above me shall roll,
No pang shall be mine, for in death as in life Thou wilt whisper Thy peace to my soul,
Thou wilt whisper thy peace to my soul.

5. But, Lord, 'tis for Thee, for Thy coming we wait, The sky, not the grave, is our goal;
Oh trump of the angel! Oh voice of the Lord! Blessed hope, blessed hope of my soul.
Blessed hope, blessed hope of my soul!

6. And Lord, haste the day when my faith shall be sight, The clouds be rolled back as a scroll;
The trump shall resound, and the Lord shall descend, Even so, it is well with my soul,
It is well, it is well with my soul.

181   It's about the cross

It's not just a-bout the man-ger Where the ba-by lay, It's not all-a-bout the an-gels who sang for him that day. It's not all a-bout the shep-herds, or the bright and shi-ning star, It's not all a-bout the wise men Who tra-velled from a - far. It's a - bout the cross, It's a-bout my sin, It's a - bout how Je - sus came to be born once So that we could be born a - gain. It's a-bout the stone That was rolled a - way So that you and I could have real life some - day; It's a - bout the cross, It's a-bout cross. It's

won-der-ful and great, But it's ___ end-ing that can save you and that's why we ce-le brate. It's a bout the cross,

___ It's a-bout my sin; It's a bout how Je - sus came to be born ___ So that we could be

___ a - gain. ___ It's a-bout God's love Nailed - to a tree, It's a-bout ev'-ry drop of blood

That flowed from Him When it should have been me. ___ It's a-bout the stone That was rolled a - way, ___

___ So that you and I could have real life some-day, It's a bout the cross, ___ It's a-bout

the cross.

182　Jesu, if still the same

Charles Wesley

2. Thou hast pronounced the mourners blest,
And lo! for thee I ever mourn.
I cannot, no, I will not rest
Till thou my only rest return;
Till thou, the Prince of Peace appear,
And I receive the Comforter.

3. Where is the blessednest bestowed
On all that hunger after thee?
I hunger now, I thirst for God!
See the poor fainting sinner, see,
And satisfy with endless peace,
And fill me with thy righteousness.

4. Ah, Lord! - if thou art in that sigh,
Then hear thyself within me pray,
Hear in my heart thy Spirit's cry,
Mark what my labouring soul would say,
Answer the deep, unmuttered groan,
And show that thou and I are one.

5. Shine on thy work, disperse the gloom;
Light in thy light I then shall see.
Say to my soul, "Thy light is come,
Glory divine is risen on thee;
Thy warfare's past, thy mourning's o'er,
Look up, for thou shalt weep no more."

6. Lord, I believe the promise sure,
And trust thou wilt not long delay;
Hungry, and sorrowful, and poor,
Upon thy Word myself I stay;
Into thine hands my all resign,
And wait till all thou art is mine!

183   Jesus alone

N.J. Clayton

Je - sus a-lone could bring sal - va - tion, And die in my stead up - on the tree,

Giv - ing re-lease from con - dem-na - tion, For time and __ e __ ter - ni - ty.

Chorus

I'm filled with joy be-cause I know He loves me, And sat - is - fied that He can

ne - ver fail, No-bo-dy else com - pares with Je - sus, No one so near, so dear as He.

2. Gracious and kind was he to save me,
And take all my burden away,
Every transgression He forgave me,
And turned all my night to day.
I'm filled with joy because I know He loves me,
And satisfied that He can never fail,
Nobody else compares with Jesus,
No one so near, so dear as he.

3. Jesus alone can take my sadness,
And give me a wonderful peace,
Jesus alone can bring me gladness,
And cause every care to cease.
I'm filled with joy because I know He loves me,
And satisfied that He can never fail,
Nobody else compares with Jesus,
No one so near, so dear as he.

Music © 2016 Harry Hicks

184   Jesus Christ, the same today

Brenda Gallant

Je-sus Christ, the - same to-day, Yes-ter-day, for - e - ver.

He will guide us on our way, He will fail us ne - ver.

2. In His person, He's the same,
His purposes are sure -
This the reason why He came;
To save and make us pure.

3. On His promises we rest,
To nurture and provide.
In His presence we are blest,
What need we ought beside?

4. He, our Saviour and our Friend
Along life's winding way,
With us, right up to the end -
The dawn of endless day.

185   Jesus died for me

I will go, I can-not stay From the arms of love a-way; O for strength of faith to say, Je-sus died for me. Can it be, O can it be, There is hope for one like me? I will go with this my plea: Je-sus died for me.

2. Though I long have tried in vain,
Tried to break the tempter's chain,
Yet tonight I'll try again,
Jesus, help thou me.
Can it be, O can it be
There is hope for one like me?
I will go with this my plea:
Jesus died for me.

3. I am lost, and yet I know
Earth can never heal my woe;
I will rise at once and go,
Jesus died for me.
Can it be, ...

4. Something whispers in my soul,
Though my sins like mountains roll,
Jesus' blood will make me whole,
Jesus died for me.
Can it be, ...

5. I obey the Saviour's call,
Now to him I yield my all,
At His feet, where others fall,
There's a place for me.
Can it be, O can it be
There is hope for one like me?
I will go with this my plea:
Jesus died for me.

186   Jesus for me

Wm. J. Kirkpatrick

Je-sus my Sav-iour is all things to me, O what a won-der-ful
Sav-iour is he; Guid-ing, pro-tect-ing o'er life's roll-ing sea,
Chorus
Migh-ty De-liv-'rer, Je-sus for me. Je-sus for me,
Je-sus for me, All the time, ev-'ry-where, Je-sus for me.

2. Jesus in sickness And Jesus in health,
Jesus in poverty, Comfort or wealth,
Sunshine or tempest, Whatever it be,
He is my safety; Jesus for me.
Jesus for me, Jesus for me,
All the time, Ev'rywhere,
Jesus for me.

3. He is my refuge, My rock and my tower,
He is my fortress, My strength and my power;
Life everlasting, My Daysman is He,
Blessed Redeemer! Jesus for me.
Jesus for me,........

4. He is my Prophet, My priest and my King,
He is my bread of life, Fountain and spring;
Bright Son of Righteousness,
Daystar is He, Blessed Redeemer!
Jesus for me.
Jesus for me,........

5. Jesus in sorrow, In joy or in pain,
Jesus my treasure In loss or in gain;
Constant companion, Where'ere I may be,
Living or dying, Jesus for me.
Jesus for me,........

187   Jesus the Saviour

G.C. Tullar

Je - sus the Sav - iour, dy - ing on Cal - v'ry, Pur - chased my par - don, set - ting me free: Love so a - bun - dant, should I not serve Him, When He so glad - ly suf - fered for me?

Chorus

Lord, I am Thine, Sav - iour Di - vine, Oh, what a joy, just to know Thou art mine!

2. Oh, what a Saviour, tender and loving,
Guarding my footsteps lest I should stray:
Love so abundant, leading me ever
Out of the darkness into the day.
Lord, I am Thine,
Saviour Divine!
Oh, what a joy,
Just to know thou art mine!

3. Constant Companion, leaving me never,
Bidding me follow close by His side:
He is my Refuge, safely I shelter,
Knowing He loves me, whate'er betide.
Lord, I am Thine,
Saviour Divine!
Oh, what a joy,
Just to know thou art mine!

Music © 2015 Harry Hicks

188   Jesus will walk with me

Haldor Lillenas

Je-sus will walk with me down through the va - lley Je-sus will walk with me ov-er the plain;

When in the sha-dow or when in the sun-shine, If He goes with me I will not com-plain.

Chorus

Je - sus my Sav-iour will walk with me, Je - sus my Sav-iour will talk with me, In

joy or sor-row - to - day or to-mor-row - I know he will walk - with me.

2. Jesus will walk with me when I am tempted,
Giving me strength as my need may demand;
When in affliction His presence in near me,
I am upheld by His almighty hand.
Jesus my Saviour will walk with me,
Jesus my Saviour will talk with me,
In joy or sorrow, today and tomorrow,
I know He will walk with me.

3. Jesus will walk with me, guarding me ever,
Giving me vict'ry through storm and through strife;
He is my comforter, counsellor, leader,
Over the uneven journey of life.
Jesus my Saviour will walk with me,
Jesus my Saviour will talk with me,
In joy or sorrow, today and tomorrow,
I know He will walk with me.

4. Jesus will walk with me in life's fair morning,
And when the shadows of evening must come;
Living or dying He will not forsake me,
Jesus will walk with me all the way home.
Jesus my Saviour will walk with me,
Jesus my Saviour will talk with me,
In joy or sorrow, today and tomorrow,
I know He will walk with me.

189   Jesus, God's Son

Richard Morgan

Jes-sus, God's Son, the cru-ci-fied, To win us peace, in an-guish died,

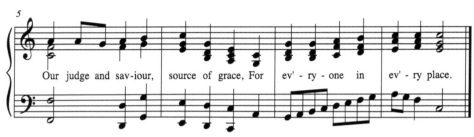

Our judge and sav-iour, source of grace, For ev'-ry-one in ev'-ry place.

Jesus, God's Son, the crucified,
To win us peace, in anguish died,
Our judge and saviour, source of grace,
For everyone, in every place.

2. In love he gave himself for us,
He paid sin's debt and bore its curse;
He plumbed the depths of human pain
That we might live and love again.

3. All rank and greatness he gave up
For suffering's universal cup,
As merely human, on the cross,
For common gain bore all our loss.

4. So let us share his openness,
Live out, ourselves, his hard won peace;
As humble sharers of his love,
May we too reconcilers prove.

190 Jesus, grant me this, I pray

Latin, 17th C., tr. H.W.Baker (1821-77)

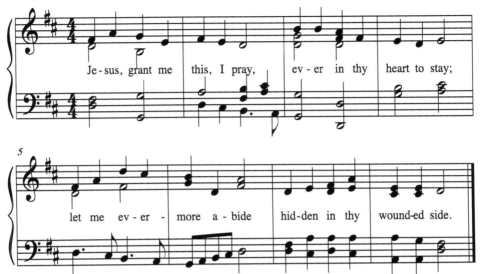

Jesus, grant me this, I pray, ev-er in thy heart to stay; let me ev-er-more a-bide hid-den in thy wound-ed side.

2. If the world or Satan lay
tempting snares about my way,
I am safe when I abide
in thy heart and wounded side.

3. If the flesh, more dangerous still,
tempt my soul to deeds of ill,
naught I fear when I abide
in thy heart and wounded side.

4. Death will come one day to me;
Jesus, cast me not from thee:
dying let me still abide
in thy heart and wounded side.

191   Jesus, my strength (1st tune)

Charles Wesley

Je-sus, my strength, my hope, On thee I cast my care, With hum-ble con-fi-dence look up, And know thou hear'st my prayer. Give me on thee to wait, Till I can all things do, On thee al-migh-ty to cre-ate, Al-migh-ty to re-new.

2. I want a sober mind,
A self-renouncing will
That tramples down and casts behind
The baits of pleasing ill:
A soul inured to pain,
To hardship, grief and loss,
Bold to take up, firm to sustain
The consecrated cross.

3. I want a godly fear,
A quick-discerning eye,
That looks to thee when sin is near
And sees the tempter fly;
A spirit still prepared,
And armed with jealous care,
Forever standing on its guard,
And watching unto prayer.

4. I want a heart to pray,
To pray and never cease,
Never to murmur at thy stay,
Or wish my suffering less;
This blessing above all,
Always to pray I want,
Out of the deep on thee to call,
And never, never faint.

5. I want a true regard,
A single, steady aim,
Unmoved by threat'ning or reward,
To thee and thy great name;
A jealous, just concern
For thine immortal praise;
A pure desire that all may learn
And glorify thy grace.

6. I rest upon thy Word,
The promise is for me;
My succour, and salvation, Lord,
Shall surely come from thee.
But let me still abide,
Nor from my hope remove,
Till thou my patient spirit guide
Into thy perfect love.

191   Jesus, my strength (2nd tune)

C. Wesley

Je - sus, my strength, my hope, On Thee I set my care, With hum-ble con - fi - dence look up, And know Thou hear'st my prayer. Give me on Thee to wait, Till I can all ___ things do: On Thee, al - migh - ty to ___ cre - ate, Al-migh-ty to ___ re - new.

2. I want a sober mind,
A self-renouncing will
That tramples down and casts behind
The baits of pleasing ill:
A soul inured to pain,
To hardship, grief and loss,
Bold to take up, firm to sustain
The consecrated cross.

3. I want a godly fear,
A quick-discerning eye,
That looks to thee when sin is near
And sees the tempter fly;
A spirit still prepared,
And armed with jealous care,
Forever standing on its guard,
And watching unto prayer.

4. I want a heart to pray,
To pray and never cease,
Never to murmur at thy stay,
Or wish my suffering less;
This blessing above all,
Always to pray I want,
Out of the deep on thee to call,
And never, never faint.

5. I want a true regard,
A single, steady aim,
Unmoved by threat'ning or reward,
To thee and thy great name;
A jealous, just concern
For thine immortal praise;
A pure desire that all may learn
And glorify thy grace.

6. I rest upon thy Word,
The promise is for me;
My succour, and salvation, Lord,
Shall surely come from thee.
But let me still abide,
Nor from my hope remove,
Till thou my patient spirit guide
Into thy perfect love.

192 Jesus, name all names above

Theoctiscus, c.890

Je-sus, name all names a-bove; Je-sus, best and dear - est; Je-sus, fount of perfect love, Hol - iest, ten - d'rest, near - est; Thou the source of grace com - ple - test, Thou the pur - est, thou the sweet-est, Thou the well of power di-vine, Make me, keep me, seal me thine!

Fin

2. Jesus, crowned with bitter thorn,
By mankind forsaken,
Jesus, who through scourge and scorn
Held thy faith unshaken,
Jesus, clad in purple raiment,
For man's evils making payment:
Let not all thy woe and pain,
Let not Calvary be in vain!

3. Jesus, open me the gate
That of old he entered
Who, in that most lost estate,
Wholly on thee ventured;
Thou, whose wounds are ever pleading,
And thy Passion interceding,
From my weakness let me rise
To a home in paradise!

193   Jesus, stand among us

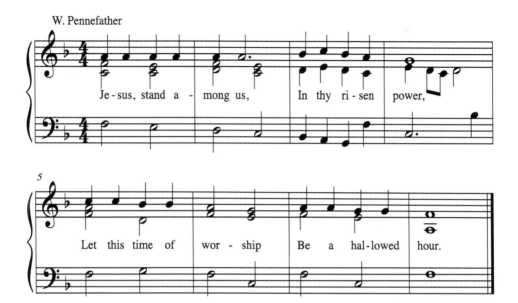

W. Pennefather

Je - sus, stand a - mong us, In thy ri - sen power,

Let this time of wor - ship Be a hal - lowed hour.

2. Breathe Thy Holy Spirit
Into every heart,
Bid the fears and sorrows
From each soul depart.

3. Thus with quickened foorsteps
We'll pursue our way,
Watching for the dawning
Of eternal day.

194   Jesus, tender shepherd

Mrs. M.L.Duncan

Je-sus, ten-der shep-herd, hear me, Bless Thy li-tle lamb to-night;

Through the dark-ness be Thou near me, Keep me safe till morn-ing light.

2. All this day Thy hand has led me,
And I thank Thee for Thy care;
Thou hast clothed me, warmed, and fed me,
Listen to my evening prayer.

3. Let my sins be all forgiven,
Bless the friends I love so well;
Take me, when I die, to heaven,
Happy there with Thee to dwell.

195   Jesus, the crucified

Rev. W.J.Sparrow-Simpson

Je-sus, the cru-ci-fied, pleads for _ me, While He is nailed to the shame-ful _ tree,

Scorned and for-sa-ken, de - ri-ded and cursed, See how His en-e-mies do their worst! _____

Yet, in the midst of the tor - ture and shame Je - sus, the cru-ci-fied, breathes my name!

Won - der of won - ders, oh! how can it be? Je - sus, the cru-ci-fied, pleads for me!

2. Lord, I have left Thee, I have denied,
Followed the world in my selfish pride;
Lord, I have joined in the hateful cry:
'Slay Him, away with Him, crucify!'
Lord, I have done it, oh! ask me not how;
Woven the thorns for Thy tortured brow;
Yet in His pity so boundless and free,
Jesus, the crucified, pleads for me!

3. Though thou hast left Me and wandered away
Chosen the darkness instead of the day;
Though thou art covered with many a stain,
Though thou hast wounded me, oft and again;
Though thou hast followed thy wayward will;
Yet, in my pity, I love thee still.
Wonder of wonders, it ever must be!
Jesus, the crucified, pleads for me!

4. Jesus is dying, in agony sore,
Jesus is suffering, more and more,
Jesus is bowed with the weight of His woe,
Jesus is faint with each bitter throe.
Jesus is bearing it all in my stead,
Pity incarnate for me has bled;
Wonder of wonders, it ever must be!
Jesus, the crucified, pleads for me!

196 Jesus, these eyes

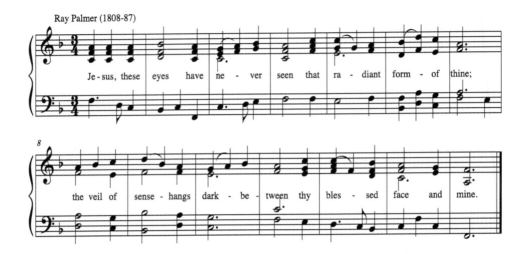

Ray Palmer (1808-87)

Je-sus, these eyes have ne-ver seen that ra-diant form of thine;

the veil of sense-hangs dark-be-tween thy bles-sed face and mine.

2. I see thee not, I hear thee not,
yet art thou oft with me;
and earth has ne'er so dear a spot
as where I meet with thee.

3. Yet, thou I have not seen, and still
must rest in faith alone,
I love the, dearest Lord, and will,
unseen, but not alone.

4. When death these mortal eyes shall seal,
and still this throbbing heart,
the rending veil shall thee reveal
all glorious as thou art.

Music © 2016 Harry Hicks

197 Jesus, thou soul

Charles Wesley

Je - sus, thou soul of all our joys, For whom we now lift up our voice, And all our strength ex - ert, Vouch - safe the grace we humb - ly claim, Com - pose in - to a thank - ful frame, And tune thy peo - ple's heart.

2. While the heavenly work we join,
Thy glory be our sole design,
Thy glory, not our own;
Still let us keep our end in view,
And still the pleasing task pursue,
To please our God alone.

3. The secret pride, the subtle sin,
Oh, let it never more steal in,
T'offend thy glorious eyes,
To desecrate our hallowed strain,
And make our solemn service vain,
And mar iur sacrifice.

4. To magnify thy awful name,
To spread the honours of the Lamb,
Let us our voices raise;
Our souls and bodies' powers unite,
Regardless of our own delight,
And dead to human praise.

5. Still let us on our guard be found,
And watch against the power of sound
With sacred jealousy;
Lest haply sense should damp our zeal,
And music's charms bewitch and steal
Our heart away from thee.

6. That hurrying strife far off remove,
That noisy burst of selfish love
Which swells the formal song;
The joy from out our heart arise,
And speak, and sparkle in our eyes,
And vibrate on our tongue.

7. Then let us praise our common Lord,
And sweetly join with one accord
Thy goodness to proclaim;
Jesus, thyself in us reveal,
And all our faculties shall feel
Thy harmonising name.

8. With calmly reverential joy,
Oh, let us all our lives employ
In setting forth thy love;
And raise in death our triumph higher,
And sing, with all the heavenly choir,
That endless song above.

198   Jesus, I will trust Thee

M.J. Walker

Je-sus, I will trust Thee, trust Thee with my soul; Guil-ty, lost and help - less, Thou canst make me whole. There is none in hea - ven or on earth like Thee; Thou hast died for sin-ners there-fore, Lord, for me.

Chorus

In thy love __ con fi __ ding I will seek Thy face, Wor - ship and __ a - dore __ Thee, for Thy wond - rous grace.

2. Jesus, I can trust Thee, trust thy written Word; Since thy voice of mercy I have often heard.
When thy Spirit teacheth, to my taste how sweet! Only may I hearken, sitting at Thy feet.
In thy love confiding I will seek Thy face,   Worship and adore thee, for Thy wondrous grace.

3. Jesus, I do trust Thee, trust thee without doubt; "Whosoever cometh, Thou wilt not cast out;"
Faithful is Thy promise, precious is thy blood - These my soul's salvation, Thou my Saviour God.
In thy love confiding I will seek Thy face,   Worship and adore thee, for Thy wondrous grace.

199 Jesus, meek and gentle

G.R. Prynne

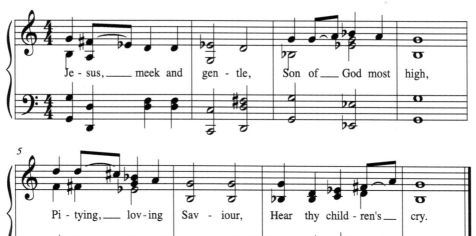

Je - sus, ___ meek and gen - tle, Son of ___ God most high,

Pi - tying, ___ lov - ing Sav - iour, Hear thy child - ren's ___ cry.

2. Pardon our offences,
Loose our captive chains,
Break down every idol
Which our soul detains.

3. Give us holy freedom,
Fill our hearts with love,
Draw us, holy Jesus,
To the realms above.

4. Lead us on our journey,
Be thyself the way
Through terrestial darkness
To celestial day.

5. Jesus, meek and gentle,
Son of God most high,
Pitying, loving Saviour,
Hear thy children's cry.

Music © 2008 Harry Hicks

200   Join all the glorious names

Isaac Watts

Join all the glor - ious names of wis - dom, love and pow'r, that ev - er mor-tals knew, that an - gels ev - er bore: All are too mean to speak his worth, too mean to set my Sav - iour forth.

2. But O what gentle terms, what condescending ways doth our Redeemer use to teach his heav'nly grace!
   Mine eyes with joy and wonder see what forms of love He bears for me.

3. Arrayed in mortal flesh he like an angel stands, and holds the promises and pardons in his hands:
   Commissioned from his Father's throne to make his grace to mortals known.

4. Great Prophet of my God, my tongue would bless thy Name; by Thee the joyful news of our salvation came.
   The joyful news of sins forgiv'n, of hell subdued, and peace with heav'n.

5. Be thou my cousellor, my pattern and my guide, and through this desert land still keep me by my side;
   O let my feet ne'er run astray nor rove nor seek the crooked way.

6. I love my shepherd's voice, his watchful eyes shall keep my wandering soul among the thousands of his sheep;
   He feeds his flock, he calls their names, his bosom bears the tender lambs.

7. To this dear surety's hand will I commit my cause; He answers and fulfills his Father's broken laws;
   Behold my soul at freedom set! My surety paid the dreadful debt.

8. Jesus my great high Priest offered his blood and died; my guilty conscience seeks no sacrifice beside;
   His powerful blood did once atone; and now it pleads before the throne.

9. My Advocate appears for my defence on high, the Father bows his ear, and lays his thunder by;
   Not all that hell or sin can say shall turn his heart, his love away.

10. My dear almighty Lord, my conquerer and my King, thy sceptre and thy sword, thy reigning grace I sing;
    Thine is the power; behold I sit in willing bonds before thy feet.

11. Now let my soul arise, and tread the tempter down, my captain leads me forth to conquest and a crown.
    A feeble saint shall win the day, though death and hell obstruct the way.

12. Should all the hosts of death and powers of hell unknown, put their most dreadful forms of rage and mischief on;
    I shall be safe, for Christ displays superior power and guardian grace.

201 Join all the names

Isaac Watts

Join all the names of love and power That ev - ver men__ or an - gels bore;
All are too mean to speak__ his worth, Or set__ Im - man - uel's glo - ry forth.

2. But O what condescending ways
He takes to teach his heavenly grace!
My eyes with joy and wonder see
What forms of love he bears for me.

3. Great Prophet let me bless thy Name:
By thee the joyful tidings came,
Of wrath appeased, of sins forgiven,
Of hell subdued, and peace with heaven.

4. Jesus, my great High Priest has died,
I seek no sacrifice beside;
His blood did once for all atone,
And now it pleads before the throne.

5. My advocate appears on high,
The Father lays his thunder by;
Not all that earth or hell can say,
Shall turn my Father's heart away.

6. My Lord, my Conqu'ror and my King,
Thy sceptre and thy sword I sing;
Thine is the victory, and I sit
A joyful subject at thy feet.

7. Should death and hell, and powers unknown
Put all their forms of mischief on,
I shall be safe; for Christ displays
Salvation in more sovereign ways.

202   Lead me to the rock

L. Hartsough

8ves in the bass

Lead me to the rock that's high-er Than the rock poor self can show; Lead me to its per-fect shel-ter, the Strong Tower from ev'-ry foe.

Chorus

In the High-er Rock I'm trust-ing, Rest-ful, peace-ful, saved, and free, 'Tis the test-ed Rock of A-ges, It's dear sha-dow shel-ters me.

2. Yes, the Higher Rock so towering Gives, amid life's rudest storms,
Perfect refuge, surest safety, Sweetest rest amid alarms.
In the Highest Rock I'm trusting, Restful, peaceful, saved, and free,
'Tis the tested Rock of Ages, Its dear shadow shelters me.

3. 'Tis the Higher Rock that gives me Faith's glad strength for ev'ry hour;
Oh to measure all it's gladness, All it's preciousness of power!

4. 'Tis the Higher Rock sustains me Joyously from day to day;
Lifting heart, and soul, and spirit, To the purer, holier way.

5. 'Tis the Higher Rock that saves me, 'Tis the Higher Rock I've found,
Where abide the crowning graces - Faith and Hope and Love abound.

6. So will I sing praises to Thee- For Thy wondrous power to save;
Daily 'neath Thy shadow resting, 'Till the victor's palm I wave.

203   Let all creation dance

Brian Wren

Let - all cre - a - tion dance in en - er-gies sub - lime, as
or - der turns with chance, un-fold-ing space - and - time; for
nat-ure's art in glo - ry grows and new - ly shows God's mind and heart.

2. God's breath each force unfurls, igniting from a spark
expanding starry swirls, with whirlpools dense and dark.
Though moon and sun seem mindless things,
each orbit sings: your will be done.

3. Our own amazing earth, with sunlight, cloud and storms,
and life's abundant growth in lovely shapes and forms
is made for praise, a fragile whole,
and from it's soul heav'n's music plays.

4. Lift heart and soul and voice: in Christ all praises meet,
and nature shall rejoice as all is made complete.
In hope be strong, All life befriend,
and kindly tend creation's song.

Music © 2011 Harry Hicks
Words: Brian Wren. Reproduced by permission of Stainer & Bell Ltd.

204　　Let all mortal flesh

Liturgy of St. James
tr. G Moultrie (1829-85)

Let all mor-tal flesh keep sil-ence and with fear and trembl-ing stand;

pon-der no-thing earth-ly-mind-ed, for with bless-ing in his hand

Christ our God to earth des-cend-eth, our full ho-mage to de-mand.

2. King of kings, yet born of Mary,
　as of old on earth he stood,
Lord of lords, in human vesture -
　in the body and the blood -
he will give to all the faithful
　his own self for heavenly food.

3. Rank on rank the host of heaven
　spreads its vanguard on the way,
as the Light of light descendeth
　from the realms of endless day,
that the powers of hell may vanish
　as the darkness clears away.

4. At his feet the six-winged seraph;
　cherubim with sleepless eye
veil their faces to the Presence,
　as with ceaseless voice they cry,
Alleluia, Alleluia,
　Alleluia, Lord most high.

205   Let earth and Heaven agree

Charles Wesley

Let earth and hea-ven a - gree, Ang - els and men be joined, To ce-le-brate with me The Sav-iour of man - kind;_____ T'a - dore the all - a - ton-ing Lamb, And bless the sound of Je - su's name.

2. Jesus, transporting sound!
The joy of earth and heaven!
No other help is found,
No other name is given
By which we can salvation have;
But Jesus came the world to save.

3. Jesus, harmonious name!
It charms the hosts above;
They evermore proclaim,
And wonder at his love;
'Tis all their happiness to gaze,
'Tis heaven to see our Jesu's face.

4. His name the sinner hears,
And is from sin set free;
'Tis music in his ears,
'Tis life and victory;
New songs do now his lips employ,
And dances his glad heart for joy.

5. Stung by the scorpion sin
My poor expiring soul
The balmy sound drinks in,
And is at once made whole.
See there my Lord upon the tree!
I hear, I feel, he died for me.

6. O unexampled love!
O all-redeeming grace!
How swiftly didst thou move
To save a fallen race!
What shall I do to make it known
What thou for all mankind hast done!

7. Oh, for a trumpet-voice
On all the world to call,
To bid their hearts rejoice
In him who died for all!
For all my Lord was crucified,
For all, for all my Saviour died!

8. To serve thy blessed will,
The dying love to praise,
Thy counsel to fulfill,
And minister thy grace.
Freely what I receive to give,
The life of heaven on earth I live.

206 Let me tell you tonight/Wonderful place

Brenda Gallant

Let me tell you to-night, Of the man-sions so bright, That the sav-iour has gone to pre-pare, There's no sick-ness or night, Faith is turned in-to sight, And the glo-ry at last we will share. Wonder-ful place, Where we see our Lord's face, There to praise Him and thank Him For His soul sav-ing grace.

2. Let me tell you tonight
Of the wonderful sight,
That the shepherds of old went to view,
God incarnate on earth,
A miraculous birth,
And the best thing of all: it is true!
God came to earth
A miraculous birth
By His coming revealing
Just how much you are worth.

3. Let me tell you tonight,
Of the sinner's sad plight,
And the God who was willing to die,
How He went to the cross,
Suffered anguish and loss
To bring rebels and sinners both nigh.
Look to the tree,
Jesus died there for thee,
Bore your sin in His body,
That your soul might go free.

4. Let me tell you tonight
Of the glorious sight,
There's a tomb with the stone rolled away,
For the Saviour arose,
Having vanquished His foes,
resurrection, Oh glorious day!
Now He's on high
Having once come to die
Seated there in the glory
Bidding us to come nigh.

5. Let me tell you tonight,
He will burst into sight
When He comes in the clouds by and by.
Have your sins been forgiven?
Are you ready for heaven?
Once there; never a tear or a sigh.
Wonderful place,
Where we see our Lord's face,
There to praise Him and thank Him
For His soul-saving grace.

207   Let saints on earth

Charles Wesley

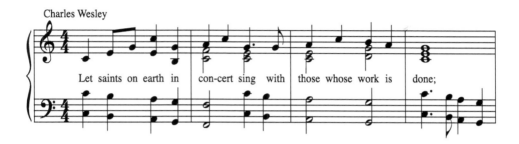

Let saints on earth in con-cert sing with those whose work is done;

for all the ser-vants of our King in heav'n and earth - are one.

2. One family, we dwell in him,
one Church, above, beneath;
though now divided by the stream,
the narrow stream of death.

3. One army of the living God,
to his command we bow:
part of the host have crossed the flood,
and part are crossing now.

4. E'en now to their eternal home
there pass some spirits blest;
while others to the margin come,
waiting their call to rest.

5. Jesu, be thou our constant guide;
then, when the word is given,
bid Jordan's narrow stream divide,
and bring us safe to heaven.

208   Let the seventh angel sound

Isaac Watts

Let the se-venth an-gel sound on high, Let shout be heard through all the sky;

Kings of the earth, with glad ac-cord Give up your king-doms to the Lord.

2. Almighty God, thy pow'r assume,
Who was, and is, and is to come;
Jesus, the Lamb who once was slain,
For ever live, for ever reign.

3. The angy nations fret and roar,
That they can slay the saints no more;
On wings of vengeance flies our God
To pay the long arrears of blood.

4. Now must the rising dead appear,
Now, the decisive sentence hear;
Now the dear martyrs of the Lord
receive an infinite reward.

209   Let the song go round the earth

Let the song go round the earth, Je-sus Christ is Lord!

Sound His prais-es, tell His worth, See His Name a - dored;

Ev - 'ry — clime and ev' - ry — tongue Join the grand, the glo-rious song!

2. Let the song go round the earth!
From the eastern sea,
Where the daylight had its birth,
Glad, and bright, and free;
China's million join the strains,
Waft them onto India's plains.

3. Let the song go round the earth!
Lands where Islam's sway
Darkly broods o'er home and hearth,
Cast their bonds away!
Let His praise from Africa's shore
Rise and swell her wide lands o'er.

4. Let the song go round the earth!
Where the summer smiles;
Let the notes of holy mirth
Break from distant isles!
Inland forests dark and dim,
Snow-bound coasts give back the hymn.

5. Let the song go round the earth!
Jesus Christ is King!
With the story of His worth
Let the whole world ring!
Him creation all adore
Evermore and evermore!

210   Let the whole creation cry

Stopford A Brooke, 1832-1916.

Let the_ whole cre - a - tion cry, 'Glo - ry be to the Lord on high!'

Heav'n and_ earth cre - a - tion sing, 'God is_ good and there-fore King!'

Praise him_ all ye hosts a - bove, Ev - er_ bright and fair in love;

Sun and_ moon, up - lift your voice, Night and_ stars, in God re-joice!

2. Warriors fighting for the Lord,
Prophets burning with his word,
Those to whom the arts belong,
Add their voices to the song.
Kings of knowledge and of law,
To the glorious circle draw;
All who work and all who wait,
Sing, 'The Lord is good and great!'

3. Men and women, young and old,
Raise the anthem manifold,
And let children's happy hearts
In this worship bear their part;
From the north and southern pole
Let the mighty chorus roll;
Holy, holy, holy One,
Glory be to God alone!

Music © 2015 Harry Hicks

211   Let them neglect

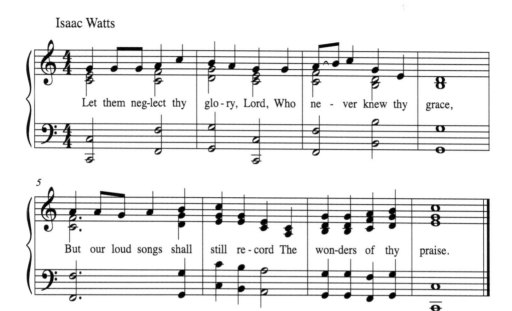

Isaac Watts

Let them neg-lect thy glo-ry, Lord, Who ne - ver knew thy grace,

But our loud songs shall still re - cord The won-ders of thy praise.

2. We raise our shouts, O God, to thee,
And send them to thy throne,
All glory to th'united Three,
The undivided One.

3. 'Twas he (and we adore his name)
That formed us by a word,
'tis he restores our ruined frame;
Salvation to the Lord!

4. Hosanna! let the earth and skies
Repeat the joyful sound,
Rocks, hills and vales, reflect the voice
In one eternal round.

212   Let us join

Charles Wesley

Let us join ('tis God com-mands), Let us join our hearts and hands;

Help to gain our cal-ling's hope, Build we each the oth-er up.

God his bless - ing shall dis-pense, God shall crown his ord - in-ance,

Meet in his ap - point-ed ways, Nour - ish us with soc - ial grace.

2. Let us then as brethren love,
Faithfully his gifts improve,
Carry on the earnest strife,
Walk in holiness of life.
Still forget the things behind;
Follow Christ in heart and mind;
Toward the mark unwearied press,
Seize the crown of righteousness!

3. Plead we thus for faith alone,
Faith which by our works is shown;
God it is who justifies,
Only faith the grace supplies,
Active faith that lives within,
Conquers earth, and hell and sin,
Sanctifies, and makes us whole,
Forms the Saviour in the soul.

4. Let us for this faith contend,
Sure salvation is its end;
Heaven already is begun,
Everlasting life is won.
Only let us persevere
Till we see our Lord appear;
Never from the rock remove,
Saved by faith which works by love.

213   Life is the time

Isaac Watts

Life is the time to serve the Lord, The time t'in-sure the great reward;
And while the lamp holds out to burn The vi-lest sin-ner may re-turn.

2. Life is the hour that God has giv'n
To 'scape from hell, and fly to heav'n,
The day of grace, and mortals may
Secure the blessings of that day.

3. The living know that they must die,
But all the dead forgotten lie,
Their mem'ry and their sense is gone,
Alike unknowing and unknown.

4. Their hatred and their love is lost,
Their envy buried in the dust;
They have no share in all that's done
Beneath the circuit of the sun.

5. Then what my thoughts design to do,
My hands, with all your might pursue,
Since no device, nor work is found,
Nor faith, nor hope beneath the ground.

6. There are no acts of pardon past
In the cold grave to which we haste,
But darkness, death and long despair
Reign in eternal silence there.

214   Light of gladness

Christopher Idle

Light of glad-ness___ Lord of glo-ry, Je-sus Christ our___ King most ho-ly,

Shine a-mong us in your mer-cy: Earth and hea-ven join their hymn.

1. Light of gladness, Lord of glory,
Jesus Christ our King most holy,
Shine among us in your mercy:
Earth and heaven join their hymn.

2. Let us sing at sun's descending
As we see the lights of evening,
Father, Son and Spirit praising
With the holy seraphim.

3. Son of God, through all the ages
Worthy of our holiest praises,
You're the light that never ceases,
Light which never shall grow dim.

215 Listen sweet dove unto my song

George Herbert

Lis - ten sweet dove un - to my song, And spread thy gol-den wings in me; Hat-ching my ten - der heart so long, Till it get wing and fly a - way with __ thee.

2. Such glorious gifts thou didst bestow
The earth did like a heav'n appear,
The stars were coming down to know
If they might mend their wages and serve here.

3.The sun which once did shine alone,
Hung down his head and wished for night.
When he beheld twelve suns for one
Going about the world and giving light.

4. Lord though we change thou art the same,
The same sweet God of love and light:
Restore this day for thy great name,
Unto his ancient and miraculous right.

216   Live out thy life

Frances R. Havergal

Live out Thy life with-in me, O Je-sus, King of kings! By Thou Thy-self the

ans-wer to all my quest-ion-ings: Live out thy life with-in me, and all things have Thy

way! I, the trans-par-ent med-ium, Thy glo-ry to dis-play.

2. The temple has been yielded, and purified of sin,
Let Thy Shekinah glory now shine forth from within,
And all the earth keep silence, the body henceforth be
Thy silent, gentle servant, moved only as by Thee.

3. Its members every moment held subject to Thy call,
Ready to have Thee use them, or not be used at all,
Held without restless longing, or strain, or stress, or fret,
Or chafings at Thy dealings, or thoughts of vain regret.

4. But restful, calm and pliant, from bend and bias free,
Awaiting Thy decision, when Thou hast need of me;
Live out Thy life within me, O Jesus, King of kings!
Be Thou the glorious answer to all my questionings.

217   Long before the world is waking

Timothy Dudley-Smith

Long be-fore the world is wa-king, mor - ning mist on Ga - li - lee,

from the shore, as dawn is brea-king, Je - sus calls a - cross the sea;

hails the boat of wea - ry men, bids them cast their net a gain.

2. So they cast, and all their heaving cannot haul their catch aboard;
   John in wonder turns, perceiving, cries aloud, "It is the Lord!"
   Peter waits for nothing more, plunges in to swim ashore.

3. Charcoal embers brightly burning, bread and fish upon them laid:
   Jesus stands at day's returning in his risen life arrayed;
   as of old his friends to greet, "Here is breakfast, come and eat."

4. Christ is risen! Grief and sighing, sins and sorrows, fall behind;
   fear and failure, doubt, denying, full and free forgiveness find.
   All the soul's dark night is past, morning breaks in joy at last.

5. Morning breaks, and Jesus meets us, feeds and comforts, pardons still;
   as his faithful friends he greets us, partners of his work and will.
   All our days, on every shore, Christ is ours for evermore!

218   Long, long ago (1st tune)

Brenda Gallant

Long, long a-go, God made a pro-mise true; Though men had sinned, the gos-pel light shone through. The wo-man's seed would bruise the ser-pent's head, The sin-less One would suf-fer in man's stead. Down through the years the pro-phets oft for-told God's lov-ing mes-sage that will not grow old.

2. This message brought a note of joy and peace,
Promised to captives freedom and release
Of victory o'er sin and death and hell,
This is the good news Christmas has to tell.
Thus in the fulness of God's time He came,
Our lovely Saviour, Jesus is His name.

3. See, now He lies in that crude bed of straw,
While from the skies the angel voices pour,
Proclaiming to the dark and slumbering world,
That now, at last, God's message in unfurled.
Peace on the earth, goodwill to sinful man,
Promised fulfillment of redemption's plan.

4. Now, look again, with wide and wondering eyes,
See, on a cross the anguished Saviour dies.
He who was born to suffer in man's stead,
Now feels the wrath of God upon His head,
He bears our sins, this sinless Son of God,
Who in the form of man this planet trod.

5. With eyes of faith then let us all behold
The One whose life and death were all foretold.
Look past the manger and the mournful tomb,
See, resurrection light has pieced the gloom.
One day He's coming back to earth to reign
The second advent - let's take up the strain!

6. Glory to God, the Father and the Son,
The Holy Spirit, blessed Three in One!
This Christmastide give praise to God alone,
Invite Him in and let Him take the throne.
Make Him your King and crown Him Lord of all,
In glad surrender at His feet to fall.

218 Long, long ago (2nd tune)

Brenda Gallant

Long, long a-go God made a pro-mise true, Though men had sinned the gos-pel light shone through. The wo-man's seed would bruise the ser-pent's head, The sin-less one would suf-fer in man's stead. Down through the years the pro-phets oft fore-told God's lov-ng mes-sage that will not grow old.

2. This message brought a note of joy and peace,
Promised to captives freedom and release
Of victory o'er sin and death and hell,
This is the good news Christmas has to tell.
Thus in the fulness of God's time he came,
Our lovely Saviour: Jesus is his name.

3. See, now he lies in that crude bed of straw,
While from the skies the angel voices pour
Proclaiming to the dark and slumbering world
That now, at last, God's message is unfurled.
Peace on the earth, goodwill to sinful man
Promised fulfillment of redemption's plan.

4. Now, look again, with wide and wondering eyes;
See, on a cross the anguished Saviour dies.
He who was born to suffer in man's stead
Now feels the wrath of God upon his head.
He bears our sins, this sinless Son of God,
Who in the form of man this planet trod.

5. With eyes of faith then let us all behold
The One whose life and death were all foretold.
Look past the manger and the mournful tomb,
See, resurrection light has pierced the gloom!
One day He's coming back to earth to reign,
The second advent: let's take up the strain.

6. Glory to God the Father and the Son,
The Holy Spirit, blessed Three in One!
This Christmastide give praise to God alone,
Invite Him in and let Him take the throne.
Make Him your King and crown Him Lord of all,
In glad surrender at His feet to fall.

219   Look, ye saints!

T. Kelly

Look, ye saints! the sight is glor-ious, See the Man of sor-rows now,

From the fight re - turned vic - tor - ious, Ev - 'ry knee to Him shall bow.

Crown Him, crown Him, crown Him, crown Him! Crowns be - come the vic-tor's brow.

2. Crown the Saviour, angels crown Him,
   Rich the trophies Jesus brings;
   In the seat of power enthrone Him,
   While the vault of heaven rings.
   Crown Him, crown Him,
   Crown Him, crown Him,
Crown the Saviour, King of kings.

3. Sinners in derision crown Him,
   Mocking thus the Saviour's claim;
   Saints and angels crowd around Him,
   Own His title, praise his name.
   Crown Him, crown Him,
   Crown Him, crown Him,
   Spread abroad the Victor's fame.

4. Hark! those bursts of acclamation;
   Hark! those loud triumphant chords;
   Jesus takes the highest station;
   O what joy the sight affords!
   Crown Him, crown Him,
   Crown Him, crown Him,
   King of kings, and Lord of lords!

220   Lord in your love we dare to speak

Colin Ferguson

Lord in your love we dare to speak, re-joic-ing in your name. Give us a voice that is not weak, for we want to pro-claim the faith that will con-vey the news of your for-giv-ing way, not filled with our small hu-man views but blessed by what you say.

2. Give us a voice that will not fear
what other people say.
Make every sentence strong and clear
and sing the Jesus way.
It is in love we dare to speak
about our Saviour's peace;
bring comfort to the poor and weak
and to the trapped release.

3. Help us to challenge what is wrong,
to lift the yearning soul,
life in its fullness is our song,
for God makes our life whole.
A voice that heals the hurting heart,
helps others to have voice,
gives to the fallen a new start
shows that we have a choice.

4. Then let our voices join as one
as we share God's praise
give thanks for Jesus Christ the Son,
let Spirit fill our days.
Then let us do the things we say
So all the world can see
Our words are not just what we pray
But what we try to be.

Music © 2012 Harry Hicks
Words © 2012 Colin Ferguson

221   Lord Jesus Christ

Martin Luther

Lord Jes-sus Christ all__ praise to Thee, That Thou wast pleased a man to be; Our low es-tate__ Thou__ didst__ not scorn; And an - gels__ sang to__ see Thee__ born.

2. The heavenly Father's only Son,
He left His rightful glorious throne;
The Lord through Whom the worlds were made
Is in the humble manger laid.

3. The brightness of the Light divine
Doth now into our darkness shine;
It breaks upon sin's gloomy night
And makes us children of the light.

4. The Father's Son, for ever blest,
Becomes in His own world a Guest,
To lead us from this vale of strife
Into the everlasting life.

222   Lord Jesus

Synesius of Cyrene tr. A.W.Chatfield

Lord Je - sus, think on me, and purge a - way my sin; from earth - born pas - sions set me free, and make me pure with - in.

2. Lord Jesus, think on me
with many a care opprest;
let me thy loving servant be,
and taste thy promised rest.

3. Lord Jesus, think on me,
nor let me go astray;
through darkness and perplexity
point thou the heavenly way.

4. Lord, Jesus, think on me,
that, when the flood is past,
I may the eternal brightness see
and share thy joy at last.

223 Lord of mercy

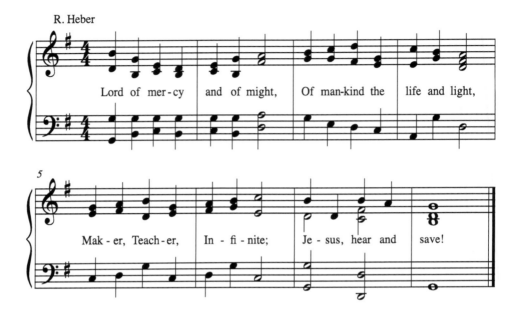

R. Heber

Lord of mer-cy and of might, Of man-kind the life and light,

Mak-er, Teach-er, In - fi - nite; Je - sus, hear and save!

2. Strong creator, Saviour mild,
Humbled to a mortal child,
Captive, beaten, bound, reviled;
Jesus, hear and save!

3. Throned above celestial things,
Borne aloft on angels' wings,
Lord of lords, and King of kings,
Jesus. hear and save!

4. Soon to come to earth again,
Judge of angels and of men;
Hear us now, and hear us then,
Jesus, hear and save!

224   Lord of the brave

Albert Bayly

Lord of the brave in ev-'ry age who, fear-ing nei-ther sword nor flame,

with-stood the cru-el ty-rant's rage; Je-ho-vah! we a-dore your Name.

Chorus

'No o-ther gods we serve, no o-ther lord-ship own;

from your com-mands we will not swerve, but wor-ship you a-lone.' *Fin*

2. Proudly the Babylonian king
before his image bids men fall;
but three will no submission bring;
upon your Name alone they call.
'No other gods we serve,
no other lordship own;
from your commands we will not swerve,
but worship you alone.'

3. Brief is the tyrant's evil hour;
no furnace flame nor lion's den
can overcome your Spirit's power,
or break the will of faithful men.
'No other gods we serve.......'

4. Give us the eyes of faith to see
like Daniel, your eternal plan
fulfilled, when all authority
is given to the Son of man.
'No other gods we serve......'

5. Ancient of days, enthroned above
the fallen images of pride;
your everlasting reign of love
shall, over all, through Christ, abide.
'No other gods we serve,
no other lordship own;
from your commands we will not swerve,
but worship you alone.'

Music © 2012 Harry Hicks   Words: 'Lord of the brave in every age' by Albert Bayly (1901-84)

225　Lord of the restless ocean

Albert Bayly

Lord of the rest-less o-cean, whose Son on Ga-li-lee a-
bove the storm's__ co-mo-tion stood mast-er of the sea;
your name for-ev-er liv-ing with grate-ful hearts we greet,
and hail with glad thanks-giv-ing the ves-sels of your fleet.

2. Lord God, whose vast creation
   is heaven's arching dome,
   your earthly habitation
   a craftman's humble home;
   for all your Spirit dowers
   accept our praises meet,
   whose grace with skill empowers
   the builders of your fleet.

3. O ruler strong, ordaining,
   your word a shining sword,
   from Calvary once reigning,
   our captain and our Lord:
   our loyalty confessing,
   we fall before your feet,
   and join our songs of blessing
   with seamen of your fleet.

4. O Lord, for ever calling
   to ventures new and bold,
   with visions still enthralling
   your servants as of old:
   O speed our high endeavour,
   we humbly you entreat,
   and send us now and ever
   the spirit of your fleet.

226   Lord of the Twelve

David Mowbray

Lord of the Twelve, you drew di-sci-ples near to-you and taught them how to pray. Our hearts with-in us burn as-fol-low-ers to — learn the path of prayer to-day

2. Prayer's dedicated task
- to seek, to knock, to ask -
is year by year the same;
the Spirit from on high
will help God's children cry
the Father's holy Name.

3. Lord, to our spirits bring
the grace of listening,
the gift to hear and heed.
Waken our eyes to see
heaven's boundless charity
and earth's unceasing need.

4. From worship send us out,
alert, resolved, devout,
to do the Father's will.
Mercy, not sacrifice
brings closer paradise,
redeeming human ill.

227   Lord, as the day begins

Timothy Dudley-Smith

Lord, as the day be - gins lift up our hearts in praise; take from us all our sins, guard us in all our ways, Our ev' - ry step di - rect and guide that Christ in all be glo - ri - fied.

2. Christ be in work and skill,   serving each other's need;
Christ be in thought and will,   Christ be in word and deed.
Our minds be set on things above   In joy and peace, in faith and love.

3. Grant us the Spirit's strength,   teach us to walk his way;
so bring us all at length   safe to the close of day.
From hour to hour sustain and bless,   And let our song be thankfulness.

4. Now as the day begins   make it the best of days;
take from us all our sins,   guard us in all our ways.
Our every step direct and guide   That Christ in all be glorified.

228   Lord, dismiss us

2. Thanks we give, and adoration,
For thy gospel's joyful sound;
May the fruits of Thy salvation
In our hearts and lives abound;
May Thy presence
With us evermore be found,
With us evermore be found.

3. So, whene'er the signal's given
Us from earth to call away,
Borne on angels' wings to heaven,
Glad the summons to obey,
May we ever
Reign with Christ in endless day,
Reign with Christ in endless day!

Music © 2008 Harry Hicks

229   Lord, that I may learn

Charles Wesley

Lord, that I may learn of thee, Give me true sim - pli - ci - ty;

Wean my soul, and keep it low, Wil - ling thee a - lone to know.

2. Let me cast my reeds aside,
All that feeds my knowing pride,
Not to man, but God submit,
Lay my reasonings at thy feet.

3. Of my boasted wisdom spoiled,
Docile, helpless as a child,
Only seeing in thy light,
Only walking in thy might.

4. Then infuse the teaching grace,
Spirit of truth and righteousness;
Knowledge, love divine impart,
Life eternal to my heart.

230 Lord, whose Son arose the victor

Albert Bayly

Lord, whose Son a-rose a vic-tor bring-ing life from cross and grave; and, as grain through death is fruit-ful, ev-er lives the world to save; through the years we trace our pur-pose per-fect-ed by giv-ing all, life laid down to find ful-fil-ment in o-be-dience to thy call.

2. For the faith of our forefathers
when thy great command they heard
to proclaim the glorious Gospel
where no voice had preached thy Word;
for their vision and devotion,
service and pure sacrifice,
thanks we give, and for the harvest
gathered at this costly price.

3. Now another summons bids us
offer this dear heritage
for thy grace from it to fashion
new designs for this new age:
ampler plans to serve thy purpose
that thy church my fully give
all her strength to her whole mission
and through Christ mankind may live.

4. Grant thy Holy Spirit's wisdom,
shape our plans to serve thy will;
and, from all laid on thine altar,
make the Church Christ's body still:
ready to be spent and broken
that in all her dying frame
Christ may live, and every people
find salvation in his Name.

231 Low in Thine agony

H. Allon

Low in Thine a-go-ny, Bear-ing Thy cross for me, Sav-iour di-vine! In the dark temp-ter's hour, Quail-ing be-neath his power, Sor-rowing yet more and more, Thou dost in-cline.

2. O Lord of heaven and earth,
   What sorrow unto death
   Doth Thou sustain?
   Thou dost in anguish bow;
   Thou art forsaken now;
   For me this cup of woe
   Thou dost now drain.

3. In deep and trembling fears,
   With crying strong and tears,
   Now Thou dost pray.
   'If it be possible
   This cup so terrible,
   Father most merciful,
   Take it away.'

4. 'Yet, Lord, Thy will be done;
   Lo, I, Thine only Son,
   This cup will drink,'
   O wondrous love of Thine,
   Unspeakable, divine;
   To save this soul of mine
   Thou wilt not shrink.

5. Saviour, give me to share
   Thy lowly will and prayer
   In all my woe;
   In my soul's agony
   Let me resemble Thee;
   An angel strengthening me,
   Let me, too, know.

6. Thy soul its travail saw,
   And in its heavy woe
   Was satisfied.
   So let Thy sorrow, Lord,
   Fulness of joy afford,
   To life and God restored,
   Through Him who died.

232   Make me a captive, Lord

Make me a cap-tive, Lord, And then I shall be free;
Force me to ren-der up my sword, And I shall con-quer'er be. I
sink in life's a-larms When by my-self I stand; Im-
pri-son me with-in Thine arms, And strong shall be my hand.

2. My heart is weak and poor
Until its master find:
It has no spring of action sure,
It varies with the wind:
It cannot freely move
Till Thou hast wrought its chain,
Enslave it with thy matchless love,
And deathless it shall reign.

3. My power is faint and low
Till I have learned to serve:
It wants the needed fire to glow,
It wants the breeze to nerve;
It cannot drive the world
Until itself be driven;
Its flag can only be unfurled
When Thou shalt breathe from heaven.

4. My will is not my own
Till Thou hast made it Thine;
It, it would reach the monarch's throne
It must its crown resign:
It only stands unbent
Amid the clashing strife,
When on Thy bosom it has leant,
And found in Thee its life.

233   Mary and Joseph

Brenda Gallant

Ma - ry and Jo___ seph were - dis - straught; Their Son they could__ not find,

A - mong their kins - folk they - both sought, But Je - sus stayed be - hind.

2. They had assumed that He was there,
As they had journeyed on.
Now to their grief and deep despair
They found they were alone.

3. Back to the temple they both went,
And there they found their Son,
The One whom God had to them sent,
But not to them alone.

4. For Mary's Son is God come down
To save mankind from sin,
And he can be your very own,
If you will let Him in.

5. Don't journey on without the Lord;
You need Him by your side,
For He has promised in His word,
To be your friend and guide.

234　May the grace of Christ

John Newton

1.May the grace of　Christ our Sav-iour,　and the fath-er's
2.Thus we may a - bide in u - nion　with each o - ther

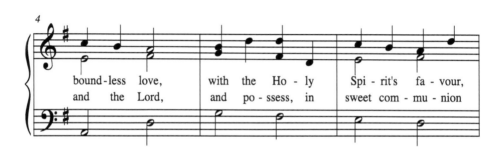

bound-less love,　with the Ho - ly　Spi - rit's fa - vour,
and the Lord,　and po - ssess, in　sweet com - mu - nion

rest　up - on　us　from a - bove.
joys which earth can - not af - ford.

235   May the words of my mouth

After Tim Hughes & Rob Hill

May the words of my mouth and the thoughts of my heart

Bless your___ name Je - sus. And the deeds of the day and the

truth in my ways speak of you, Je - sus. Lord, will you be my vi - sion,

Lord, be my guide, Lord, be my hope, my light and my way,

Lord, be the first in my heart.

236 Meet and right

Charles Wesley

Meet and right it is to sing In ev'-ry time and place.
Glo-ry to our heav'n-ly King, The God of truth and grace.
Join we then with sweet ac-cord, All in one thanks-giv-ing join:
Ho-ly, ho-ly, ho-ly, Lord! E-ter-nal praise be thine!

2. Thee the firstborn sons of light,
In choral symphonies,
Praise by day, day without night.
And never, never cease;
Angels and archangels all
Praise the mystic Three in One,
Sing, and stop, and gaze, and fall
O'erwhelmed before thy throne.

3. Vying with that happy choir
Who chant thy praise above,
We on eagles' wings aspire,
The wings of faith and love;
Thee they sing with glory crowned,
We extol the slaughtered Lamb;
Lower if our voices sound
Our subject is the same.

4. Father, God, thy love we praise
Which gave thy Son to die;
Jesus, full of truth and grace,
Alike we glorify;
Spirit, Comforter divine,
Praise by all to thee be given,
Till we in full chorus join,
And earth is turned to heaven.

237   Mine eyes have seen (1st tune)

Mine— eyes have seen the dawn-ing of a com-ing glor-ious morn, Mine—
eyes have heard the an - gels' song they sang when Christ was born, I have
caught the word of pro-mise un-to wea-ry hearts and worn, That God is march-ing on.

2. I can hear the steady tramping of ten thousand marching feet;
True men and women moving on through highway, lane and street,
They will never pause nor falter till the triumph is complete,
With God they're marching on.

3. Let the sobs of helpless children, crushed by crime as law allows,
Let the blighted lives of women, lost through mankind's broken vows,
Let the sighs of hopeless sorrow every free man's heart arouse,
Since God is marching on.

4. The cries of all earth's little ones have reached the great white Throne,
And the King himself has hearkened, He has made their griefs His own,
He is come to help the helpless, He will make His judgements known,
His strength is marching on.

5. Though the chains of sin be heavy, and they bind our native land,
Though the curse be on the nations, yet our God has raised his hand,
He is calling us to follow, we advance at His command,
With Him we're marching on.

6. No multitude is mighty that has made a league with sin,
Nor wealth nor wisdom can defend, when evil rules within,
For the meek shall overcome them, and the right the day must win,
Since God is marching on.

Music © 2016 Harry Hicks

237 Mine eyes have seen (2nd tune)

R.H. Thomas

Mine eyes have seen the dawn-ing of a com-ing glor-ious morn, Mine
ears have heard the an-gels' song they sang when Christ was born, I have caught the word of
pro-mise un-to wea-ry hearts and worn, That God is march - ing on.

2. I can hear the steady tramping of ten thousand marching feet;
True men and women moving on through highway, lane and street,
They will never pause nor falter till the triumph is complete,
With God they're marching on.

3. Let the sobs of helpless children, crushed by crimes the law allows,
Let the blighted lives of women, lost through manhood's broken vows,
Let the sighs of hopeless sorrow every free man's heart arouse,
Since God is marching on.

4. The cries of all earth's little ones have reached the great white Throne,
And the King Himself has hearkened, He has made their griefs His own,
He is come to help the helpless, He will make His judgements known,
His strength is marching on.

5. Though the chains of sin be heavy, and they bind our native land,
Though the curse be on the nations, yet our God has raised His hand,
He is calling us to follow, we advance an His command;
With Him we're marching on.

6. No multitude is mighty that has made a leaugue with sin,
Now wealth nor wisdom can defend, when evil rules within,
For the meek shall overcome them, and the right the day must win,
Since God is marching on.

238   Most high and holy Lord

Albert Bayly

Most high and ho-ly Lord, by heav'n-ly choirs a-dored, poor is the wor-ship of our heart's de-vo-tion, Thy truth must light our mind, else to thy glo-ry blind; thy love re-vive the em-bers of e-mo-tion.

2. Kindle our tongues with fire,
   words of true praise inspire,
   tune them to heaven's songs of adoration.
   Take the musician's art,
   grace to his soul impart
   to move our hearts to willing consecration.

3. Silence shall praise thee still,
   when, musing on thy will,
   thought fails at mysteries beyond our knowing.
   Faith shall our worship be,
   offered in truth to thee,
   by lowly souls in love's obedience growing.

4. Fulness of perfect praise,
   Father, alone we raise
   when all our powers confess that we adore thee.
   Help us that praise to give
   as for thy will we live;
   all life is worship offered up before thee.

Music © 2012 Harry Hicks   Words: 'Most high and holy Lord' by Albert Bayly (1901-84)

239 My faith looks up to Thee

Ray Palmer

2. May Thy rich grace impart   Strength to my fainting heart
My zeal inspire;
As Thou hast died for me,   Oh may my love to Thee
Pure, warm, and changeless be   A living fire.

3. While life's dark maze I tread,   And griefs around be spread,
Be Thou my Guide:
Bid darkness turn to day,   Wipe sorrow's tears away;
Nor let me ever stray   From Thee aside.

4. When ends life's transient dream,   When death's cold sullen stream
Shall o'er me roll,
Blest Saviour, then in love,   Fear and distress remove;
Oh, bear me safe above,   A ransomed soul.

240 My God, accept my heart this day

Matthew Bridges

My God, ac-cept my heart this day, and make it al-ways thine,_____ that
I from thee no more may stray, no more from thee de-cline.

2. Before the Cross of him who died,
   behold, I prostrate fall;
   let every sin be crucified,
   and Christ be all in all.

3. Anoint me with thy heavenly grace,
   and seal me for thine own;
   that I may see thy glorious face,
   and worship near thy throne.

4. Let every thought and work and word
   to thee be ever given;
   then life shall be thy service, Lord,
   and death the gate of heaven.

5. All glory to the Father be,
   all glory to the Son,
   all glory, Holy Ghost, to thee,
   while endless ages run.

241   My God, my King

H.F. Lyte

My God, my King,— Thy praise— I sing,

My heart is all— thine own; My high-est pow'rs—

My choic-est hours, I yield to Thee a - lone.

2. My voice awake,
Thy part to take;
My soul, the concert join;
Till all around
Shall catch the sound,
And mix their hymns with mine.

3. But man is weak
Thy praise to speak;
Your God, ye angels, sing:
'Tis yours to see,
More near then we,
The glories of our King.

4. His truth and grace
Fill time and space;
As large His honours be
Till all that live
Their homage give,
And praise my God with me.

242 My God, my life, my love

Isaac Watts

My God, my life, my love, To thee, to thee I call, I
can-not live if thou re-move, For thou art all - in all.

2. Thy shining grace can cheer,
This dungeon where I dwell;
'tis paradise when thou art here;
If thou depart, 'tis hell.

3. The smilings of thy face,
How amiable they are!
'tis heav'n to rest in thine embrace,
And nowhere else but there.

4. To thee, and thee alone,
The angels owe their bliss;
They sit around thy gracious throne,
And dwell where Jesus is.

5. Not all the harps above
Can make a heavenly place,
If God his residence remove,
Or but conceal his face.

6. Nor earth nor all the sky
Can one delight afford;
No not a drop of real joy,
Without thy presence, Lord.

7. Thou art the sea of love,
Where all my pleasures roll,
The circle where my passions move,
And centre of my soul.

8. To thee my spirits fly
With infinite desire;
And yet how far from thee I lie!
Dear Jesus, raise me higher!

243   My God, the spring of all

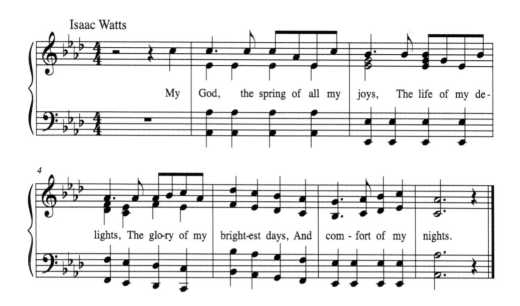

Isaac Watts

My God, the spring of all my joys, The life of my de-lights, The glo-ry of my bright-est days, And com-fort of my nights.

2. In darkest shades if He appear,
My dawning has begun;
He is my soul's sweet morning star
And He my rising sun.

3. The opening heavens around me shine
With beams of sacred bliss,
While Jesus shows his heart is mine,
And whispers, "I am his!"

4. My soul would leave this heavy clay
At that transporting word,
Run up with joy the shining way
T'embrace my dearest Lord.

5. Fearless of hell and ghastly death!
I'd break through ev'ry foe;
The wings of love, the arms of faith
Should bear me conquerer through.

244 My God, what endless pleasures dwell

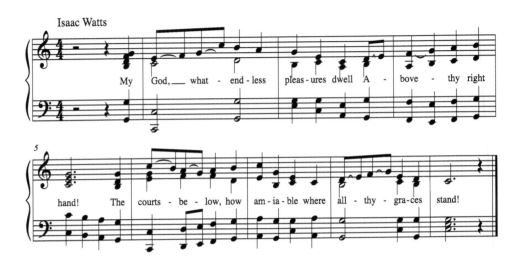

Isaac Watts

My God,— what - end - less pleas - ures dwell A - bove— thy right hand! The courts - be - low, how am - ia - ble where all - thy - gra - ces stand!

2. The swallow near thy temple lies,
   And chirps a cheerful note;
   The lark mounts upward to thy skies,
   And tunes her warbling throat.

3. And we, when in thy presence, Lord,
   We shout with joyful tongues,
   Or sitting round our Father's board,
   We crown the feast with songs.

4. While Jesus shines with quick'ning grace,
   We sing and mount on high;
   But if a frown becloud his face,
   We faint, and tire, and die.

5. Just as we see the lonesome dove
   Bemoan her widowed state,
   Wandering she flies through all the grove,
   And mourns her loving mate.

6. Just so our thoughts from thing to thing
   In restless circles rove,
   Just so we drop, and hang the wing,
   When Jesus hides his love.

245   My heavenly home

Wm. Hunter

My heav'n-ly home is bright and fair; nor pain, nor death can en-ter there;

It's glit-t'ring towers the sun out-shines; that heav'n-ly man-sion shall be mine.

Chorus

go-ing home to die no more! I'm go-ing home to die no more!

2. My Father's house is built on high,   far, far above the starry sky;
When from this earthly prison free,   that heav'nly mansion mine shall be.
I'm going home to die no more!
I'm going home to die no more!

3. Let others seek a home below,   which flames devour, or waves o'erflow;
Be mine a happier lot to own   a heav'nly mansion near the throne.
I'm going home to die no more!
I'm going home to die no more!

246   My latest sun is sinking

Rev. J. Haskell

Verse 4:
Oh, bear my longing heart to Him who bled and died for me;
Whose blood now cleanses from all sin, and gives me victory.

247   My Shepherd leads

Mary S. Leonard

In-to the val-leys of bless-ing My Shep-herd leads; Peace is my spi-rit pos-sess-ing, My soul He feeds. Pas-tures so green are a-round me, Wat-ers of life shall flow; Fair-est of flow-ers sur-round me, Ev-er I on ward go.

Chorus

My Shep-herd leads a-long the way; Kept by His care, I can-not stray; In ten-der love, to realms a-bove, My Shep-herd leads me home!

2. Into the ways that are weary,
My Shepherd leads;
Dark though the skies be, and dreary,
He knows my needs.
Heavy the load I am bearing,
Love hath my pathway planned;
Trusting, I'm still forward faring,
Led by my Shepherd's hand.

Refrain:
My Shepherd leads along the way;
Kept by His care, I cannot stray;
In tender love,
To realms above,
My Shepherd leads me home!

3. Into the land all immortal,
My Shepherd leads;
Unto the glorious portal
My way He heeds.
Mansions of heavenly splendor,
Wait me when I shall come,
Led by the Shepherd so tender,
Unto my Father's home.

248 My song shall be of Jesus

Fanny J. Crosby

My song shall be of Je-sus; His mer-cy crowns my days, He fills my cup with bless-ings, And tunes my heart with praise: My song shall be of Je-sus, The pre-cious Lamb of God, Who gave Him-self my ran-som, And bought me with His blood.

2. My song shall be of Jesus;
   When, sitting at His feet,
   I call to mind His goodness,
   In meditation sweet:
   My song shall be of Jesus,
   Whatever ill betide;
   I'll sing the grace that saves me,
   And keeps me at His side.

3. My song shall be of Jesus,
   While pressing on my way
   To reach the blissful region
   Of pure and perfect day:
   And when my soul shall enter
   The gate of Eden fair,
   A song of praise to Jesus
   I'll sing for ever there.

249 My spirit longs for Thee

J. Byrom

My spi - rit longs for Thee with - in my trou-bled breast,

though I un - wor - thy be of so di-vine a guest.

2. Of so divine a guest
   unworthy thou I be,
   yet has my heart no rest
   unless it come from thee.

3. Unless it come from thee,
   in vain I look around;
   in all that I can see
   no rest is to be found.

4. No rest is to be found
   but in thy blessed love:
   O let my wish be crowned,
   and send it from above!

250 My whole world was lost

My whole world was lost in the darkness of sin, The light of the world is Je-sus. Like sunshine at noonday His glory shone in, The Light of the world is Je-sus.

Chorus

Come to the light, 'tis shining for thee; Sweet-ly the light has dawned up-on me, Once I was blind, but— now I can see: The light of the world is: Jes-sus!

2. No darkness have we who in Jesus abide, The Light of the world is Jesus.
We walk in the light if we follow our guide. The Light of the world is Jesus.
Come to the light, 'tis shining for thee; Sweetly the Light has dawned upon me,
Once I was blind, but now I can see; The Light of the world is: Jesus!

3. You dwellers in darkness, with sin-blinded eyes, The Light of the world is Jesus.
Go, wash at his bidding, and light will arise, The Light of the world is Jesus.
Come to the light, 'tis shining for thee; Sweetly the Light has dawned upon me,
Once I was blind, but now I can see; The Light of the world is: Jesus!

4. No need of the sunlight in heaven, we're told, The Light of the world is Jesus.
The Lamb is the Light in the City of God, The Light of the world is Jesus.
Come to the light, 'tis shining for thee; Sweetly the Light has dawned upon me,
Once I was blind, but now I can see; The Light of the world is: Jesus!

251 Nature with all her powers

Isaac Watts

Nat-ture with all her pow-ers shall sing; God, the Cre-a-tor and the King;

Nor air, nor earth, nor skies nor seas de-ny the tri-bute of their praise.

Be-gin to make his glo-ries known, ye se-raphs that sit near his throne;

Tune your harps high, and spread___ the sound to the cre-a-tion's ut-most bound.

2. All mortal things of meaner frame, exert your force and own His name;
Whilst with our souls and with our voice we sing his honours and our joys.
To him be sacred all we have from the young cradle to the grave;
Our lips shall his loud wonders tell and every word a miracle.

3. This northern isle, our native land lies safe in God th'almighty's hand;
Our foes of victory dream in vain, and wear the captivating chain.
He builds and guards the British throne, and makes it gracious like his own,
Makes our successive princes kind, and gives our dangers to the wind.

4. Raise monumental praises high to his that thunders through the sky,
And with an awful nod or frown shakes and opposing tyrant down.
Pillars of lasting brass proclaim the triumphs of th'eternal Name;
While trembling nations read from far the honours of the God of war.

5. Thus let our flaming zeal employ our loftiest thoughts and loudest songs
Britain pronounce with warmest joy hosanna from ten thousand tongues.
Yet, mighty God, our feeble frame attempts in vain to reach thy Name;
The strongest notes that angels raise faint in the worship and the praise.

252 Near the Cross Col. 1:20

F. J. Crosby

W.H.Doane

Je - sus, keep me near the cross: There a pre - cious foun - tain,

Free to all a hea - ling stream Flows from Cal - v'ry's moun - tain.

Chorus

In the Cross, in the Cross, Be my glo - ry ev - er;

Till my rap - tured soul shall find Rest be - yond the ri - ver.

2. Near the Cross, a trembling soul, love and mercy found me;
There the Bright and Morning Star shed its beams around me.
In the Cross, in the Cross, Be my glory ever;
Till my raptured soul shall find rest beyond the river.

3. Near the Cross! O Lamb of God, bring its scenes before me;
Help me walk from day to day, with its shadow o'er me.
In the cross......

4. Near the cross I'll watch and wait, hoping, trusting ever,
Till I reach the golden strand, just beyond the river.
In the cross......

253 Nearer, still nearer

C.H.Morris

Near - er, still near - er, close to my heart, Draw me, my Sav - iour, so prec - ious Thou art; Fold me, O fold me close to Thy breast, Shel - ter me close in that "Ha - ven of rest."

2. Nearer, still nearer, nothing I bring,
Naught as an off'ring to Jesus my King;
Only my sinful, now contrite heart;
Grant me the cleansing Thy blood doth impart.

3. Nearer, still nearer, Lord, to be Thine,
Sin with its follies I gladly resign,
All of its pleasure, pomp and its pride;
Give me but Jesus, my Lord crucified.

4. Nearer, still nearer, while life shall last,
Till safe in glory my anchor is cast;
Through endless ages ever to be,
Nearer, my Saviour, still nearer to Thee!

254 No other way

Oh hear-ken now to God's own Word This mes-sage comes to you,
Down through the years it has been heard, An-cient, yet ev - er new.

2. No other way to get to heav'n,
No matter what men say,
Only the one that had been giv'en
Jesus, Himself, the Way.

3. No other truth on which to rest,
For Christ alone is true,
God's promises have stood the test,
So you may trust Him too.

4. No other life can e'er compare
What Christ offers you,
He is the life, and you may share
In all its blessings too.

5. No other name can meet your need,
Jesus alone will save,
This warning message you must heed,
So solemn and so grave.

6. Oh follow Him who is the Way,
Trust Him, so wise and true,
Give Him your life as from today
And He will live in you.

7. Take Jesus as your Saviour now,
He'll cleanse you from your sin,
Before His Kingship gladly bow
And let Him reign within.

8. Then bear that blessed holy name
With deep humility,
And live to spread abroad His fame
Wherever you may be.

255   No tramp of soldiers' marching feet

Timothy Dudley-Smith

No tramp of sold-iers' mar-ching feet with ban-ners and with drums,

no sound of mu-sic's mar-tial beat: 'The King of glo-ry comes!'

To greet what pomp and king-ly pride no bells of tri-umph ring_____

no ci-ty gates swing op-en wide: 'Be-hold, behold your King!'

2. And yet he comes. The children cheer; with palms his path is strown.
With every step the cross draws near - The King of glory's throne.
Astride a colt he passes by As loud hosannas ring,
or else the very stones would cry 'Behold, behold your King!'

3. What fading flowers his road adorn; the palms, how soon laid down!
No bloom or leaf but only thorn The King of Glory's crown.
The soldiers mock, the rabble cries, the streets with tumult ring,
as Pilate to the mob replies, 'Behold, behold your King!'

4. Now he who bore for mortals' sake the cross and all its pains
and chose a servant's form to take, the King of glory reigns.
Hosanna to the Saviour's Name Till heaven's rafters ring,
And all the ransomed host proclaim 'Behold, behold your King!'

256 Nor eye has seen

Isaac Watts

Nor eye has seen, nor ear — has heard, Nor sense — nor - rea-son known What joys — the — Fa-ther hath — pre - pared For those — that love the Son.

2. But the good Spirit of the Lord
Reveals a heaven to come:
The beams of glory in his word
Allure and guide us home.

3. Pure are the joys above the sky,
And all the region peace;
No wanton lips, nor envious eye
Can see or taste the bliss.

4. Those holy gates for ever bar
Pollution, sin, and shame;
None shall obtain admittance there
But followers of the Lamb.

5. He keeps the Father's book of life,
There all their names are found;
The hypocrite in vain shall strive
To tread the heavenly ground.

257 Not to condemn

Not to con-demn the sons of men did Christ, the Son of
God, ap-pear; No weapons in his hands are seen,
No fla - ming sword, nor thun - der there.

2. Such was the pity of our God,
He loved the race of man so well,
He sent his Son to bear our load
Of sins, and save our souls from hell.

3. Sinners, believe the Saviour's word,
Trust in his mighty name and live;
A thousand joys his lips afford,
His hands a thousand blessings give.

4. But vengeance and damnation lies
On rebels who refuse the grace;
Who God's eternal Son despise
The hottest hell shall be their place.

Music © 2013 Harry Hicks

258 Not to us be glory given <small>based on Psalm 115</small>

Timothy Dudley-Smith

Not to us be glo-ry gi - ven but to him who reigns a-bove; Glo-ry to the
God of hea - ven for his faith - ful - ness and love! What though un - be -
lie-ving voi - ces hear no word and see no sign, still in God my
heart re - joi - ces, work-ing out his will di - vine.

2. Not what human fingers fashion, gold and silver, deaf and blind,
dead to knowledge and compassion, having neither heart nor mind -
lifeless gods, yet some adore them, nerveless hands and feet of clay;
all become, who bow before them, lost indeed and dead as they.

3. Not in them the hope of blessing - hope is in the living Lord!
High and low, his name confessing, find in him their shield and sword.
Hope of all whose hearts revere him, God is Israel, still the same!
God of Aaron! Those who fear him, he remembers them by name.

4. Not the dead, but we the living praise the Lord with all our powers;
of his goodness freely giving - his is heaven, earth is ours.
Not to us be glory given but to him who reigns above;
glory to the God of heaven for his faithfulness and love!

Music © 2011 Harry Hicks   Words: 'Not to us be glory given' by Timothy Dudley-Smith (b. 1926)
© Timothy Dudley-Smith in Europe and Africa. © Hope Publishing Company in the United States of America and the rest of the world.
Reproduced by permission of Oxford University Press. All rights reserved.

259   Nothing but the blood of Jesus

Rev. R. Lowry

What can wash a - way my stain? No-thing but the blood of Je - sus!

What can make me whole a - gain? No-thing but the blood of Je - sus!.

Refrain

Oh, pre-cious, pre-cious is the flow that makes me white as snow!

No o-ther fount I know;___ no-thing but the blood of Je - sus!

2. For my cleansing this I see, nothing but the blood of Jesus!
For my pardon this my plea - nothing but the blood of Jesus!
Oh, precious, precious is the flow that makes me white as snow!
No other fount I know - nothing but the blood of Jesus!

3. Nothing can for sin atone - nothing but the blood of Jesus!
Nought of good that I have done - nothing but the blood of Jesus!
Oh, precious, precious is the flow that makes me white as snow!
No other fount I know - nothing but the blood of Jesus!

4. This is all my hope and peace - nothing but the blood of Jesus!
This is all my righteousness - nothing but the blood of Jesus!
Oh, precious, precious is the flow that makes me white as snow!
No other fount I know - nothing but the blood of Jesus!

260   Nothing to pay!

Frances Havergal

No-thing to pay! ah, no-thing to pay! Ne-ver a word of ex-cuse to say!

Year af-ter year thou hast filled the score, Ow-ing the Lord still more and more.

Hear the voice of Je-sus say, "Ve-ri-ly thou hast no-thing to pay!

Ru-ined,— lost art thou, and yet I for-gave thee all that debt!"

2. Nothing to pay! the debt is so great;
What will you do with the awful weight?
How shall the way of escape be made?
Nothing to pay! yet it must be paid!
Hear the voice of Jesus say,
"Verily thou hast nothing to pay!
All has been put to My account,
I have paid the full amount."

3. Nothing to pay! yes, nothing to pay.
Jesus has cleared all the debt away,
Blotted it out with His bleeding hand!
Free and forgiven, and loved, you stand.
Hear the voice of Jesus say,
"Verily thou hast nothing to pay!
Paid is the debt and the debtor free!
Now I ask thee, Lov'st thou Me?"

261 Now be the God

Isaac Watts

Now be the God of Is-rael blessed Who makes the truth ap - pear,

His migh-ty hand ful - fils his word, and all the oaths he sware.

2. Now he bedews old David's root
   With blessings from the skies;
He makes the branch of promise grow,
   The promised horn arise.

3. John was the prophet of the Lord
   To go before his face,
The herald which our Saviour God
   Sent to prepare his ways.

4. He makes the great salvation known,
   He speaks of pardon'd sins;
While grace divine and heavenly love
   In its own glory shines.

5. "Behold the Lamb of God," he cries,
   "That takes our guilt away:
I saw the Spirit o'er his head
   On his baptizing day.

6. "Be every vale exalted high,
   Sing every mountain low,
The proud must stoop, and humble souls
   Shall his salvation know.

7. "The heathen realms in Israel's land
   Shall join in sweet accord;
And all that's born of man shall see
   The glory of the Lord.

8. "Behold the morning star arise,
   Ye that in darkness sit;
He marks the path that leads to peace,
   And guides our doubtful feet."

262   Now for a tune

Now for a tune - of - lof-ty praise To great Je-ho-vah's e - qual Son!

A-wake my voice - in - heav'n-ly lays Tell loud the won-ders he hath done.

2. Sing how he left the worlds of light
And the bright robes he wore above,
How swift and joyful was his flight
On wings of everlasting love.

3. Down to this base, this sinful earth
He came to raise our nature high;
He came t'atone almighty wrath;
Jesus the God was born to die.

4. Hell and its lions roared around,
His precious blood the monsters split,
While weighty sorrows pressed him down,
Large as the loads of all our guilt.

5. Deep in the shades of gloomy death
Th'almighty Captive pris'ner lay;
Th'almighty Captive left the earth,
And rose to everlasting day.

6. Lift up your eyes, ye sons of light,
Up to his throne of shining grace,
See what immortal glories sit
Round the sweet beauties of his face.

7. Amongst a thousand harps and songs
Jesus the God exalted reigns,
His sacred Name fills all their tongues
And echoes through the heav'nly plains!

Music © 2014 Harry Hicks

263 Now I belong to Jesus

Norman J. Clayton

1. Jesus my Lord will love me for-ev-er, from Him no pow'r of ev-il can sev-er, He gave His life to ran-som my soul, Now I be-long to Him;

Chorus

Now I be-long to Je-sus, Je-sus belongs to me, Not for the years of time a-lone, but for e-ter-ni-ty.

2. Once I was lost to sin's degredation,
Jesus came down to bring me salvation,
Lifted me up from sorrow and shame,
Now I belong to Him;
Now I belong to Jesus, Jesus belongs to me,
Not for the years of time alone, but for eternity.

3. Joy floods my soul for Jesus has saved me,
Freed me from sin that long had enslaved me,
His precious blood He gave to redeem,
Now I belong to Him;
Now I belong to Jesus, Jesus belongs to me,
Not for the years of time alone, but for eternity.

264 Now the green blade (1st tune)

Now the green blade ris - eth from the bur - ied grain, wheat that in the dark earth ma-ny days has lain; love lives a - gain, that with the dead has been; love is come a - gain like wheat the spring-eth green.

2. In the grave they laid Him, love whom we had slain,
thinking that never would He wake again.
Laid in the earth like grain that sleeps unseen;
love is come again like wheat that springeth green.

3. Forth he came at Easter like the risen grain.
He that for three days in the grave had lain.
Quick from the dead my risen Lord is seen;
love is come again like wheat that springeth green.

4. When our hearts are wintry, grieving or in pain,
thy touch can call us back to life again.
Fields of our heart that dead and bare have been;
love is come again like wheat that springeth green.

Music © 2014 Harry Hicks

264 Now the green blade (2nd tune)

Now the green blade ris-eth from the bur-ied grain,
wheat that in the dark earth ma-ny days - has lain;
love lives - a - gain, that with the dead - has been.
love is come a - gain like wheat that spring - eth green.

2. In the grave they laid him, love whom we had slain,
thinking that never would he wake again.
Laid in the earth like grain that sleeps unseen;
love is come again like wheat that springeth green.

3. Forth he came at Easter like the risen grain.
He that for three days in the grave had lain.
Quick from the dead my risen Lord is seen;
love is come again like wheat that springeth green.

4. When our hearts are wintry, grieving or in pain,
thy touch can call us back to life again.
Fields of our heart that dead and bare have been;
love is come again like wheat that springeth green.

Music © 2014 Harry Hicks

265   Now to the Lord a noble song

Now to the Lord a no-ble song! A-wake, my soul, a-wake my tongue;

Ho-san-na to th'e - ter - nal Name, And all his bound-less love pro-claim.

2. See where it shines in Jesus' face,
The brightest image of his grace;
God, in the person of his Son,
Has all his mightiest works outdone.

3. The spacious earth and spreading flood
Proclaim the wise, the powerful God;
And thy rich glories from afar
Sparkle in every rolling star.

4. But in his looks a glory stands,
The noblest labour of thine hands:
The pleasing lustre of his eyes
Outshines the wonders of the skies.

5. Grace, 'tis a sweet, a charming theme;
My thoughts rejoice at Jesus' name:
Ye angels, dwell upon the sound,
Ye heavens, reflect it to the ground!

6. O, may I live to reach the place
Where he unveils his lovely face,
Where all his beauties you behold,
And sing his Name to harps of gold!

266 Now to the Lord we bring the child

Timothy Dudley-Smith

Now to the Lord we bring the child he gave us, for rain or shine, for laugh-ter and for tears; pledged to his ser-vice, who was born to save us, rich with the pro-mise of the fu-ture years.

2. Into the threefold Name we here baptise you
as Jesus bids by water and the Word;
fast in his grace, when Satan sifts and tries you,
child of the covenant of Christ the Lord!

3. True to believe and trust our living Master
from life's bright morning to the twilight dim,
firm in the face of evil or disaster,
Christ's faithful soldier, turned to follow him.

4. One with his church, though all the world deride you,
signed with his cross, who once was sacrificed;
strong in his strength, for Jesus walks beside you,
world without end, in company with Christ!

Music © 2011 Harry Hicks
Words: 'Now to the Lord we bring the child he gave us' by Timothy Dudley-Smith (b. 1926)
© Timothy Dudley-Smith in Europe and Africa. © Hope Publishing Company in the United States of America
and the rest of the world. Reproduced by permission of Oxford University Press. All rights reserved.

267   Now to the power

Isaac Watts

Now to the power of God __ su-preme Be ev-er-las-ting ho-nours giv'n,

He saves from hell __ (we __ bless his Name) He calls our wan-d'ring feet to heav'n.

2. Nor for our duties or deserts,
But of his own abounding grace,
He works salvation in our hearts,
And forms a people for his praise.

3. 'Twas his own purpose that begun
To rescue rebels doomed to die;
He gave us grace in Christ his Son
Before he spread the starry sky.

4. Jesus the Lord appears at last,
And makes his Father's counsels known;
Declares the great transactions past,
And brings immortal blessings down.

5. He dies; and in that dreadful night
Did all the powers of hell destroy;
Rising he brought our heaven to light,
And took possession of the joy.

268 O day of rest and gladness

C. Wordsworth

O day of rest and glad-ness, O day of joy and light, O balm of care and sad - ness, Most beau-ti-ful, most bright; On thee, the high and low - ly, Through ag - es joined in tune, Sing 'ho-ly, ho-ly, ho - ly,' To the great God Tri - une!

2. On thee, at the creation,
The light first had its birth;
On thee, for our salvation,
Christ rose from depths of earth;
On thee our Lord victorious
The Spirit sent from heaven;
And thus on thee most glorious
A triple light was given.

3. Thou art a port protected
From storms that round us rise;
A garden intersected
With streams of paradise;
Thou art a cooling fountain
In life's dry dreary sand;
From thee, like Pisgah's mountain,
We view our promised land.

4. Today on weary nations
The heavenly manna falls;
To holy convocations
The silver trumpet calls,
Where gospel-light is glowing
With pure and radiant beams;
And living water flowing
With soul-refreshing streams.

5. May we, new graces gaining
From this our day of rest,
Attain the rest remaining
To spirits of the blest,
And there our voice upraising,
To Father and to Son
And Holy Ghost, be praising
Ever the Three in One.

269   O for a closer walk

William Cowper (1731-1800)

O for a clo-ser walk with God, a calm and

heav'n-ly frame; a light to shine up-on-the

road that leads me to-the Lamb.

2. What peaceful hours I once enjoyed,
    how sweet their memory still!
  but they have left an aching void
    the world can never fill.

3. Return, O holy Dove, return,
    sweet messenger of rest:
  I hate the sins that made thee mourn,
    and drove thee from my breast.

4. The dearest idol I have known,
    whate'er that idol be,
  help me to tear it from thy throne,
    and worship only thee.

5. So shall my walk be close with God,
    calm and serene my frame;
  so purer light shall mark the road
    that leads me to the Lamb.

270   O for a heart

C. Wesley

O for a heart to praise my God, A heart from sin set free! A
heart that al - ways feels Thy blood So free - ly spilt for me!

2. A heart resigned, submissive, meek,
My great Redeemer's throne,
Where only Christ is heard to speak,
Where Jesus reigns alone;

3. A humble, lowly, contrite heart,
Believing, true, and clean;
Which neither life nor death can part
From Him that dwells within:

4. A heart in every thought renewed,
And full of love divine;
Perfect, and right, and pure, and good,
A copy, Lord, of Thine!

5. My heart, Thou know'st, can never rest,
Till Thou create my peace;
Till, of my Eden re-possessed,
From every sin I cease.

6. Thy nature, gracious Lord, impart!
Come quickly from above;
Write Thy new name upon my heart,
Thy new, best name of love.

Music © 2016 Harry Hicks

271　　O give thanks

J. Conder

O give thanks to Him who made Morn - ing light and eve'n-ing shade; Source and giv-er of all good, Night-ly sleep and dai-ly food; Quick'n - er of our wear - ied powers; Guard of our un - con - cious hours.

2. O give thanks to nature's King,
Who made every breathing thing;
His, our warm and sentient frame,
His, the mind's immortal flame.
O how close the ties that bind
Spirits to eternal Mind!

3. O give thanks with heart and lip,
For we are His workmanship;
And all creatures are his care;
Not a bird that cleaves the air
Falls unnoticed; but who can
Speak the father's love to man?

4. O give thanks to Him who came
In a mortal, suffering frame -
Temple of the deity -
Came for rebel man to die;
In the path Himself hath trod,
Leading back His saints to God.

272   O God of truth

Thomas Hughes

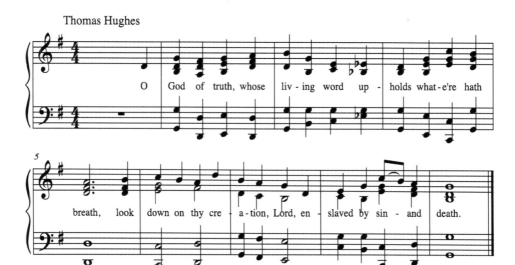

O God of truth, whose liv-ing word up-holds what-e're hath breath, look down on thy cre - a-tion, Lord, en - slaved by sin - and death.

2. Set up thy standard, Lord, that we
who claim a heavenly birth
may march with thee to smite the lies
that vex thy groaning earth.

3. Ah, would we join that blest array,
and follow in the might
of him, the Faithful and the True,
in raiment clean and white?

4. We fight for truth? we fight for God?
poor slaves of lies and sin!
he who would fight for thee on earth
must first be true within.

5. Then, God of truth, for whom we long,
thou who wilt hear our prayer,
do thine own battle in our hearts,
and slay the falsehood there.

6. Yea, come! then, tried as in the fire,
from every lie set free,
thy perfect truth shall dwell in us,
and we shall live in thee.

273   O happy day

Philip Doddridge

O hap-py day, that fixed my choice on Thee, my Sav-iour and my God! Well may this glow-ing heart re - joice and tell it's rap-tures all a - broad!

Chorus

O hap-py day! O hap-py day! When Je-sus washed my sins a - way! He taught me how to watch and pray, and live re - joic-ing ev - 'ry day! O hap-py day! O hap-py day! When Je-sus washed my sins a - way!

2. 'Tis done, the great transaction's done,   I am the Lord's, and He is mine;
He drew me, and I followed on,   charmed to confess the voice divine.
O happy day! O happy day!   When Jesus washed my sins away!
He taught me how to watch and pray,   and live rejoicing every day!
O happy day! O happy day!   When Jesus washed my sins away.

3. Now rest, my long divided heart,   fixed on this blissfull centre, rest;
nor ever from my Lord depart,   with Him of ev'ry good possessed.
O happy day! O happy day!   When Jesus washed my sins away!
He taught me how to watch and pray,   and live rejoicing every day!
O happy day! O happy day!   When Jesus washed my sins away.

274   O Jesus, Jesus

Frederick W. Faber (1814-1863)

O Je-sus, Je-sus, dear—est Lord! For-give me if I say,

For ve-ry love,— Thy sa-cred Name A thou-sand times— a day.

Refrain

O Je-sus, Lord, with me a-bide; I rest in Thee,— what e'er be-tide:

Thy gra-cious smile— is my re-ward; I love, I love— Thee, Lord!—

2. O love Thee so I know not how
My transports to control;
Thy love is like a burning fire
Within my very soul.
O Jesus, Lord, with me abide;
I rest in Thee, whate'er betide;
Thy gracious smile is my reward;
I love, I love Thee, Lord!

3. Burn, burn, O love, within my heart,
Burn fiercely night and day,
Till all the dross of earthly loves
Is burned, and burned away.
O Jesus, Lord, with me abide;
I rest in Thee, whate'er betide;
Thy gracious smile is my reward;
I love, I love Thee, Lord!

4. O light in darkness, joy in grief,
O heav'n begun of earth;
Jesus, my Love, my Treasure, who
Can tell what Thou art worth?
O Jesus, Lord, with me abide;
I rest in Thee, whate'er betide;
Thy gracious smile is my reward;
I love, I love Thee, Lord!

5. What limit is there to this love?
Thy flight, where wilt thou stay?
O, on! our Lord is sweeter far
Today than yesterday.
O Jesus, Lord, with me abide;
I rest in Thee, whate'er betide;
Thy gracious smile is my reward;
I love, I love Thee, Lord!

275 O Lamb of God

J.D. Deck

O Lamb of God, still keep me near to thy wound-ed side;
'Tis on-ly there in sa___fety and peace I can a-bide.
What foes and snares sur-round me! What doubts and fears with-in!
The grace that sought and found__ me a-lone can keep me clean.

2. "Tis only in Thee hiding, I feel my life secure;
Only in Thee abiding, the conflict can endure.
Thine arm the vict'ry gaineth o'er ev'ry hurtful foe;
Thy love my heart sustaineth in all its care and woe.

3. Soon shall mine eyes behold Thee, with rapture, face to face;
One half hath not been told me of all Thy pow'r and grace;
Thy beauty, Lord, and glory, the wonders of Thy love
Shall be the endless story of all Thy saints above.

276   O Love divine

Charles Wesley

O Love di - vine, what hast thou done! The Christ of God for us hath bled; The Fa-ther's co - e - ter-nal Son Had all our sins up - on Him laid. The Son of God for us hath died, Our Lord, our Life was cru - ci - fied.

2. Was crucified for us in shame
To bring us rebels back to God.
So we may glory in His Names,
As those redeemed by precious blood.
Pardon and life flowed from His side,
When He our Lord was crucified.

3. Then let us glory in the cross,
Make Christ our boast, our constant theme;
All things for him account but loss,
And now for him despise our shame.
Let nought with Him our hearts divide
Since He for us was crucified.

Music © 2016 Harry Hicks

277   O love how deep

Words ascribed to Thomas a Kempis,
translated by Benjamin Webb.

O love, how deep, how broad, how high! It fills the heart___ with ec - sta - sy, that God, the Son of God - should take our mor - tal form - for mor - tals' sake.

2. He sent no angel to our race
of higher or of lower place,
but wore the robe of human frame
himself, and to this lost world came.

3. For us he was baptised, and bore
his holy fast, and hungered sore;
for us temptations sharp he new;
for us the tempter overthrew.

4. For us the wicked men betrayed,
scourged, mocked, in purple robe arrayed,
he bore the shameful cross and death;
for us at length gave up his breath.

5. For us he rose from death again,
for us he went on high to reign,
for us he sent his Spirit here
to guide, to strengthen, and to cheer.

6. To him whose boundless love has won
salvation for us through his Son,
to God the Father, glory be
both now and through eternity.

278   O Love of God

H. Bonar

O love of God, how strong and true! E-ter-nal and yet e-ver new; Un-com-pre-hen-ded and un-bought, Be-yond all know-ledge and all thought!

2. O love of God, how deep and great!
Far deeper than man's deepest hate;
Self-fed, self-kindled, like the light,
Changeless, eternal, infinite!

3. O heavenly love, how precious still
In days of weariness and ill;
In nights of pain and helplessness,
To heal, to comfort, and to bless!

4. O wide-embracing, wondrous Love!
We read Thee in the sky above,
We read Thee in the earth below,
In seas that swell, and streams that flow.

5. We read Thee best in Him who came
To bear for us the cross of shame;
Sent by the Father from on high,
Our life to live, our death to die.

6. We read Thy power to bless and save,
E'en in the darkness of the grave;
Still more in resurrection light,
We read the fulness of Thy might.

7. O Love of God, our shield and stay
Through all the perils of our way,
Eternal Love, in Thee we rest,
For ever safe, for ever blessed!

279   O Love that will not let me go (1st tune)

George Matheson (1842-1906)

O Love that wilt not let me go, I rest my wea-ry soul - in thee: I give thee back the life I owe, that in thine o - cean depths its flow may ri - cher - full - er be.

2. O Light that followest all my way,
I yield my flickering torch to thee:
my heart restores its borrowed ray
that in thy sunshine's blaze its day
my brighter, fairer be.

3. O Joy that seekest me through pain,
I cannot close my heart to thee:
I trace the rainbow through the rain,
and feel the promise not in vain,
that morn shall tearless be.

4. O Cross that liftest up my head,
I dare not ask to fly from thee:
I lay in dust life's glory dead,
and from the ground there blossoms red
life that shall endless be.

279 O Love that will not let me go (2nd tune)

George Matheson

O love that will not let me go, I rest my wea-ry soul in thee; I give thee back the life I owe, that in thine o-cean depths its flow may rich-er full - er be.

2. O Light that follow'st all my way,
I yield my flick'ring torch to thee;
my heart restores it's borrowed ray,
that in thy sunshine's blaze its day
may brighter, fairer be.

3. O Joy that seekest me through pain,
I cannot close my heart to thee;
I trace the rainbow through the rain,
and feel the promise is not vain
that morn shall tearless be.

4. O Cross that liftest up my head,
I dare not ask to fly from thee;
I lay in dust life's glory dead,
and from the ground there blossoms red
life that shall endless be.

280   O Prince of peace

Timothy Dudley-Smith

1. O Prince of peace whose promised birth the angels sang with 'Peace of earth',
   peace be to us and all besides,
   peace to us all
   peace to the world this Christmastide.

2. O child who found to lay your head no place but in a manger bed,
   come where our doors are open wide,
   peace to us all,
   peace to the world
   peace in our homes this Christmas tide

3. O Christ whom shepherds came to find, their joy be ours in heart and mind;
   let grief and care be laid aside,
   peace to us all
   peace to the world
   peace in our homes
   peace in our hearts this Christmastide.

4. O Saviour Christ, ascended Lord, our risen Prince of life restored,
   our Love who one for sinners died,
   peace to us all
   peace to the world
   peace in our homes
   peace in our hearts
   peace with our God this Christmastide.

Music © 2011 Harry Hicks
Words: 'O Prince of peace whose promised birth' by Timothy Dudley-Smith (b. 1926) © Timothy Dudley-Smith in Europe
and Africa. © Hope Publishing Company in the United States of America and the rest of the world.
Reproduced by permission of Oxford University Press. All rights reserved.

281   O the Almighty Lord!

Isaac Watts

O the Al migh ty Lord! How match less is his power! Trem

ble, O earth, be neath his word, And all the heavens a dore.

2. Let proud imperious kings,
Bow low before his throne,
Crouch to his feet, ye haughty things,
Or he shall tread you down.

3. Above the skies he reigns,
And with amazing blows
he deals insufferable pains
On his rebellious foes.

4. Yet, everlasting God,
We love to speak thy praise;
Thy sceptre's equal to thy rod,
The sceptre of thy grace.

5. The arms of mighty love
defend our Sion well,
And heavenly mercy walls us round
From Babylon and hell

6. Salvation to the King
That sits enthroned above;
Thus we adore the God of might,
And bless the God of love.

282   O Thou from whom

T. Haweis (1734-1820) and others

O Thou from whom all good - ness flows, I lift my heart to Thee;

In all my sor - rows, con - flicts, woes, Dear Lord, re - mem - ber me.

2. When on my poor distressed heart
   My sins lie heavily,
Thy pardon grant, new peace impart:
   Dear Lord, remember me.

3. When trials sore obstruct my way,
   And ills I cannot flee,
O let my strength be as my day:
   Dear Lord, remember me.

4. If, for thy sake, upon my name
   Shame and reproaches be,
All hail reproach, and welcome shame!
   Dear Lord, remember me.

5. If worn with pain, disease, or grief
   This feeble spirit be;
Grant patience, rest, and kind relief:
   Dear Lord, remember me.

6. So that, when comes the hour of death,
   My earthly fears may flee:
This song of praise be my last breath -
   Thou wilt remember me.

283 Oh flee as a bird

Brenda Gallant

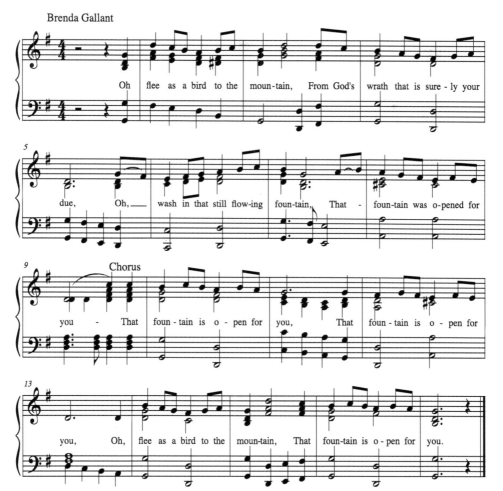

Oh flee as a bird to the moun-tain, From God's wrath that is sure-ly your due, Oh,___ wash in that still flow-ing foun-tain, That - foun-tain was o-pened for you -

Chorus

That foun-tain is o-pen for you, That foun-tain is o-pen for you, Oh, flee as a bird to the moun-tain, That foun-tain is o-pen for you.

2. There's refuge and shelter in Jesus,
   He died that you might enter in,
   For He is the Rock of Salvation,
   The answer to all of your sin.
   That fountain is open for you,
   That fountain is open for you,
   Oh, flee as a bird to the mountain,
   That fountain is open for you.

3. There's refuge and shelter in Jesus,
   Enough to supply every need,
   He offers you cleansing and pardon,
   And guidance if you let Him lead.
   That fountain.......

4. There's refuge and shelter in Jesus,
   For time and eternity too,
   That wonderful, infinite mercy,
   Sufficient to see you right through.
   That fountain.....

5. There's refuge and shelter in Jesus,
   He died and is living again,
   One day He will come back to take you,
   Triumphant for ever to reign.
   That fountain is open for you,
   That fountain is open for you,
   Oh, flee as a bird to the mountain,
   That fountain is open for you.

284   Oh who is this

Brenda Gallant

Oh who is this who prays and weeps In dark Geth-se-me-

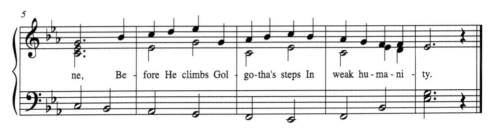

ne, Be - fore He climbs Gol - go-tha's steps In weak hu-ma-ni - ty.

2. Just see him now, as bending low
   He wrestles long in prayer,
   With drops of blood upon His brow
   He agonises there.

3. The battle fought is hardly won,
   He bows himself to bear,
   Redemption's work at last begun
   For all mankind to share.

4. Oh who is this in robes arrayed
   And with a thorny crown?
   Forsaken, mocked, by friends betrayed,
   With pain and grief weighed down.

5. Oh who is this, his visage marred,
   Condemned at last to die?
   His hands and feet with nail prints scarred,
   As He is lifted high.

6. He hangs in shame twixt earth and sky,
   Abused and sore reviled,
   That man to God might be brought nigh,
   Forever reconciled.

7. Oh who is this in linen shroud,
   Now numbered with the dead?
   To take God's wrath He meekly bowed,
   And suffered in our stead.

8. It is the Lord, it is the Lord,
   He burst from sin's dread chains!
   The living and exalted Word,
   Once more in heaven reigns.

9. Oh have you seen the risen Christ,
   How at His feet to fall,
   His sacrifice for sin sufficed,
   Now yield to Him your all.

10. One day He's coming back again,
    To call to Him His own,
    This message echoes loud and plain,
    And should be widely known.

11. Will you be ready for that day,
    Whenever that may be,
    Oh do not trust to anything,
    But gladly bow the knee.

Music © 2013 Harry Hicks
Words © 1992 Brenda Gallant

285 Oh, safe to the Rock

2. In the calm of the noontide, in sorrow's lone hour,
In times when temptation casts o'er me its power;
In the tempests of life, on its wide, heaving sea,
Thou blest "Rock of Ages," I'm hiding in Thee.
Hiding in Thee, hiding in Thee,
Thou blest "Rock of Ages," I'm hiding in Thee.

3. How oft in the conflict, when pressed by the foe,
I have fled to my Refuge and breathed out my woe;
How often, when trials like sea-billows roll,
Have I hidden in Thee, O Thou Rock of my soul.
Hiding in Thee, hiding in Thee,
Thou blest "Rock of Ages," I'm hiding in Thee.

286 Once more, my soul

Once more, my soul, the ri - sing day sa-lutes thy wa - king eyes.

Once more, my voice, thy tri - bute pay to him that rolls - the skies.

2. Night unto night his name repeats,
The day renews the sound,
Wide as the heav'n on which he sits
to turn the seasons round.

3. 'tis he supports my mortal frame,
My tongue shall speak his praise;
My sins would rouse his wrath to flame,
And yet his wrath delays.

4. On a poor worm thy power might tread,
And I could ne'er withstand;
Thy justice might have crushed me dead,
But mercy held thine hand.

5. A thousand wretched souls are fled
Since the last setting sun,
And yet thou length'n'est out my thread,
And yet my moments run.

6. Dear God, let all my hours be thine
Whilst I enjoy the light,
Then shall my sun in smiles decline,
And bring a pleasing night.

287   Only trust Him

J.H.Stockton

Come, ev-ry soul by sin op-pressed, There's mer - cy with___ the
Lord,___ And He___ will sure - ly give you rest By
trust - ing in___ His word.

Chorus - not too fast

On - ly trust___ Him, On - ly trust___ Him,
He will save___ you from___ your sins, He will wel-come you now.

2. For Jesus shed His precious blood
   Rich blessings to bestow;
   Plunge now into the crimson flood
   That washes white as snow.
   Only trust Him, Only trust Him,
   He will save you from your sins,
   He will welcome you now.

3. Yes, Jesus is the Truth, the Way,
   That leads you into rest;
   Believe in Him without delay,
   And you are fully blest.
   Only trust Him, Only trust Him,
   He will save you from your sins,
   He will welcome you now.

4. Come, then, and join the holy band,
   And on to glory go,
   To dwell in that celestial land,
   Where joys immortal flow.
   Only trust Him, Only trust Him,
   He will save you from your sins,
   He will welcome you now.

Music © 2016 Harry Hicks

288   Our Father in heaven

289 Our Lord is risen

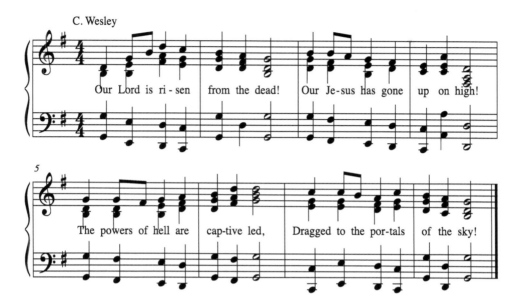

C. Wesley

Our Lord is ri-sen from the dead! Our Je-sus has gone up on high!

The powers of hell are cap-tive led, Dragged to the por-tals of the sky!

2. There the triumphal chariot waits,
And angels chant the solemn lay:
Lift up your heads, ye heavenly gates;
Ye everlasting doors, give way!

3. Loose all your bars of massy light,
And wide unfold the ethereal scene;
He claims these mansions as His right
Receive the King of Glory in!

4. Who is this King of Glory? Who?
The Lord, that all our foes o'ercame;
The world, sin, death, and hell o'erthrew,
And Jesus is the Conqueror's name.

5. Lo! His triumphal chariot waits,
And angels chant the solemn lay;
Lift up your heads, ye heavenly gates;
Ye everlasting doors, give way!

6. Who is this king of Glory? Who?
The Lord, of glorious power possessed,
The King of saints, and angels too,
God over all, for ever blest!

290   Our Saviour

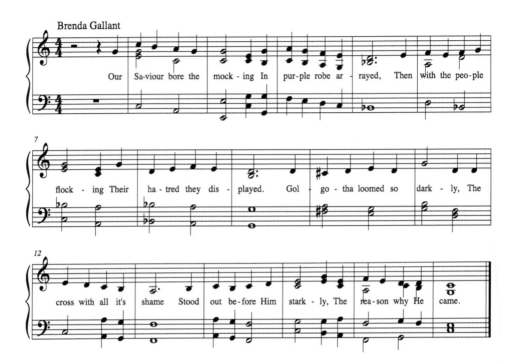

Brenda Gallant

Our Sa-viour bore the mock-ing In pur-ple robe ar-rayed, Then with the peo-ple flock-ing Their ha-tred they dis-played. Gol-go-tha loomed so dark-ly, The cross with all it's shame Stood out be-fore Him stark-ly, The rea-son why He came.

2. Then myrrh and wine they proffered,
A cup He would not drink,
But His own self He offered,
From suff'ring did not shrink.
They crucified the Saviour,
Then gambled by His cross,
Such ignorant behaviour
To their eternal loss.

3. The superscription written
Proclaimed the King of Jews,
The sinless One was smitten,
His life to gladly lose.
In order to save others,
Himself He would not save,
He died to make men brothers,
And triumph o'er the grave.

4. Then as He hung suspended
Betwixt the earth and sky,
The daylight swift was ended
When Jesus bowed to die.
He felt himself forsaken
By God in that dread hour,
The temple court was shaken
By His almighty power.

5. This man was truly God's Son,
One watching Him then cried,
And now with that dread deed done,
It could not be denied.
Those standing by observing
Acknowledged God, made man,
And we, though undeserving
Are part of His great plan.

291   Our sins, alas

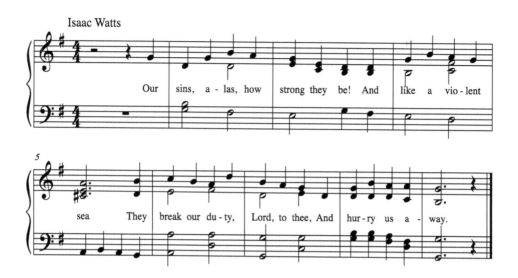

Isaac Watts

Our sins, a-las, how strong they be! And like a vio-lent sea They break our du-ty, Lord, to thee, And hur-ry us a-way.

2. The waves of trouble, how they rise!
How loud the tempests roar!
But death shall land our weary souls
Safe on the heavenly shore.

3. There to fulfill his sweet commands
Our speedy feet shall move,
No sin shall clog our winged zeal,
Or cool our burning love.

4. There shall we sit, and sing, and tell
The wonders of his grace,
Till heavenly raptures fire our hearts,
And smile in every face.

5. For ever his dear sacred Name
Shall dwell upon our tongue,
And Jesus and salvation be
The close of every song.

292 Our souls shall magnify the Lord

solo

Isaac Watts

Our souls____ shall mag-ni - fy the Lord, In
God__ the Sav-iour we re - joice;____ While we re-peat the
Vir - gin's__ song, May the same Spi - rit__ tune our__ voice.

2. The highest saw her low estate,
And mighty things his hand hath done;
His overshadowing power and grace
Makes her the mother of his Son.

3. Let every nation call her blessed,
And endless years prolong her fame;
But God alone must be adored;
Holy and reverend in his Name.

4. To those that fear and trust the Lord
His mercy stands for ever sure:
From age to age his promise lives,
And the performance is secure.

5. He spake to Abra'm and his seed,
"In thee shall all the earth be blessed;"
The memory of that ancient word
Lay long in his eternal breast.

6. But now no more shall Israel wait,
No more the Gentiles lie forlorn;
Lo, the desire of nations comes,
Behold the promised seed is born.

293 Peace, peace is mine!

J. Denham Smith

God's al-migh-ty arms are round me; peace, peace is mine!

Judge-ment scenes need not con-found me; peace, peace is mine!

Je - sus came Him - self and sought me, Sold to death, he found and bought me,

then my bless-ed free - dom taught me; peace, peace is mine!

2. While I hear life's rugged billows, peace, peace is mine!
Why suspend my harp on willows, peace, peace is mine!
I may sing, with Christ beside me,
Though a thousand ills betide me,
Safely he hath sworn to guide me; peace, peace is mine!

3. Every trial draws him nearer: peace, peace is mine!
All his strokes but make him dearer: peace, peace is mine!
Bless I then the hand that smiteth
Gently, and to heal delighteth,
'tis against my sins he fighteth: peace, peace is mine!

4. Welcome every rising sunlight, peace, peace is mine!
Nearer home each rolling midnight: peace, peace is mine!
Death and hell cannot appall me;
Safe in Christ whate'er befall me;
Calmly wait I till he calls me: peace, peace is mine!

294   Poor and needy

D.A.Thrupp

Poor and nee-dy though I be, God Al-migh-ty cares for me;

Gives me cloth-ing, shel-ter, food, Gives me all I have of good.

2. He will hear me when I pray,
He is with me night and day;
When I sleep and when I wake,
For my Lord and Saviour's sake.

3. He who reigns above the sky
Once became as poor as I;
He whose blood for me was shed
Had not where to lay his head.

4. Though I labour here awhile,
He will bless me with His smile,
And when this short life is past
I shall rest with Him at last.

5. Then to him I'll tune my song,
Happy as the day is long;
This my joy for ever be,
God Almighty cares for me.

295   Praise Him! Praise Him!

F.J.Crosby

296   Praise the God of truth and love

Brenda Gallant

Praise the God of truth and love - Lif - ted high. He who stoops from
heav'n a - bove - Draws - us nigh. See the beau-ty all a-round, Mi - ra-cles of
skill a-bound, All cre - a - tion joins the sound - Give - Him praise

2. Mark the beauty of the skies, Gaze in awe.
View the stars with wondering eyes And adore
See the everlasting hills,
Note the sparkling fountain rills,
Hear how all creation thrills,
Give Him praise.

3. God's creation shouts His name, Clear and plain.
Far and wide it spreads His fame, And again.
All mankind can hear His voice
He has given each the choice,
To believe Him and rejoice,
Give Him praise.

4. "What is man,' the psalmist cried, Long ago.
Overcome with awe he tried God to know.
All creation speaks His worth
Azure skies and friendly earth,
These all set the Godhead forth
Give him praise.

5. These all speak, their voices one, Of His might.
But He speaks now through His son; His delight.
He who left the heav'n above,
Object of His Father's love,
Comes our sin and guilt to move,
Give Him praise.

6. Jesus Christ surpasses all, He will save.
All the souls who on Him call Life shall have.
He who died and rose again
Brings salvation in His train
Let each heart take up the strain,
Give Him praise.

297 Praise the Lord and bless his Name

Timothy Dudley-Smith

Praise the Lord and bless his Name, life and peace in him are found.

All his be-ne-fits pro-claim, grace with love and mer-cy crowned;

sins for-giv-en, strength re-stored! Sing, my soul, and praise the Lord!

2. High as heaven's furthest star, vaster than the shores of space,
so he bears our sins afar, so he brings us to his grace.
He who hears his children's prayer Ever keeps us in his care.

3. Swifter than the winds that pass, fading as the summer flowers,
what though all our days are grass? Faith and hope shall still be ours.
God's unchanging love is sure And endures for evermore.

4. Praise the Lord of earth and heaven, Angel hosts about his throne,
Sinners by his grace forgiven, Saints who his dominion own;
God of all, by all adored! Sing, my soul, and praise the Lord!

298   Praise the Lord of heaven

Timothy Dudley-Smith

Praise the Lord of heav-en, Praise him in the height;
Praise him, all his an-gels Praise him, hosts of light.
Sun and moon to-geth-er, shin-ing stars a-flame,
Plan-ets in their cour-ses, Mag-ni-fy his Name!

2. Earth and ocean praise him; mountains, hills and trees;
   fire and hail and tempest, wind and storm and seas,
   Praise him, fields and forests, Birds on flashing wings,
   Praise him, beasts and cattle, All created things.

3. Now by prince and people let his praise be told;
   praise him, men and maidens, praise him, young and old.
   He, the Lord of glory! We, his praise proclaim!
   High above all heavens Magnify his name!

299 Praise the Lord!

vv 1&2: Foundling Hospital Collection (1796)
v2: E. Osler 1798-1863

Praise the Lord! Ye heavens a-dore him; Praise, him, an-gels in the height;

Sun and moon, re-joice be-fore him; Praise him, all ye stars and light:

Praise, the Lord, for he hath spok-en; Worlds his migh-ty voice o-beyed;

Laws, which ne-ver shall be bro-ken, For their guid-ance hath he made.

2. Praise the Lord, for he is glorious!
Never shall his promise fail;
God hath made his saints victorious;
Sin and death not prevail.
Praise the God of our salvation;
Hosts on high, his power proclaim;
Heaven and earth, and all creation,
Laud and magnify his name!

3. Worship, honour, glory, blessing,
Lord, we offer to thy name;
Young and old, thy praise expressing,
Join their Saviour to proclaim.
As the saints in heaven adore thee,
We would bow before thy throne;
As thine angels serve before thee,
So on earth thy will be done.

300 Praise ye the Lord

Isaac Watts

Praise ye the Lord; 'tis good — to raise Our hearts and voi - ces in His praise;

His na - ture and His works in - vite To make this du - ty our de - light.

2. He formed the stars, those heavenly flames;
He counts their numbers, calls their names:
His wisdom's deep and knows no bound,
A deep where all our thoughts are drowned.

3. Sing to the Lord, exalt Him high,
Who spreads the clouds around the sky;
There He prepares the fruitful rain,
Nor lets the drops descend in vain.

4. He makes the grass the hills adorn,
And clothes the smiling fields with corn;
The beasts with food His hands supply,
And the young ravens when they cry.

5. What is a creature's skill or force?
The sprightly man, or warlike horse?
The piercing wit, the active limb?
All are too mean delights for Him.

6. But saints are precious in His sight:
He views His children with delight;
He sees their hope, He knows their fear,
And looks, and loves His image there.

301 Praise, everlasting praise

Isaac Watts

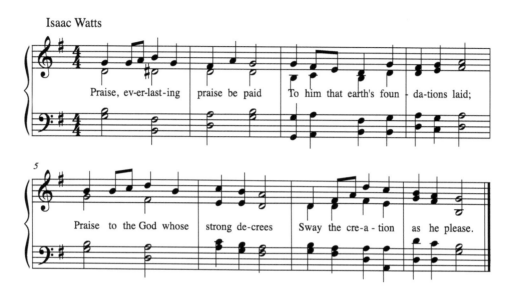

Praise, ev-er-last-ing praise be paid To him that earth's foun - da-tions laid;

Praise to the God whose strong de-crees Sway the cre-a-tion as he please.

2. Praise to the goodness of the Lord
Who rules his people by his word,
And there as strong as his decrees
He sets his kindest promises.

3. Firm are the words his prophets give,
Sweet words on which his children live;
Each of them is the voice of God,
Who spoke and spread the skies abroad.

4. Each of them powerful as that sound
That bid the new-made heavens go round;
And stronger than the solid poles,
On which the wheel of nature rolls.

5. Whence then should doubts and fears arise,
Why trickling sorrows drown our eyes?
Slowly, alas, our mind receives
the comfort that our Maker gives.

6. O for a strong, a lasting faith
to credit what th'almighty saith!
T' 'embrace the message of the Son,
And call the joys of heaven our own.

7. Then should the earth's old pillars shake,
And all the wheels of nature break,
Our steady souls should fear no more
Than solid rocks when billows roar.

8. Our everlasting hopes arise
Above the ruinable skies,
Where the eternal Builder reigns,
And his own courts his power sustains.

Music © 2013 Harry Hicks

302 Precious, precious blood

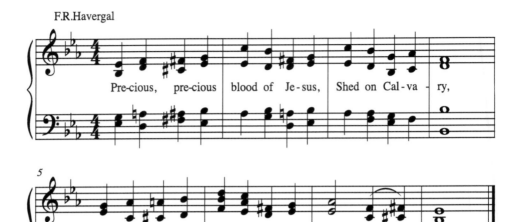

F.R.Havergal

Pre-cious, pre-cious blood of Je-sus, Shed on Cal-va - ry,

Shed for re-bels and for sin-ners, Shed for ____ me.

2. Precious blood that hath redeemed us,
   All the price is paid!
   Perfect pardon now is offered,
   Peace is made.

3. Precious, precious blood of Jesus,
   Let it make thee whole,
   Let its mighty power in cleansing
   Reach thy soul.

4. Though thy sins are red like crimson,
   Deep as scarlet glow,
   Jesus' blood can make them
   White as snow.

303 Precious, precious

Frances R. Havergal

Pre-cious, pre-cious blood of Je-sus, Shed on Cal-va - ry; Shed for re-bels,

shed for sin-ners, Shed for thee and me! O the pre-cious blood of Je-sus,

Refrain

Shed on Cal-va - ry! O be-lieve it, O re-ceive it, 'Tis for thee and me!

2. Though my sins are red like crimson,
Deep in scarlet glow,
Jesus' precious blood shall wash thee
White as snow, as snow.
O the precious blood of Jesus,
Shed on Calvary!
O believe it, O receive it,
'Tis for thee and me!

3. Precious blood that hath redeemed us!
All the price is paid;
Perfect pardon now is offered,
Peace is made, is made.
O the precious blood of Jesus,
Shed on Calvary!
O believe it, O receive it,
'Tis for thee and me!

4. Precious blood, by this we conquer
In the fiercest fight;
Sin and Satan overcoming
By its might, its might.
O the precious blood of Jesus,
Shed on Calvary!
O believe it, O receive it,
'Tis for thee and me!

304　Present in creation

Pres-ent in cre - a - tion, Was Je - sus Christ, our Lord,
He, the re - ve - la - tion Of God the liv - ing Word.

2. Perfected through suffering
As He fulfilled God's will,
His life, a fragrant offering,
Efficacious still.

3. Praying in the glory
For those who are his own,
This, the blessed story
Presented at the throne.

4. Dying for Redemption,
His blood, it paid the price,
Reconciliation;
The perfect sacrifice.

5. Resurrection splendour
O'er sin and death and hell,
Praises we should render,
Christ has done all things well!

305   Put thou thy trust

P. Gerhardt, tr. John Wesley and others.

Put thou thy trust in God, in duty's path go on; walk in his strength with faith and hope, so shall thy work be done.

2. Commit thy ways to him,
thy works into his hands,
and rest on his unchanging word,
who heaven and earth commands.

3. Though years and tears roll on,
his covenant shall endure;
though clouds and darkness hide his path,
the promised grace is sure.

4. Give to the winds thy fears;
hope, and be undismayed:
God hears thy sighs and counts thy tears;
God shall lift up thy head.

5. Through waves and clouds and storms
his power will clear thy way:
wait thou his time: the darkest night
shall end in brightest day.

6. Leave to his sovereign sway
to choose and to command;
so shalt thou, wondering, own his way,
how wise, how strong his hand.

306 Raise your triumphant songs

Isacc Watts

Raise your tri-um-phant songs
To an im-mor-tal tune,
Let the wide earth re - sound the deeds Ce - les-tial grace___ has done.

Fin

2. Sing, how eternal love
It's chief beloved chose
And bid him raise our wretched race
From their abyss of woes.

3. His hand no thunder bears,
Nor terror clothes his brow,
No bolts to drive our guilty souls
To fiercer flames below.

4. 'Twas mercy filled the throne,
And wrath stood silent by,
When Christ was sent with pardons down
To rebels doomed to die.

5. Now, sinners, dry your tears,
Let hopeless sorrow cease;
Bow to the sceptre of his love,
And take the offered peace.

Music © 2016 Harry Hicks

307   Rise, rise, my soul

Isaac Watts

Rise, - rise my soul, and leave the ground, Stretch - all thy thoughts a - broad,

And - rouse up ev' - ry tune - ful sound To - praise th'e - ter - nal - God

2. Long ere the lofty skies were spread
Jehovah filled his throne;
Or Adam formed, or angels made,
The Maker lived alone.

3. His boundless years can ne'er decrease,
But still maintain their prime;
Eternity's his dwelling place,
And ever is his time.

4. While like a tide our minutes flow,
The present and the past,
He fills his own immortal now,
And sees our ages waste.

5. The sea and sky must perish too,
And vast destruction come.
The creatures - look, how old they grow,
And wait their fiery doom.

6. Well, let the sea shrink all away,
And flame melt down the skies,
My God shall live an endless day,
When th'old creation dies.

Music © 2013 Harry Hicks

308   Save me at the cross

F.J.Crosby

Lo-ving Sav - iour, hear my cry, hear my cry___ hear my cry; Trem'-bling to ___ Thine

arms I fly, save me at ___ the cross. I have sinned ___ but Thou hast died,

Thou hast died, ___ Thou hast died. In Thy mer - cy let me hide; save me at ___ the

cross.   Chorus   Lord, Je-sus, re - ceive me, no more would I grieve thee.

Now, bles-sed re - dee - mer, Oh save me at the cross.

2. Though I perish, I will pray, I will pray, I will pray;
Thou of life the Living Way; save me at the cross.
Thou hast said Thy grace is free, grace is free, grace is free,
Have compassion, Lord, on me, save me at the cross.
Lord Jesus, receive me, no more would I grieve thee.
Now, blessed redeemer, Oh save me at the cross.

3. Wash me in thy cleansing blood, cleansing blood, cleansing blood;
Plunge me now beneath the flood; save me at the cross.
Only faith will pardon bring, pardon bring, pardon bring;
In that faith to thee I cling, save me at the cross.
Lord Jesus, receive me, no more would I grieve thee.
Now, blessed redeemer, Oh save me at the cross.

Music © 2008 Harry Hicks

309   Saved through Jesus' blood

J.W.VanDeVenter

J.W.VanDeVenter

Some-time we'll stand be-fore the judg-ment bar, The quick, the ris-en dead; The Lord will then make known the rec-ord there; Our names will all be read.

Chorus

I'll be pres-ent when the roll is called, Pure and spot-less through the crim-son flood; I will ans-wer when they call my name: Saved through Je-sus' blood.

2. I'll then receive a bright and starry crown,
As only God can give;
And when I've been with Him ten thousand years,
I'll have no less to live.
I'll be present when the roll is called,
Pure and spotless through the crimson flood;
I will answer when they call my name;
Saved through Jesus' blood.

3. Then we shall meet to never part again;
Our toil will then be o'er;
We'll lay our burdens down at Jesus' feet,
And rest for evermore.
I'll be present when the roll is called,
Pure and spotless through the crimson flood;
I will answer when they call my name;
Saved through Jesus' blood.

310　　Saviour Christ

Timothy Dudley-Smith

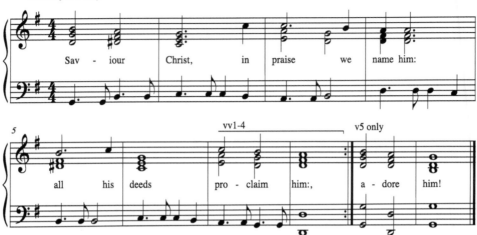

vv1-4　　v5 only

(Each verse could finish at bar 8, returning to the start
and ignoring the repeated last three syllables,
and using bars 9 and 10 for the last time only.)

1. Saviour Christ,　in praise we name him;
   All his deeds　proclaim him,

2. Lamb of God　for sinners dying;
   All our need　supplying,

3. Risen Lord　in glory seated;
   All his work　completed,

4. King of kings　ascended, reigning;
   All the world,　sustaining,

5. Christ is all!　Rejoice before him;
   Evermore　adore him!

311   Saviour, again

J. Ellerton

after Rev. Dr. J.B. Dykes

Sav - iour, a - gain to Thy dear Name we raise With one ac-

cord our part - ing hymn of praise: We stand to bless Thee

ere our wor-ship cease, Then low-ly kneel-ing wait Thy word of peace.

2. Grant us Thy peace upon our homeward way;
With Thee began, with Thee shall end the day;
Guard thou the lips from sin, the hearts from shame,
That in this house have called upon Thy name.

3. Grant us Thy peace, Lord, through the coming night,
Turn Thou for us its darkness into light;
From harm and danger keep Thy children free,
For dark and light are both alike to Thee.

4. Grant us Thy peace throughout our earthly life,
Our balm in sorrow, and our stay in strife.
Then, when Thy voice shall bid our conflicts cease,
Call us, O Lord, to Thine eternal peace!

312   Saviour, blessed Saviour

G. Thring

Sav-iour, bles-sed Sav___iour, List-en while we sing,
Hearts and voi-ces rais - ing Prais-es to our King;___
All we have to off - er, All our hope to be,
Bo-dy, soul and spi___rit, All we yield to Thee. King.

2. Nearer, ever nearer, Christ, we draw to Thee.
Deep in adoration Bending low the knee:
Thou, for our redemption, Cam'st on earth to die;
Thou, that we might follow Hast gone up on high.

3. Clearer still and clearer, Dawns the light from heav'n,
In our sadness bringing News of sin forgiv'n;
Life has lost it's shadows, Pure the light within;
Thou hast shed Thy radiance On a world of sin.

4. Onward ever onward, Journeying o'er the road
Worn by saints before us, Journeying on to God:
Leaving all behind us, May we hasten on,
Backward never looking Till the prize is won.

5. Higher, then and higher Bear the ransomed soul,
Earthly toils forgotten, Saviour to its goal;
Where, in joys unthought of, Saints with angels sing,
Never weary, raising Praises to their King.

313   Saviour, Thy dying love

S.D. Phelps

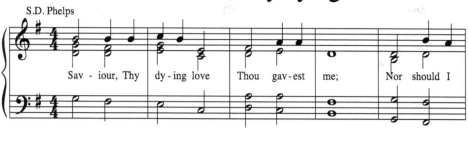

Sav - iour, Thy dy - ing love Thou gav - est me; Nor should I

aught with - hold, My Lord, from Thee. In love my

soul would bow, My heart ful - fill its vow, Some offer - ing

Fin

bring Thee now, Some - thing for thee.

2. At the blest mercy-seat
Pleading for me -
My feeble faith looks up,
O Lord, to Thee;
Help me the cross to bear,
Thy wondrous love declare,
Some song to raise, or prayer,
Something for Thee.

3. Give me a faithful heart,
Likeness to Thee,
That each departing day
Henceforth may see
Some work of love begun,
Some deed of kindness done,
Some wonderer sought and won -
Something for Thee.

4. All that I am and have -
Thy gifts so free -
In joy, in grief, through life,
O Lord, for Thee!
And when Thy face I see
My ransomed soul shall be
Through all eternity
Living for Thee.

314   See the Conqueror

Christopher Wordsworth

See the Con-queror mounts in tri-umph see the King in royal state rid-ing on the clouds his char-iot to his heav'n-ly pa-lace gate; hark, the choirs of an-gel voi-ces joy-ful al-le-lu-ias sing, and the por-tals high are lif-ted to re-ceive their heav'n-ly King.

2. Who is this that comes in glory
with the trump of jubilee?
Lord of Battles, God of armies,
he has gained the victory;
he who on the Cross did suffer,
he who from the grave arose,
he has vanquished sin and Satan,
he by death has spoiled his foes.

3. He has raised our human nature
on the clouds to God's right hand;
there we sit in heavenly [places
there with him in glory stand:
Jesus rigns, adored by angels;
man with God is on the throne;
mighty Lord, in thine ascension
we by faith behold our own.

4. See him who is gone before us
heavenly mansions to prepare,
see him who is ever pleading
for us with prevailing prayer,
see him who with sound of trumpet
and with his angelic train,
summoning the world to judgement,
on the clouds will come again.

5. Glory be to God the Father;
glory be to God the Son,
dying, ris'n, ascending for us,
who the heavenly realm has won;
glory to the Holy Spirit:
to One God in Persons Three
glory both in earth and heaven,
glory, endless glory be.

Music © 2016 Harry Hicks   Words: Christopher Wordsworth (1807-85)

315   See, to us a child is born

Timothy Dudley-Smith

vv1-4 1.See, to us a child is born. Glo-ry breaks on Christ - mas morn!

vv5-8 5.Migh-ty God, who mer - cy brings Lord of lords and King of kings!

2. Now to us a Son is giv'n -
Praise to God in highest heav'n!

3. On his shoulder rule shall rest -
In him all the earth be blest!

4. Wise and wonderful his Name -
Heaven's Lord in human frame!

5. Mighty God, who mercy brings -
Lord of lords and King of kings!

6. Father of eternal days -
Ev'ry creature sing his praise!

7. Everlasting Prince of Peace -
Truth and righteousness increase!

8. He shall reign from shore to shore -
Christ is King for evermore!

Music © 2011 Harry Hicks   Words: 'See, to us a child is born' by Timothy Dudley-Smith (b. 1926)
© Timothy Dudley-Smith in Europe and Africa. © Hope Publishing Company in the United States of America and the rest of the world.
Reproduced by permission of Oxford University Press. All rights reserved.

316   Seek, oh seek the Lord

Brenda Gallant

Seek, oh seek the Lord - of - Glo - ry, While He may be found,

Heed re - demp - tion's won - drous - sto - ry, Hear the joy - ful sound;

Seek ye, seek ye, Turn un - to the Lord, Hear the lov - ing ex - hor - ta - tion In the pre - cious Word.

2. Call upon the Lord of Glory,
   While He still is near,
Throw yourself upon His mercy,
   There is nought to fear.
   Call ye, call ye,
   While the Lord is near,
Take the living invitation;
   Love that casts out fear.

3. Forsake, forsake all your own way,
   And unrighteous thought,
For the Lord will truly welcome
   One He long has sought.
   Forsake ye, forsake ye,
   Turn from your own way,
God is willing to receive thee;
   Come to Him today.

4. Return to God, who then will pardon,
   More abundantly,
Do not let your spirit harden,
   Come, He calls for thee.
   Return ye, return ye,
   Return unto the Lord,
He is waiting to receive thee,
   Welcome is assured.

Music © 2013 Harry Hicks
Words © 2013 Brenda Gallant

317   Seeking for me

Je - sus my Sav-iour to Beth-le-hem came, born in a man-ger to sor-row and shame; oh, it was won-der-ful, blest be His name! seek - ing for me, for me. Seek - ing for me! Seek - ing for me! Oh, it was won-der-ful, blest be His name!

2. Jesus, my Saviour, on Calvary's tree,   paid a great debt, and my soul set free;
Oh, it was wonderful, how could it be?   Dying for me, for me.
Dying for me! Dying for me! Oh, it was wonderful, how could it be?

3. Jesus, my Saviour, the same as of old,   while I was wandering afar from the fold,
Gently and long did he plead with my soul,   calling for me, for me.
Calling for me! Calling for me! Gently and long did he plead with my soul.

4. Jesus, my Saviour, shall come from on high,   sweet is the promise as weary years fly;
Oh, I shall see him descend from the sky,   coming for me, for me.
Coming for me! Coming for me! Oh, I shall see him descend from the sky!

Music © 2012 Harry Hicks

318 Shall we go

Isaac Watts

Shall we go on to ___ sin Be - cause thy grace a - bounds, Or
cru - ci - fy the Lord a - gain, and o - pen all his wounds?

2. Forbid it, mighty God,
Nor let it e'er be said
That we whose sins were crucified
Should raise them from the dead.

3. We will be slaves no more,
Since Christ has made us free,
Has nailed our tyrants to his cross,
And bought our liberty.

Music © 2015 Harry Hicks

319   Shout to the Lord

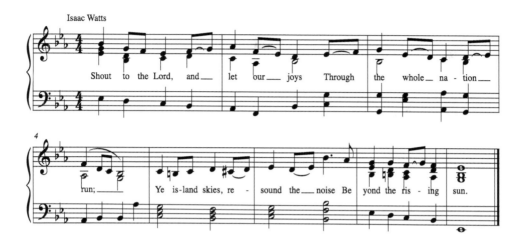

Shout to the Lord, and let our joys Through the whole nation run; Ye is-land skies, re-sound the noise Be-yond the ris-ing sun.

2. Thee, mighty God, our souls admire,
Thee our glad voices sing,
And join with the celestial choir
To praise th'eternal King.

3. Thy power the whole creation rules,
And on the starry skies
Sits smiling at the weak designs
Thine envious foes devise.

4. Thy scorn derides their feeble rage,
And with an awful frown
Flings vast confusion on their plots,
And shakes their babel down.

5. Their secret fires in caverns lay,
And we the sacrifice:
But gloomy caverns strove in vain
To 'scape all-searching eyes

6. Their dark designs were all revealed,
Their treason all betrayed:
Praise to the God that broke the snare
Their cursed hands had laid.

7. In vain the busy sons of hell
Still new rebellions try,
Their souls shall pine with envious rage,
And vex away and die.

8. Almighty grace defends our land
From their malicious power,
Let us with united songs
Almighty grace adore.

320 Simply trusting

321 Sing to the Lord

Isaac Watts

Sing to the Lord, ye heav'n — ly — hosts, And thou, O earth a - dore,

Let death and hell through all their coasts, Stand - trem' bling at his pow'r.

2. His sounding chariot shakes the sky,
He makes the clouds his throne,
There all his stores of lightning lie,
Till vengeance dart them down.

3. His nostrils breathe out fiery streams,
And from his awful tongue
A sovereign voice divides the flames,
And thunder roars along.

4. Think, O my soul, the dreadful day
When this incensed God
Shall rend the sky and burn the sea,
And fling his wrath abroad.

5. What shall the wretch the sinner do?
He once defied the Lord:
But he shall dread the Thunderer now,
And sink beneath his word.

6. Tempests of angry fire shall roll
To blast the rebel-worm,
And beat upon his naked soul
In one eternal storm.

(Written during a great sudden storm of thunder, August 20, 1697.)

322 Sing unto the Lord

J.H. Johnston

Sing unto the Lord, O ye saints of His!
Sing unto the Lord;
and at the remembrance of His holiness,
Oh, give thanks to the Lord!

1. O Lord, thy loving kindness   doth compass all our ways,
and thy compassions fail not   through all the passing days;
To Thee, O great Jehovah,   in time of need we cry,
And all who call upon Thee   shall find Thee ever nigh.
Sing unto the Lord, O ye saints of His!
Sing unto the Lord;
and at the remembrance of His holiness,
Oh, give thanks to the Lord!

2. Thy goodness we remember,   we praise Thy holiness;
We look to Thee, O Saviour,   to save, and heal, and bless;
'Tis by thy loving favour   thy trusting children stand
Upheld, and kept, and guided,   by Thy protecting hand.
Sing unto the Lord, O ye saints of His!
Sing unto the Lord;
and at the remembrance of His holiness,
Oh, give thanks to the Lord!

3. Let saints recount His mercies,   and fill his courts with praise;
Let all who know his goodness   their hallelujahs raise;
Praise God, the loving Father,   and Jesus Christ His Son,
With God the Holy Spirit,   the Glorious Three in One.
Sing unto the Lord, O ye saints of His!
Sing unto the Lord;
and at the remembrance of His holiness,
Oh, give thanks to the Lord!

Music © 2012 Harry Hicks

323   Singing for Jesus

Frances R. Havergal

Sing - ing for Je - sus, our Sav - iour and king,
Sing - ing for Je - sus, the Lord — whom we love;
All ad-or-a - tion we joy - ous-ly bring,
Long - ing to praise as they praise Him a-bove.

2. Singing for Jesus, and trying to win
Many to love Him, and join in the song;
Calling the weary and wandering in,
Rolling the chorus of gladness along.

3. Singing for Jesus, our shepherd and guide,
Singing for gladness of heart that He gives,
Singing for wonder and praise that he died,
Singing for blessing and joy that He lives.

4. Singing for Jesus, yes, singing for joy;
Thus will we praise Him and tell out His love,
Till He shall call us to brighter employ,
Singing for Jesus, for ever above.

324 Slumbering in a manger

Brenda Gallant

Slumb'-ring in a man - ger, Ho-ly, meek, and un - de -
filed, All the God-head cap-tured, In a ti-ny new-born child.

2. Watching on the hillside,
Humble shepherds hear the word,
Spoken by the angels
A Saviour, which is Christ the Lord.

3. Travelling from the east land,
Come the watchers of the sky,
Following the Natal star,
Of the baby born to die.

4. Pondering the mystery,
Mary tends the infant Lord,
Promised by the angel,
God made flesh, the living Word.

5. Shepherds bow in homage,
Wise men bring their gifts of worth
To their God incarnate,
He who came from heaven to earth.

6. Ah, we must not linger,
By the manger and the hay,
For the Lord our Saviour,
Came to bear our sins away.

7. We must view Him hanging
Bearing all our sin and loss,
Gone the rustic manger,
Now a cursed Roman cross.

8. This the wondrous reason
Why we celebrate today,
He has paid the ransom,
He has borne our sins away.

9. Past the lowly manger,
Gone the anguish of the tree,
For our Lord now reigneth
In pow'r and majesty.

10. Come we then to worship,
Bring our hearts, our lives, our all,
Praise Him and adore him,
At His feet in wonder fall.

325 Some day

Fanny J. Crosby

Some day the sil-ver cord will break, And I no more as now shall sing;
But, oh, the joy when I shall wake With-in the pa-lace of the King!

Chorus
And I shall see, and I shall see, and tell the sto-ry: saved by grace!

vv 1-3
And tell the sto-ry: saved by grace!

last verse only
saved by grace, by grace, by grace, by grace!

2. Some day my earthly home shall fall,
   I cannot tell how soon 'twill be;
   But this know: my All-in-all
   Has now a place in heav'n for me.
   And I shall see,
   And I shall see,
   And tell the story: saved by grace!
   And tell the story: saved by grace!

3. Some day, when fades the golden sun
   Beneath the rosy-tinted west,
   My blessed Lord shall say "Well done!"
   And I shall enter into rest.
   And I shall see......

4. Some day; till then I'll watch and wait,
   My lamp all trimmed and burning bright,
   That when my Saviour opes the gate,
   My soul to Him may take it's flight.
   And I shall see,
   And I shall see,
   And tell the story: saved by grace!
   And tell the story: saved by grace!
   By grace, by grace, by grace!

326 Some happy day

John James

Some hap-py day_____ mine eyes shall see_____ The face of Him_____ who died for me;_____ I'll praise Him through_____ e-ter-ni-ty,_____ Some hap-py day.

Refrain

Some hap-py day,_____ some hap-py day_____ The Lord will wipe_____ our tears a - way._____ And we will see_____ Him as he is,_____ Some hap-py day,_____ some hap-py day.

2. Some happy day I too shall sing
The song that makes all heaven ring;
Worthy the Lamb, our Lord and King,
Some happy day, some happy day.
Some happy day, some happy day,
The Lord will wipe our tears away,
And we shall see him as he is,
Some happy day, some happy day.

3. Some happy day O blessed thought,
The race is won, the battle fought,
We'll join the throng with His blood bought
Some happy day, some happy day.
Some happy day, some happy day,
The Lord will wipe our tears away,
And we shall see him as he is,
Some happy day, some happy day.

4. Some happy day - 'tis drawing near,
The thought my fainting soul doth cheer,
Sweet welcome from His lips to hear,
Some happy day, some happy day.
Some happy day, some happy day,
The Lord will wipe our tears away,
And we shall see him as he is,
Some happy day, some happy day.

Music © 2016 Harry Hicks

327   Songs of praise the angels sang (1st tune)

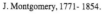

J. Montgomery, 1771- 1854.

Songs of praise the an - gels sang, Heav'n with al - le - lu - ias — rang,

When cre -a - tion was be-gun, When God spake and it was done.

2. Songs of praise awoke the morn
When the Prince of Peace was born;
Songs of praise arose when he
Captive led captivity.

3. Heav'n and earth must pass away,
Songs of praise shall crown that day;
God will make new heav'ns and earth,
Songs of praise shall hail their birth.

4. And will man alone be dumb
Till that glorious kingdom come?
No, the church delights to raise
Psalms and hymns and songs of praise.

5. Saints below, with heart and voice,
Still in songs of praise rejoice,
Learning here by faith and love
Songs of praise to sing above.

6. Hymns of glory, songs of praise,
Father, unto the thee we raise;
Jesus, glory unto thee,
With the Spirit ever be.

327　Songs of praise the angels sang (2nd tune)

J. Mongomery

Songs of___ praise___ the___ an-gels sang, Heav'n with___ ha___ le - lu-jahs rang,

When Je___ ho - vah's - work be-gun, When He___ spoke___ and___ it was done.

2. Songs of praise awoke the morn,
When the Prince of Peace was born;
Songs of praise arose when he
Captive led captivity.

3. Heav'n and earth must pass away
Songs of praise shall crown that day:
God will make new heav'ns and earth;
Songs of praise shall hail their birth.

4. And can man alone be dumb,
Till that glorious kingdom come?
No: the church delights to raise
Psalms and hymns and songs of praise.

5. Saints below, with heart and voice,
Still in songs of praise rejoice:
Learning here, by faith and love,
Songs of praise to sing above.

6. Hymns of glory, songs of praise,
Father, unto thee we raise;
Jesus, glory unto thee,
With the Spirit ever be.

327 Songs of praise the angels sang (3rd tune)

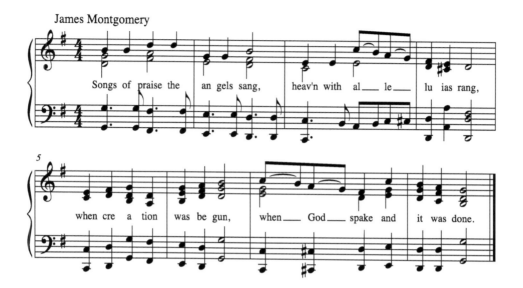

James Montgomery

Songs of praise the an gels sang, heav'n with al le lu ias rang,
when cre a tion was be gun, when God spake and it was done.

2. Songs of praise awoke the morn
when the Prince of Peace was born;
songs of praise arose when he
captive led captivity.

3. Heaven and earth must pass away;
songs of praise will crown that day:
God will make new heavens and earth;
songs of praise shall hail their birth.

4. And will man alone be dumb
till that glorious kingdom come?
No, the Church delights to raise
psalms and hymns and songs of praise.

5. Saints below, with heart and voice,
still in songs of praise rejoice;
learning here, by faith and love,
songs of praise to sing above.

6. Hymns of glory, songs of praise,
Father, unto thee we raise,
Jesu, glory unto thee,
with the Spirit, ever be.

328   Sound the angel's clarion trumpet

Colin Ferguson

Sound the an-gel's cla-rion trum-pet, bang the cym-bal, ring the bell.

Christ has ri-sen from di-sas-ter; he hath con-quered death and hell.

2. Let the choirs sing Allelulia,
this is our salvation day.
God in heaven, Christ among us,
leading the celestial way.

3. By the cross and our rejection,
Jesus suffered for our sins;
dead and buried by our evil,
now he rises, glory wins.

4. Life in all its rich abundance;
faith expressed in wine and bread;
hope of justice for his people;
joy for those who thought him dead.

5. Come and follow, love is calling,
God is with us all our days,
he forgives us, Christ is risen,
come and join his people's praise!

329   Spirit of Faith

Charles Wesley

Spi-rit of faith - come down, Re-veal the things - of God,
And make to us - the God - head known, And wit-ness with - the blood:
'Tis thine the blood - t'ap-ply, And give us eyes — to see,
Who did for ev-'ry sin - ner die Hath sure-ly died — for me.

2. No man can truly say
That Jesus is the Lord
Unless thou take the veil away,
And breathe the living word;
Then, only when we feel
Our interest in his blood,
And cry with joy unspeakable,
Thou art my Lord, my God!

3. Oh, that the world might know
The all-atoning Lamb!
Spirit of faith, descend, and show
The virtue of his name;
The grace which all may find,
The saving power impart,
And testify to all mankind,
And speak in every heart!

4. Inspire the living faith
(Which whosoe'er receives,
The witness in himself he hath,
And consciously believes),
The faith that conquers all,
And doth the mountain move,
And saves whoe'er on Jesus call,
And perfects them in love.

330 Spirit of God within me

Timothy Dudley-Smith

Spi - rit of God__ with - in me, pos-sess my hu - man frame; fan the dull em - bers of my heart, stir up the li - ving flame. Strive till that i-mage that A - dam lost, new min - ted and re-stored, in shi -ning sple - dour bri - ghtly bears the like ness of - the Lord.

2. Spirit of truth within me, possess my thought and mind;
lighten anew the inward eye by Satan rendered blind;
shine on the words that wisdom speaks and grant me power to see
the truth made known to men in Christ and in that truth be free.

3. Spirit of love within me, possess my hands and heart;
break through the bonds of self-concern that seeks to stand apart:
grant me the love that suffers long, that hopes, believes and bears,
the love fulfilled in sacrifice that cares as Jesus cares.

4. Spirit of life within me, possess this life of mine;
come as the wind of heaven's breath, come as the fire divine!
Spirit of Christ, the living Lord, reign in this house of clay,
till from its dust with Christ I rise to everlasting day.

331   Stand up, my soul

Isaac Watts

Stand up, my soul, shake off thy fears, And gird the gos - pel ar-mour on,

8ves in the bass

March to the gates of end - less joy Where thy great Cap - tain Sav-iour's gone.

2. Hell and thy sins resist thy course,
But hell and sin are vanquished foes,
Thy Jesus nailed them to the cross,
And sung the triumph when he rose.

3. What though the prince of darkness rage,
And waste the fury of his spite,
Eternal chains confine him down
To fiery deeps, and endless night.

4. What though thine inward lusts rebel,
'tis but a struggling gasp for life,
The weapons of victorious grace
Shall slay thy sins and end the strife.

5. Then let my soul march boldly on,
Press forward to the heavenly gate,
There peace and joy eternal reign,
And glittering robes for conquerors wait.

6. There shall I wear a starry crown,
And triumph in almighty grace,
While all the armies of the skies
Join in my glorious leader's praise.

Music © 2013 Harry Hicks

332   Stand up!

G. Duffiela

Stand up! stand up for Je - sus! Ye sol-diers of the cross; Lift high His ro - yal ban - ner, It

must not suf-fer loss: From vic-t'ry un - to vic-t'ry His ar - my shall he lead, Till ev - 'ry foe is

van-quished, And Christ is Lord in - deed. Stand up, stand up for Je - sus! Ye sol - diers of the

Refrain

cross; Lift high His ro - yal ban - ner, It must not suf - fer loss.

2. Stand up! Stand up for Jesus!
The trumpet call obey;
Forth to the mighty conflict
In this His glorious day!
Ye that are men, now serve Him
Against unnumbered foes;
Let courage rise with danger,
And strength to strength oppose.
Stand up, stand up for Jesus!
Ye soldiers of the cross;
Lift high His royal banner,
It must not suffer loss.

3. Stand up! stand up for Jesus!
Stand in His strength alone;
The arm of flesh will fail you;
Ye dare not trust your own.
Put on the Gospel armour,
And, watching unto prayer,
Where duty calls, or danger,
Be never wanting there.
Stand up, stand up for Jesus!
Ye soldiers of the cross;
Lift high His royal banner,
It must not suffer loss.

4. Stand up! stand up for Jesus!
The strife will not be long;
This day the noise of battle -
The next the victor's song;
To him that overcometh
A crown of life shall be;
He, with the King of glory,
Shall reign eternally.
Stand up, stand up for Jesus!
Ye soldiers of the cross;
Lift high His royal banner,
It must not suffer loss.

333 **Stars of heaven, clear and bright**

Timothy Dudley-Smith

Stars of - heav-en, clear and bright, Shine up - on this Christ-mas night.

Vast - er - far than mid - night skies are its - time - less mys - ter - ies.

Tramp-led - earth and sta - ble floor Lift the - heart to hea-ven's door:

God has - sent to us his Son, Earth and hea - ven meet as one.

2. Sleepy sounds of beast and byre, Mingle with the angel choir.
Highest heaven bends in awe Where he lies amid the straw,
Who from light eternal came Aureoled in candle-flame-
  God has sent to us his Son, Earth and heaven meet as one.

3. Wide-eyed shepherds mutely gaze At the child whom angels praise.
Threefold gifts the wise men bring, To the infant priest and king:
To the Lord immortal, myrrh For an earthly sepulchre-
  God has sent to us his Son, Earth and heaven meet as one.

4. Heaven of heavens hails his birth, King of glory, child of earth,
Born in flesh to reign on high, Prince of life to bleed and die.
Throned on Mary's lap he lies, Lord of all eternities-
  God has sent to us his Son, Earth and heaven meet as one.

5. 'Glory be to God on high, peace on earth,' the angels cry.
Ancient enmities at rest, Ransomed, reconciled and blest,
In the peace of Christ we come, come we joyful, come we home -
  God has sent to us his Son, Earth and heaven meet as one.

334 Summer suns are glowing

William Walsham How

Sum - mer suns are glow - ing ov - er land and sea; hap - py light is flow _ ing boun - ti - ful and free. Ev - 'ry-thing re - joic - es in the mel-low rays; all earth's thou - sand voi - ces _ swell the psalm of praise.

2. See God's mercy streaming
over all the world,
and his banner streaming
everywhere unfurled.
Broad and deep and glorious
an the herav'n above,
shines in mighty victorious
his eternal love.

3. Lord, upon our blindness
your pure radiance pour;
for your loving kindness
make us love you more.
And, when clouds are drifting
dark across the sky,
then, the veil uplifting,
Father, still be nigh.

4. We will never doubt you,
though you veil your light;
life is dark without you,
death with you is bright.
Light of light, shine o'er us
on our pilgrim way;
still go on before us
to the endless day.

335 Sun of my soul

John Keble

Sun of my soul, thou Sa - viour dear, it is not night if thou __ be near: O may no earth - born cloud __ a - rise to hide thee from thy ser - vant's eyes.

2. When the soft dews of kindly sleep
my wearied eyeslids gently steep,
be my last thought, how sweet to rest
for ever on my Saviour's breast.

3. Abide with me from morn till eve,
for without thee I cannot live;
abide with me when night is nigh,
for without thee I dare not die.

4. If some poor wandering child of thine
have spurned today the voice divine,
now, Lord, the gracious work begin;
let him no more lie down to sin.

5. Watch by the sick; enrich the poor
with blessings from thy boundless store;
be every mourner's sleep tonight
like infant's slumbers, pure and light.

6. Come near and bless us when we wake,
ere through the world our way we take;
till in the ocean of thy love
we lose ourselves in heaven above.

336   Tell me the story of Jesus

Fanny J. Crosby

Tell me the sto-ry of Je - sus, Write on my heart ev'-ry word!

Tell me the sto-ry most pre-cious, Sweet-est that ev-er was heard.

Tell how the an-gels in cho - rus Sang, as they wel-comed His birth,

"Glo-ry to God in the high - est, Peace and good ti-dings to earth."

2. Fasting alone in the desert,
Tell of the days that He passed;
How He was tried and was tempted,
Yet was triumphant at last.
Tell of the years of His labours,
Tell of the sorrows He bore;
He was despised and afflicted,
Homeless, rejected, and poor.

3. Tell of the cross where they nailed Him,
Hanging in anguish and pain;
Tell of the grave where they laid Him;
Tell how He liveth again.
Love, in that story so tender,
Clearer and clearer I see;
Stay, let me weep while you whisper
Love paid the ransom for me.

Music © 2015 Harry Hicks

337   Tell the world

Brenda Gallant

Tell the world the gos-pel-sto-ry: Je-sus Christ has come to save!
He. who left His Fa-ther's-glo-ry Died and tri-umphed o'er the grave!
Tell the home-less of a dwell-ing Christ pre-pares for them a-bove,
Show com-pas-sion with the tell-ing, Act - tion shown to them in love.

2. Tell the ones who bow in anguish
Of a loving Saviour's care,
Those who in sore bondage languish
Can this peace and pardon share.
Tell the masses of salvation,
Children, middle-aged and old,
Tell them, 'Heed the invitation,
All are welcomed to the fold.'

3. Tell each government and nation,
'Seek your guidance from above.'
Those of lowly rank and station;
All included in God's love.
Tell the rich, the poor, the needy
Of the treasure laid in store;
Tell those tempted to be greedy
God can give them so much more.

4. Tell the world God loves and longs for
All to turn to Him today.
For He's standing at the heart's door,
He who is Life, Truth and Way.
Tell the world in darkness lying
Of the One who is the Light -
Tell the living and the dying,
Faith gives way to glorious sight!

Music © 2014 Harry Hicks
Words © 2014 Brenda Gallant

338 Ten thousand thanks

2. Ten thousand hearts to Jesus, how gladly we would give;
Ten thousand lives to Jesus, had we so long to live.
Ten thousand tongues shall praise Him, ten thousand songs ascend
To Him, our blest Redeemer, to Him, our dearest friend!
Ten thousand thanks, ten thousand thanks,
We'll praise Him o'er and o'er;
And for the life with Him to live,
Ten thousand thousand more!

3. Ten thousand hearts to Jesus, for blessing every hour
Ten thousand times ten thousand, for love's redeeming power:
And when we hear His welcome beyond the rolling sea,
His love through endless ages our sweetest song shall be!
Ten thousand thanks, ten thousand thanks,
We'll praise Him o'er and o'er;
And for the life with Him to live,
Ten thousand thousand more!

Music © 2016 Harry Hicks

339   Tenderly the shepherd

Ten-der-ly the shep-herd, O'er the moun-tains cold, Goes to bring his

lost one Back to the fold. **Refrain** Seek - ing to save, Seek - ing to

save, Lost one, 'tis Je - sus See - king to save!

2. Patiently the owner
Seeks, with earnest care,
In the dust and darkness,
Her treasures rare.
Seeking to save,
Seeking to save;
Lost one, 'tis Jesus,
Seeking to save!

3. Lovingly the father
send the news around,
"He once dead, now liveth,
Once lost, is found."
Seeking to save,
Seeking to save;
Lost one, 'tis Jesus,
Seeking to save!

Music © 2015 Harry Hicks

340 The billows swell

W. Cowper

The bil-lows swell, the winds — are high, Clouds o - ver -

cast — the win - try sky; Out of the depths to Thee we

call; Our fears are great, our strength is small.

2. O Lord, the pilot's part perform,
And guide and guard us through the storm,
Defend us from each threatening ill,
Control the waves: say, 'Peace, be still.'

3. Amidst the roaring of the sea
Our souls still hang their hope on Thee;
Thy constant love and faithful care
Support, and save us from despair.

341 The blessed Saviour

W.A.Ogden

The bles-sed Sav-iour died for me, On the cross! On the cross! He bore my sins at Cal - va-ry, On the rug - ged cross! Be-hold His hands and feet and side, The crown of thorns, the crim-son tide! "For-give them, Fath-er!" loud He cried, On the rug - ged - cross, - On the rug - ged - cross.

2. He is now calling unto me, In His word! In His word!
He bids me drink life's water's free, in His blessed word!
For me his life He freely gave, My guilty soul from sin to save;
His precious promises I have, In His blessed word, in His blessed word!

3. O Saviour, touch my heart of sin, With thy love! With thy love!
And let the light of glory in, With thy precious love!
Then I will join to praise thy name, To spread abroad thy wondrous fame;
And all thy promises will claim, With thy precious love, with thy precious love!

Music © 2009 Harry Hicks

342   The glories of my Maker God

Isaac Watts

The glo-ries of my Ma-ker God, My joy-ful voice shall sing, And

call - the - na-tions to - a - dore Their For-mer and - their King.

2. 'Twas his right hand that shaped our clay,
And wrought this human frame,
But from his own immediate breath
Our nobler spirits came.

3. We bring our mortal powers to God,
And worship with our tongues;
We claim some kindred with the skies
And join th'angelic songs.

4. Let groveling beats of every shape,
And fowls of every wing,
And rocks, and trees, and fires, and seas,
Their various tributes bring.

5. Ye planets, to his honour shine,
And wheels of nature roll,
Praise him in your unwearied course
Around the steady pole.

6. The brightness of our Maker's Name
The wide creation fills,
And his unbounded grandeur flies
Beyond the heavenly hills.

Music © 2013 Harry Hicks

343   The heavens are singing

Timothy Dudley-Smith

The hea-vens are sing-ing, are sing-ing and prais-ing, the depths of the heart and the moun-tains re - joice; the trees of the fo-rests are prais-ing, are rais-ing the song of cre - a - tion in thun - der - ous roar!

2. The sun in his rising, his rising and setting,
the stars in their courses, their maker proclaim.
We only, his children, forgetting, forgetting
The love of our Father, have turned to our shame.

3. For he is the Father, the Father who made us,
who founded and fashioned the earth and the sky;
who stooped from his glory to aid us, to aid us
when we were yet sinners deserving to die.

4. O Father eternal, eternally living,
resplendent in glory, the Lord on his throne,
we praise and adore you, forgiving, forgiving,
none other beside you, in mercy alone!

Music © 2011 Harry Hicks   Words: 'The heavens are singing' by Timothy Dudley-Smith (b. 1926)
© Timothy Dudley-Smith in Europe and Africa. © Hope Publishing Company in the United States of America and the rest of the world.
Reproduced by permission of Oxford University Press. All rights reserved.

344   The heavens declare thy glory

Isaac Watts

The heav'ns de-clare Thy glo - ry, Lord! In ev'-ry star Thy wis - dom shines;

But when our eyes be - hold Thy Word, we read Thy Name in fair - er lines.

2. The rolling stars, the changing light,
and nights and day thy pow'r confess;
But the blest volume thou hast writ
reveals thy justice and thy grace.

3. Sun, moon and stars convey thy praise
round the whole earth, and never stand:
so, when thy truth began its race,
it touched and glanced on ev'ry land.

4. Nor shall thy spreading gospel rest,
till through the world thy truth has run;
till Christ has all the nations blest
that see the light, or feel the sun.

345   The Holy Trinity

Frederick William Faber

O Bless-ed Tri - ni-ty! Thy child-ren dare to lift their hearts to

Thee, And bless Thy tri - ple ma - jes - ty! Ho - ly Tri - ni-

Refrain

ty! Bless - ed E - qual Three, One God, we praise Thee.

2. O Blessed Trinity!
Holy, unfathomable, infinite,
Thou art all Life and Love and Light.
Holy Trinity!
Blessed Equal Three,
One God, we praise Thee.

3. O Blessed Trinity!
God of a thousand attributes! we see
That there is no one good but Thee.

4. O Blessed Trinity!
In our astonished reverence we confess
Thine uncreated loveliness.

5. O Blessed Trinity!
O simplest Majesty! O Three in One!
Thou art for ever God alone.

6. O Blessed Trinity!
The Fountain of the Godhead, in repose,
For ever rests, for ever flows.

7. O Blessed Trinity!
O Unbegotten Father! give us tears
To quench our love, to calm our fears.

8. O Blessed Trinity!
Bright Son! who art the Father's mind displayed,
Thou art begotten and not made.

9. O Blessed Trinity!
Coequal Spirit! wondrous Paraclete!
By Thee the Godhead is complete.

10. O Blessed Trinity!
We praise Thee, bless Thee, worship Thee as one.
Yet Three are on the single Throne.

11. O Blessed Trinity!
In the deep darkness of prayer's stillest night
We worship Thee blinded with light.

12. O Blessed Trinity!
Oh would that we could die of love for Thee,
Incomparable Trinity!

346   The King of love

H.W.Baker

The King of love my shep - herd is, Whose good - ness fail - eth ne - ver; I no-thing lack if I am His, And He is mine for ev - er.

2. Where streams of living water flow
My ransomed soul He leadeth,
And where the verdant pastures grow,
My ransomed soul He leadeth.

3. Perverse and foolish oft I strayed,
But yet in love He sought me,
And on His shoulder gently laid,
And home rejoicing brought me.

4. In death's dark vale I feel no ill
With Thee, dear Lord, beside me;
Thy rod and staff me comfort still,
Thy cross before to guide me.

5. Thou spread'st a table in my sight;
Thy unction grace bestoweth;
And oh, what transport of delight
From Thy pure chalice floweth!

6. And so through all the length of days
Thy goodness failest never;
Good Shepherd, may I sing thy praise
Within Thy house for ever.

347　The Lamb of God

S.M. Luxmoore

The Lamb of God upon the tree, Was slain to set poor sinners free; He bore the dreadful penalty, That we might life obtain.

Chorus

The Lamb for sinners slain Will come to earth again, The Holy One, God's mighty Son, As King of kings will reign.

2. A Man of sorrows, undefiled,
He died that e'en a guilty child
By nature wilful, selfish, wild,
Might endless life obtain.
The Lamb for sinners slain
Will come to earth again,
The Holy One, God's mighty Son,
As King of kings will reign.

3. Yes, when the Lord was crucified,
When He to save poor sinners died;
E'en God His face from Him did hide,
That we might life obtain.
The Lamb for sinners slain
Will come to earth again,
The Holy One, God's mighty Son,
As King of kings will reign.

4. The Lamb of God will come again,
In majesty and might to reign,
And they who endless life obtain
Will follow in His train.
The Lamb for sinners slain
Will come to earth again,
The Holy One, God's mighty Son,
As King of kings will reign.

Music © 2016 Harry Hicks

348   The lands that long in darkness lay

Isaac Watts

The lands that long in dark-ness lay Now have be-held a heav'n-ly light;

Na-tions that sat in death's cold shade Are blessed with beams di - vine-ly bright

2. The virgin's promised Son is born,
Behold th'expected Child appear;
What shall his names or titles be?
The Wonderful, the Counsellor.

3. This infant is the mighty God
Come to be suckled and adored
Th'eternal Father, Prince of Peace,
The son of David, and his Lord.

4. The government of earth and seas
Upon his shoulders shall be laid,
His wide dominions still increase,
And honours to his name be paid.

5. Jesus the holy child shall sit
High on his father David's throne,
Shall crush his foes beneath his feet,
And reign to ages yet unknown.

349 The Lord bless you and keep you

350   The Lord is here

Brenda Gallant

The Lord is here His word to __ bless In this most ho - ly

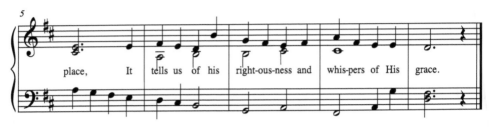

place, It tells us of his right-ous-ness and whis-pers of His grace.

2. The Lord is here, he sees your need
Just as in days of old,
And unto all who will take heed
He will His love unfold.

3. The Lord is here, He knows your sin,
But loves you just the same,
He wants to cleanse your heart within,
Through faith in His dear name.

4. The Lord is love in all His power,
To strengthen and to heal,
Oh hear his voice this very hour,
And tell Him how you feel.

5. The Lord is here, your soul to save,
It was for you He died,
To save you from a hopeless grave
God's Son was crucified.

6. The Lord is here, the price is paid,
More precious still than gold,
Accept the sacrifice he made
To win you for His fold.

7. Arise and go with grateful heart,
Trusting in Christ alone,
He'll make you whole in every part,
Your life shall be His throne.

351   The Lord is King!

Harry Hicks

The Lord is King! He's ris'n a-gain, sin's lost it's pow'r o'er us!

Up from the grave! He lives a-gain, and ne-ver___more will die!

He came to earth a ti-ny___babe. Born in a way-side inn.

He grew___up like you and me, Now we are freed from sin!

Written for the youngsters of Mundesley Free Church, Norfolk. 18/12/15

352 The Lord is King

J. Conder

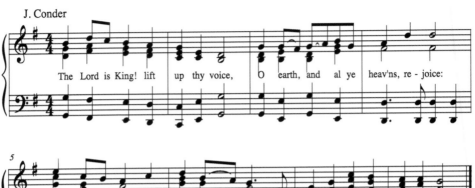

The Lord is King! lift up thy voice, O earth, and al ye heav'ns, re - joice:

from world to world the joy shall ___ ring; 'The Lord om - ni - po - tent is King.'

2. The Lord is King! who then shall dare
resist his will, distrust his care,
or murmur at his wise decrees,
or doubt his royal promises?

3. He reigns! ye saints, exalt your strains;
your God is King, your Father reigns;
and he is at the Father's side,
the Man of love, the Crucified.

4. Alike pervaded by his eye
all parts of his dominion lie:
this world of ours and worlds unseen,
and thin the boundary between.

5. One Lord one empire all secures;
he reigns, and life and death are yours;
through earth and heaven one song shall ring,
'The Lord omnipotent is King'.

353 The Lord Jehovah reigns

Isaac Watts

The Lord Je-ho-vah reigns, His throne is built on high; The gar-ments He as-sumes Are light and ma-je-sty; No glo-ries shine with beams so bright, No mor-tal eye can bear the sight.

2. The thunders of His hand
Keep the wide world in awe;
His wrath and justice stand
To guard His holy law;
And where His love resolves to bless,
His truth confirms and seals the grace.

3. Through all His ancient works
His perfect wisdom shines;
Confounds the powers of hell,
And breaks their dark designs;
Strong is His arm, and shall fulfil
His great decrees, His sovereign will.

4. And will this mighty King
Of glory condescend?
And will He write His name
My Father and my Friend?
I love His name, I love His word;
Join all my powers and praise the Lord!

354   The Lord my shepherd is

2. If e'er I go astray, he doth my soul reclaim:
and guides me in his own right way for his most holy name.
While He affords his aid I cannot yield to fear;
Though I should walk through death's dark shade my shepherd's with me there.

3. In spite of all my foes, thou dost my table spread;
My cup with blessings overflows and joy exalts my head.
The bounties on thy love shall crown my future days;
Nor from thy house will I remove nor cease to speak thy praise.

355 The Lord of heaven has come to earth

Bill Anderson

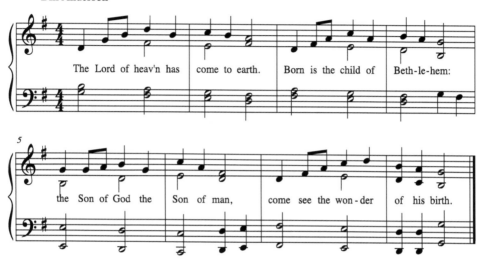

The Lord of heav'n has come to earth. Born is the child of Beth-le-hem: the Son of God the Son of man, come see the won-der of his birth.

2. The angels sang; the shepherds heard,
'The Saviour of the world is born
this night in David's royal town',
the message clear, their hearts were stirred.

3. The star shone bright, the wise men saw,
they followed and they journeyed far;
with gold and frankincense and myrrh,
gifts for the Prince of Peace they bore.

4. God's law of love he came to live:
Jesus his name and Mary's child.
We worship him, the 'King of kings',
And with the angels glory give.

5. 'Glory to God' shall be our song,
and 'peace on earth', it pleases him,
who to us all his Son has given,
Glory to God all ages long.

356   The Lord on high proclaims

Isaac Watts

The Lord on high pro - claims His God-head from his throne; "Mer - cy and jus-tice are the names By which I will __ be known.

2. "Ye dying souls that sit
In darkness and distress,
Look from the borders of the pit
To my recovering grace."

3. Sinners shall hear the sound;
Their thankful tongues shall own,
"Our righteousness and strength is found
In thee, the Lord, alone."

4. In thee shall Israel trust,
And see their guilt forgiv'n;
God will pronounce the sinners just,
And take the saints to heav'n.

357   The old account was settled

Mrs. C.D. Martin

O how dark the way be-fore me, And how hea-vy was my load, How I
dread-ed com-ing judg-ment, How I feared the wrath of God; Since I heard the old, old sto-ry, I am
v2: par - don -
(v3) hap-py, for I know That the old ac-count was sett-led long a - go.

Chorus
O the old ac-count was set-tled long a - go, long a - go, long a - go, and the
blood that brought re-demp-tion came, I know, from His side, long a - go.

2. Long my weary heart was trying
To make peace with God in heav'n,
Knowing not that peace and pardon
Would be freely giv'n;
Then I heard how Jesus suffered,
How His blood could make like snow,
How the old account was settled long ago.
O the old account was settled long ago,
Long ago, long ago,
And the blood that brought redemption came,
I know, from His side, long ago.

3. I'm rejoicing in salvation,
Jesus' blood my only plea,
All the past has been forgiven
From all sin, praise God, I'm free!
This sweet story of redemption
I would tell all below,
How the old account was settled long ago.
O the old account was settled long ago,
Long ago, long ago,
And the blood that brought redemption came,
I know, from His side, long ago.

Music © 2016 Harry Hicks

358 The Saviour Christ

Brenda Gallant

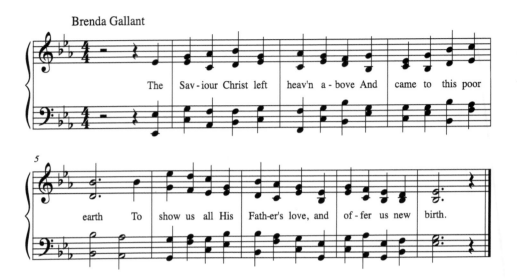

2. He came right down to reach the lost,
   To bear the shame and sin;
   Salvation at tremendous cost
   That He your love might win.

3. Oh, have you glimpsed Him hanging there
   Upon that awful tree,
   And can you feel His tender care,
   Who died, to make you free.

4. Tonight He speaks through His own Word,
   To those who will take heed,
   And if His voice is truly heard,
   He'll meet the deepest need.

5. So come to Him and do not wait,
   He'll make your heart His home,
   Tomorrow may be just too late,
   Oh, hear Him pleading "Come."

359 The Sea

1. The sea, it is a wondrous sight,
Of colour, shade and hue,
The children paddle with delight,
And adults love it too.

2. The sea was ordered in it's place;
God issued the command,
This in creation we can trace,
For then appeared dry land.

3. The sea has moods we can't control,
Calm and tempestuous too,
But it God's wonders doth extol -
Old, yet ever new.

4. The sea, it yields abundant food,
And marvels rarely seen,
But it can also rage and flood,
Nor can we intervene.

5. But there is One who slept through storm,
Then heard disciples call,
He rose and banished their alarm,
And ordered waves to fall.

6. There are still storms that come our way,
They bring much fear and woe;
Wrecking ships and homes and lives,
Causing us to know

7. How weak and vulnerable we are,
How frail life's little span,
But God is not aloof and far,
For He became a man.

8. Experiencing the storms we face,
Sinless and undefiled.
He has borne this in our place,
On him our sins are piled.

9. So, as we look out on the sea,
Observing it's great might,
Let's heed this voice: "Come unto Me
And I will set things right."

10. Just as He calmed disiples' fears
Within their storm-tossed boat,
So He will hear your earnest prayers
And give us grace to float

11. Above the tossing waves of fear
That seek to drag us down,
He will lift us from despair
And give the victor's crown.

360　The solid rock

Edward Mote

My hope is built on noth-ing less Than Je-sus' blood and righ-teous-ness.
I dare not trust the sweet-est frame, But whol-ly lean on Jes-us' name.

Refrain
On Christ, the sol-id rock I stand, All oth-er ground is sink-ing sand.

2. When darkness veils His lovely face
   I rest on His unchanging grace;
   In every high and stormy gale,
   My anchor holds within the veil.
   On Christ, the solid rock I stand;
   All other ground is sinking sand.

3. His oath, His covenant, His blood,
   Support me in the whelming flood;
   When all around my soul gives way,
   He then is all my hope and stay.
   On Christ, the solid rock I stand;
   All other ground is sinking sand.

4. When He shall come with trumpet sound,
   O may I then in Him be found;
   Dressed in His righteousness alone,
   Faultless to stand before the throne!
   On Christ, the solid rock I stand;
   All other ground is sinking sand.

Music © 2016 Harry Hicks

361   The strife is o'er

Tr. from the Latin by Rev. F. Pott

The strife is o'er, the bat - tle done; The vic - to -

8ves in the bass

ry of life is won; The song of tri - umph

has__ be - gun. Al - le - lu - ia! Al - le - lu - ia!

2. The powers of death have done their worst,
But Christ their legions hath dispersed;
Let shouts of holy joy outburst.
Alleluia! Alleluia!

3. The three sad days have quickly sped:
He rises glorious from the dead;
All glory to our risen Head!
Alleluia! Alleluia!

4. He brake the bonds of death and hell;
The bars from heaven's high portals fell;
Let hymns of praise His triumph tell.
Alleluia! Alleluia!

5. Lord, by the stripes which wounded Thee,
From death's dread sting Thy servants free,
That we may live, and sing to Thee.
Alleluia! Alleluia!

362   The sun is sinking fast

Latin, c18th Cent. Trans. E.Caswall

The sun is sink-ing fast, the day - light dies; let love a - wake, and pay her even - ing sac - ri - fice.

2. As Christ upon the cross
his head inclined,
and to his Father's hands
his parting soul resigned,

3. so now herself my soul
would wholly give
into his sacred charge
in whom all spirits live;

4. so now beneath his eye
would calmly rest,
without a wish or thought
abiding in the breast,

5. save that, his will be done,
whate'er be tide,
dead to himself, and dead
in him to all betide.

6. Thus would I live; yet now
not I, but he,
in all his power, and love
henceforth alive in me.

7. One sacred Trinity,
one Lord divine,
may I be ever his,
and he for ever mine.

Music © 2015 Harry Hicks

363   The true Messiah

Isaac Watts

The true Mes-si-ah now ap-pears, The types are all with-drawn;

So fly the sha-dows the stars___ Be-fore the ri - sing dawn.

2. No smoking sweets, nor bleeding lambs,
   Nor kid, nor bullock slain,
   Incense and spice of costly names
   Would all be burnt in vain.

3. Aaron must lay his robes away;
   His mitre and his vest,
   When God himself comes down to be
   The offering and the priest.

4. He took our mortal flesh to show
   The wonders of his love;
   For us he paid his life below,
   And prays for us above.

5. "Father," he cries, "forgive their sins,
   For I myself have died,"
   And then he shows his opened veins,
   And pleads his wounded side.

364   The will of God

Timothy Dudley-Smith

The will of God - to mark my way, The word of God for light; E - ter - nal jus - tice

vv1-3   last time only   fin

to o - bey in e - ver - las - ting right.   righ teous - ness and love.

2. Your eyes of mercy keep me still,
   your gracious love be mine;
   so work in me your perfect will
   and cause your face to shine.

3. With ordered step secure and strong,
   from sin's oppression freed,
   redeemed for ev'ry kind of wrong
   in thought and word and deed.

4. So set my heart to love your word
   and ev'ry promise prove,
   to walk with truth before the Lord
   in righteousness and love.

Music © 2009 Harry Hicks   Words: 'The will of God to mark my way' by Timothy Dudley-Smith (b. 1926)
© Timothy Dudley-Smith in Europe and Africa. © Hope Publishing Company in the United States of America and the rest of the world.
Reproduced by permission of Oxford University Press. All rights reserved.

365   Thee will I love

Robert Seymour Bridges (1844-1930)

Thee will I love, my God and King, Thee will I sing, My strength and tow-er: For ev-er-more thee will I trust, O God most just Of truth and power; Who all things hast In or-der placed, Yea, for thy plea-sure hast cre-a-ted; And on thy throne Un seen-un-known, Reign-est a-lone In glo-ry seat ed.

2. Set in my heart thy love I find;
My wandering mind
To thee thou leadest:
My trembling hope, my strong desire
With heavenly fire
Thou kindly feedest.
Lo, all things fair
Thy path prepare,
The beauty to thy spirit calleth,
Thine to remain
In joy or pain
And count it gain
Whate'er befalleth.

3. O more and more thy love extend,
My life befriend
With heavenly pleasure;
That I may win thy paradise,
Thy pearl of price,
Thy countless treasure;
Since but in thee
I can go free
From earthly care and vain oppression,
This prayer I make
For Jesus' sake
That thou me take
In thy posession.

366   There is a house

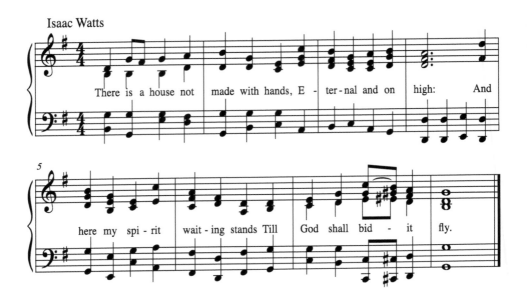

Isaac Watts

There is a house not made with hands, E - ter - nal and on high: And
here my spi - rit wait - ing stands Till God shall bid - it fly.

2. Shortly this prison of my clay
Must be dissolved and fall,
Then, O my soul, with joy obey
They heavenly Father's call.

3. 'tis He by his almighty grace
That forms thee fit for heav'n,
And as an earnest of the place,
Has his own Spirit giv'n.

4. We walk by faith of joys to come,
Faith lives upon his word;
But while the body is our home
We're absent from the Lord.

5. 'tis pleasant to believe thy grace,
But we would rather see;
We would be absent from the flesh,
And present, Lord, with thee.

Music © 2013 Harry Hicks

367   There is a land of pure delight

Isaac Watts

There - is a land of pure de-light Where saints im - mor-tal reign,
In - fi-nite day ex - cludes the night, and pleas-ures ban - ish pain.

2. There everlasting spring abides,
And never withering flowers;
Death like a narrow sea divides
This heavenly land from ours.

3. Sweet fields beyond the swelling flood,
Stand dressed in living green
So to the Jews old Canaan stood,
While Jordan rolled between.

4. But timorous mortals start and shrink
To cross this narrow sea,
And linger shivering on the brink,
And fear to launch away.

5. O! could we make our doubts remove,
These gloomy doubts that rise,
And see the Canaan that we love,
With unbeclouded eyes!

6. Could we but climb where Moses stood,
And view the landscape o'er,
Not Jordan's stream, nor death's cold flood,
Should fright us from the shore.

368   There's a spirit in the air

Brian Wren

There's a spi-rit in the air, Tel-ling Christ-ians ev-er-y-where:

'Praise the love that Christ re-vealed, Liv-ing, work-ing, in our world!'

2. Lose your shyness, find your tongue,
tell the world what God has done:
God in Christ has come to stay.
Live tomorrow's life today!

3. When believers break the bread,
when a hungry child is fed,
praise the love that Christ revealed,
living, working, in our world.

4. Still the Spirit gives us light,
seeing wrong and setting right:
God in Christ has come to stay.
Live tomorrow's life today!

5. When a stranger's not alone,
where the homeless find a home,
praise the love that Christ revealed,
living, working, in our world.

6. May the spirit fill our praise,
guide our thoughts and change our ways,
God in Christ has come to stay.
Live tomorrow's life today!

7. There's a spirit in the air,
calling people ev'rywhere:
praise the love that Christ revealed,
living, working, in our world.

369   These glorious minds

Isaac Watts

"These gor - ious minds, how bright they shine Whence all their bright ar - ray? How come they to the hap - py seats Of ev - er las - ting day?"

2. From torch'ring pains to endless joys
On fiery wheels they rode,
And strangely washed their raiment white
In Jesus' dying blood.

3. Now they approach a spotless God,
And bow before his throne
Their warbling harps and sacred songs
Adore the Holy One.

4. The unveiled glories of his face
Amongst his saints reside,
While the rich treasure of his grace
Sees all their wants supplied.

5. Tormenting thirst shall leave their souls,
And hunger flee as fast;
The fruit of life's immortal tree
Shall be their sweet repast.

6. The Lamb shall lead his heavenly flock
Where living fountains rise,
And love divine shall wipe away
The sorrows of their eyes.

370   They bound the hands of Jesus

2. Upon His precious head they placed a crown of thorns;
They laughed and said "Behold the King,"
They struck Him and they cursed Him and mocked His holy Name,
All alone He suffered everything.
He could have called ten thousand angels
To destroy the world and set Him free.
He could have called ten thousand angels,
But He died alone for you and me.

3. When they nailed Him to the cross, His mother stood nearby;
He said "Woman, behold thy son!"
He cried "I thirst for water,' but they gave Him none to drink,
Then the sinful work of man was done.
He could have called ten thousand angels
To destroy the world and set Him free.
He could have called ten thousand angels,
But He died alone for you and me.

4. To the howling mob He yielded; He did not for mercy cry,
The cross of shame He took alone.;
And when he cried "'Tis finished," He gave himself to die;
Salvation's wondrous plan was done.
He could have called ten thousand angels
To destroy the world and set Him free.
He could have called ten thousand angels,
But He died alone for you and me.

371 This awesome world

Andrew Pratt

This awe some world that fills us with a maze ment: your Spi rit breathed and

all things came to be; each stun ning scene ex tends i ma gin a tion, the fruit ful land and

ev' ry spread ing sea. your Spi rit's force and pre sence through our days.

2. The seasons change, predictable and constant,
   the rolling sun, the moon and stars above
   are witness to that same creative Spirit;
   we read in this the constancy of love.

3. And in this light we sing your praise forever,
   in word and action tune our works and ways
   to echo in a mighty celebration
   your Spirit's force and presence through our days.

372   This cherished child

Timothy Dudley-Smith

1. This che-rished child of God's cre - a - tion, heir to a
2. Lord, as of old the chil - dren found you, when to your

world of joy __ and pain, free - ly in thank - ful ded - i -
side with joy __ they pressed, so may our chil - dren ga - ther

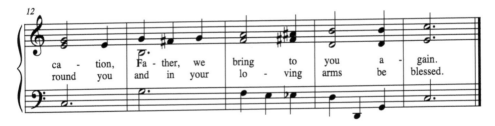

ca - tion, Fa - ther, we bring to you a - gain.
round you and in your lo - ving arms be blessed.

*him/her

3. Spirit of holiness, descending,
Grant them* to grow, as years increase,
Closer to Christ and his befriending,
Filled with your love and joy and peace.

4. God ever One, whose care unsleeping
watches about your children's way,
take now this child within your keeping,
whom here we dedicate today.

Music © 2012 Harry Hicks   Words: 'This cherished child' by Timothy Dudley-Smith (b. 1926)
© Timothy Dudley-Smith in Europe and Africa. © Hope Publishing Company in the United States of America and the rest of the world.
Reproduced by permission of Oxford University Press. All rights reserved.

373 This day above all days

Timothy Dudley-Smith

This day a-bove all days glad hymns of tri-umph bring; lift ev-'ry heart to love and praise and ev-'ry voice to sing: for Je-sus is ri-sen our glor-ious Lord and King! for Je-sus is ri-sen our glor-ious Lord and King!

2. Christ keeps his Eastertide!
The Father's power descends;
the shuttered tomb is open wide,
the rock-hewn grave he rends;
For Jesus is risen
our glorious Lord and King!
For Jesus is risen
our glorious Lord and King!

3. What sovereign grace is found
in Christ for all our need!
The powers of sin and death are bound,
the ransomed captives freed;
For Jesus is risen
and death's dominion ends!
For Jesus is risen
and death's dominion ends!

4. So lift your joyful songs
with all the hosts on high,
where angel and archangel throngs
his ceaseless praises cry:
for Jesus is risen
and lives no more to die!
for Jesus is risen
and lives no more to die!

374   This happy Christmas Day

Brenda Gallant

On this hap-py Christ-mas day, Tune your hearts in joy-ful lay,
Praise the Fa-ther and the Son, With the Spi-rit, Three in One.
God's great pro-mise has come true, Gos-pel grace is shi-ning through.

2. Like the shepherds long ago,
May we to the manger go,
See the Infant lying there,
Our humanity to share.
See Him as the promised One,
God's beloved only Son.

3. Long ago God gave His Word,
And the hearts of men were stirred,
For One promised at the fall
Would release from sins enthrall.
The Messiah soon would come,
God's beloved only Son.

4. Thus it was that Jesus came,
Though men scorned His precious Name,
As a little Babe was born
In a stable all forlorn.
When He came to this poor earth
Very few perceived His worth.

5. Only shepherds went to see
At His manger bowed the knee,
And the wise men travelled far,
Following His natal star.
These rejoiced and spread abroad
All that they had seen and heard.

6. When He grew to be a man,
He fulfilled the Father's plan,
Chose to suffer in our stead,
On the cross He hung and bled.
Jesus died our souls to save,
Rose in triumph o'er the grave.

7. That first Advent showed God's face,
Ushered in this day of grace.
May we give Him all our love,
He who left the heav'n above,
Welcome Him with hearts aglow;
Live for Him while here below.

375   This is the day of light

J. Ellerton

This is the day of light: let there be light to-day; O
Day-spring, rise up-on our night, and chase its gloom a-way.

2. This is the day of rest:
our failing strength renew;
on weary brain and troubled breast
shed thou thy freshening dew.

3. This is the day of peace:
thy peace our spirits fill;
bid thou the blasts of discord cease,
the waves of strife be still.

4. This is the day of prayer:
let earth to heaven draw near;
lift up our hearts to seek thee there,
come down and meet us here.

5. This is the first of days:
send forth thy quickening breath,
and wake dead souls to love and praise,
O vanquisher of death.

Music © 2015 Harry Hicks

376   This is the day

Isaac Watts

This is the day that the Lord hath made, He calls the hours his own;
Let heav'n re - joice, let earth be glad And praise sur - round the throne.

2. Today He rose and left the dead,
And Satan's empire fell;
Today the saints His triumphs spread,
And all His wonders tell.

3. Hosanna to the anointed King,
To David's holy Son!
Make haste to help us, Lord, and bring
Salvation from Thy throne.

4. Blest be the Lord, who comes to men
With messages of grace;
Who comes, in God His Father's Name,
To save our sinful race.

5. Hosanna to the highest strains
The church on earth can raise;
The highest heavens in which he reigns
Shall give Him nobler praise.

377 This is the threefold truth

John Barnard

This is the three-fold___ truth On which our faith de - pends: And with this joy ful cry___ Wor - ship be - gins___ and ends!

Chorus

Christ has died! Christ is ri - sen! Christ will come a - gain!

2. Made sacred by long use, new-minted for our time,
our liturgies sum up the hope we have in Him:
Christ has died! Christ is risen! Christ will come again!

3. On this we fix our minds as, kneeling side by side,
we take our bread and wine from Him, the crucified:
Christ has died! Christ is risen! Christ will come again!

4. By this we are upheld when doubt and grief assails
our Christian fortitude, and only grace avails:
Christ has died! Christ is risen! Christ will come again!

5. This is the threefold truth which, if we hold it fast,
changes the world and us and brings us home at last.
Christ has died! Christ is risen! Christ will come again!

378　Thou art the Way

G.W.Doane

Thou art the Way: by thee — a - lone from sin and

death we flee; and he who would the Fa - ther

seek must seek him, Lord, — by thee.

2. Thou art the Truth: thy word alone
   true wisdom can impart;
   thou only canst inform the mind
   and purify the heart.

3. Thou art the life: the rending tomb
   proclaims thy conquering arm;
   and those who put their trust in thee
   nor death nor hell shall harm.

4. Thou art the Way, the truth, the life:
   grant us that Way to know,
   that truth to keep, that Life to win,
   whose joys eternal flow.

379 Thou Hidden Source

Charles Wesley

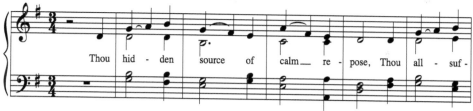

Thou hid-den source of calm_ re-pose, Thou all-suf-

fi-cient love_ di-vine, My help and ref-uge from_ my

foes, Se-cure I am,_ if thou_ art mine; And lo! from

sin, and grief, and shame, I hide me, Je-sus, in_ thy name.

2. Thy mighty name salvation is,
And keeps my happy soul above;
Comfort it brings, and power, and peace,
And joy, and everlasting love;
To me with thy dear name are given
Pardon, and holiness, and heaven.

3. Jesu, my all in all thou art,
My rest in toil, my ease in pain;
My med'cine of my broken heart,
In war my peace, in loss my gain;
My smile beneath the tyrant's frown,
In shame my glory and my crown.

4. I want my plentiful supply,
In weakness my almighty power;
In bonds my perfect liberty,
My light in Satan's darkest hour;
In grief my joy unspeakable,
My life in death, my heaven in hell.

380   Thou whom my soul admires

Isaac Watts

Thou whom my soul ad - mires a - bove, all -
earth - ly __ joy, and __ earth - ly - love, Tell me dear Shep - herd,
let me - know, - Where - doth thy sweet - est pas - ture grow?

2. Where is shadow of that rock
That from the son defends his flock?
Fain would I feed among thy sheep,
Among them rest, among them sleep.

3. Why should thy bride appear like one
That turns aside to paths unknown?
My constant feet would never rove,
Would never seek another love.

4. The footsteps of thy flock I see;
Thy sweetest pastures here they be;
A wondrous feast thy love prepares,
Bought with thy wounds, and groans, and tears.

5. His dearest flesh he makes my food,
And bids me drink his richest blood;
Here to these hills my soul will come,
Till my beloved leads me home.

381   Throned upon the awful tree

John Ellerton

Throned up - on the aw - ful tree. King of grief, I watch with thee;

Dark-ness veils thine an-guished face, None its line of woe can trace.

None can tell what pangs un-known Hold thee si - lent and a - lone.

2. Silent through those three dread hours,
   wrestling with the evil powers,
   Left alone with human sin,
   Gloom around thee and within,
   Till th'appointed time is nigh,
   Till the Lamb of God may die.

3. Hark that cry that peals aloud
   Upward through the whelming cloud!
   Thou, the Father's only Son,
   Thou, His own Anointed One,
   Thou dost ask him (can it be?)
   "Why hast thou forsaken me?"

4. Lord, should fear and anguish roll
   Darkly o'er my sinful soul,
   Thou, who once was thus bereft,
   That this own should ne'er be left,
   Teach me by that bitter cry
   In the gloom to know thee nigh.

382 Through good report

H. Bonar

Through good re - port and ev - il, Lord, Still guid - ed by Thy faith-ful

word, Our staff, our buck-ler, and our sword, We fol-low thee.

2. In silence of the lonely night,
In the full glow of day's clear light,
Through life's strange windings, dark or bright,
We follow Thee.

3. Strengthened by Thee we forward go,
'Mid smile, or scoff, or friend or foe,
Through pain or ease, through joy or woe,
We follow Thee.

4. With enemies on every side,
We lean on Thee, the Crucified;
Forsaking all on earth beside,
We follow Thee.

5. O Master! point Thou out the way,
Nor suffer thou our steps to stray;
Then in the path that leads the way,
We follow Thee.

6. Thou hast passed on before our face;
Thy footsteps on the way we trace;
O keep us, aid us by Thy grace!
We follow Thee.

7. Whom have we in the heaven above,
Whom on this earth, save Thee, to love?
Still in Thy light we onward move,
We follow Thee.

Music © 2016 Harry Hicks

383 Through the love of God (1st tune)

Mary Peters (1813-1856)

Through the love of God our Sa-viour, All will be well;
Free and change-less is His fa-vour, All, all is well.
Pre-cious is the blood that healed us, Per-fect is the grace that sealed us,
Strong the hand stretched out to shield us, All____ must be well.

2. Though we pass through tribulation,
   All will be well;
Ours is such a full salvation
   All, all is well;
Happy still in God confiding,
Fruitful, if in Christ abiding,
Holy, through the Spirit's guiding,
   All must be well.

3. We expect a bright tomorrow,
   All will be well;
Faith can sing, through days of sorrow,
   All, all is well:
On our Father's love relying,
Jesus every need supplying,
Or in living or in dying,
   All must be well.

Music © 2015 Harry Hicks

383 Through the love of God (2nd tune)

Mary Peters (1813-1856)

Through the love of God, our Sav-iour, all - will be well.
Free and change-less is his fa-vour; all,— all is well.
Pre-cious is the blood that healed us, per-fect is the grace that sealed us,
strong the hand stretched forth to shield us; all— must be well.

2. Though we pass through tribulation,
all will be well.
Ours is such a full salvation,
all, all is well.
Happy still in God confiding,
fruitful, if in Christ abiding,
holy, through the Spirit's guiding;
all must be well.

3. We expect a bright tomorrow;
all will be well.
Faith can sing through days of sorrow,
'All, all is well.'
On our Father's love relying,
Jesus every need supplying,
in our living, in our dying,
all must be well.

384   Thus far the Lord

Isaac Watts

Thus far the Lord has led me on, Thus far his pow'r prolongs my days, And ev'ry ev'ning shall make known Some fresh memorial of his grace.

2. Much of my time has run to waste,
And I perhaps am near my home;
But he forgives my follies past,
He gives me strength for days to come.

3. I lay my body down to sleep,
Peace is the pillow for my head,
While well-appointed angels keep
Their watchful station round my bed.

4. In vain the sons of earth or hell
Tell me a thousand frightful things,
My God in safety makes me dwell
Beneath the shadow of his wings.

5. Faith in his name forbids my fear:
O may thy presence ne'er depart!
And in the morning make me hear
the love and kindness of thy heart.

6. Thus when the night of death shall come,
My flesh shall rest beneath the ground,
And wait thy voice to rouse my tomb,
With sweet salvation in the sound.

385   Thy way, not mine, O Lord

H. Bonar

Thy way, not mine, O Lord, How - ev - er dark it

be, Lead me by Thine own hand, Choose out the path for me

2. Smooth let it be, or rough,
  It will be still the best;
Winding or straight, it leads
  Right onward to Thy rest.

3. I dare not choose my lot;
  I would not if I might;
Choose Thou for me my God,
  So shall I walk aright.

4. The kingdom that I seek
  Is Thine; so let the way
That leads to it be Thine;
  Else I must surely stray.

5. Take Thou my cup, and it
  With joy or sorrow fill,
As best to Thee may seem;
  Choose Thou my good and ill.

6. Choose Thou for me my friends,
  My sickness or my health;
Choose Thou my cares for me,
  My poverty or wealth.

7. Not mine, not mine the choice,
  In things or great or small;
Be Thou my Guide, my Strength,
  My Wisdom, and my All!

386   To God be glory

From the Greek, tr. by N. Tate & N. Brady

To God be glo - ry, peace on earth, To all man - kind, __ good - will; We

bless, we praise, we wor - ship Thee, And glo - ri - fy __ Thee still.

2. And thanks for Thy great glory give,
That fills our souls with light;
O Lord, our heavenly king, the God
And Father of all might:

3. And Thou begotten Son of God,
Before all time begun,
Thou Lord and God, Thou Lamb of God,
The Father's only Son.

4. Have mercy, Thou that takes the sins
Of all mankind away:
Have mercy, Saviour of mankind,
And hear us when we pray.

5. O Thou, who sits at God's right hand,
Upon the Father's throne;
Have mercy on us, Thou, O Christ,
The everlasting Son:

6. Thou, Lord, who, with the Holy Ghost,
Whom heaven and earth adore,
In glory of the Father, art
Most high for evermore.

387   To God the only wise

Isaac Watts

To God the on-ly wise, Our Sa - viour and our King, Let all the saints be-low the skies Their hum - ble prais - es bring.

2. 'Tis his almighty love,
His counsel, and his care,
Preserves us safe from sin and death,
And every hurtful snare.

3. He will present our souls
Unblemished and complete,
Before the glory of his face,
With joys divinely great.

4. Then all the chosen seed
Shall meet around the throne,
Shall bless the conduct of his grace,
And make his wonders known.

5. To our Redeemer God
Wisdom and power belongs,
Immortal crowns of majesty,
And everlasting songs.

Music © 2012 Harry Hicks

388   To Him that chose us first

Isaac Watts

To Him that chose us first Be - fore the world be - gan, To

Him that bore the curse To save re - bell - ious man, To

Him that formed Our hearts a - new, Is end - less praise And glo - ry due.

2. The Father's love shall run
Through our immortal songs,
We bring to God the Son
Hosannas on our tongues:
Our lips address
The Spirit's Name
With equal praise,
And zeal the same.

3. Let every saint above
And angel round the throne,
For ever bless and love
The sacred Three in One:
Thus heaven shall raise
His honours high
When earth and time
Grow old and die.

4. To God the father's throne
Perpetual honours raise;
Glory to God the Son,
To God the Spirit praise:
And while our lips
Their tribute bring,
Our faith adores
The name we sing.

5. To our eternal God,
The Father and the Son,
And Spirit all divine,
Three mysteries in one,
Salvation, power,
And praise be given
By all on earth
And all in heaven.

389   To us a child

Charles Wesley

To us a child of royal birth. Heir of the
promises is giv'n, the invisible
appears on earth, The Son of man the God of
heav'n, The Son of man the God of heav'n.

2. A Saviour born, in love supreme
He comes our fallen souls to raise;
He comes his people to redeem
With all His plenitude of grace.
With all His plenitude of grace.

3. The Christ, by raptured seers foretold,
Filled with the 'ternal spirit's pow'r,
Prophet, and priest, and king behold,
And Lord of all the worlds adore.
And Lord of all the worlds adore.

4. The Lord of Hosts, the God most High,
Who quits His throne on earth to live,
With joy we welcome from the sky,
With faith into our hearts receive.
With faith into our hearts receive.

Music © 2008 Harry Hicks

390 To us in Bethlem city

Colner Psalter, 1638.

To us in Beth - lem ci - ty Was born a lit - tle son; In him all

gen - tle gra - ces Were gath-ered in - to one.

2. And all our love and fortune
Lie in his mighty hands;
Our sorrows, joys, and failures,
He sees and understands.

3. O Shepherd ever near us,
We'll go where thou dost lead;
No matter where the pasture,
With thee at hand to feed.

4. No grief shall part us from thee,
However sharp the edge;
We'll serve, and do thy bidding -
O take our hearts in pledge!

391   To you, O Christ

2. As once you walked in Galilee   and learned its paths and valleys,
or met within Jerusalem   the crowds from streets and alleys;
so help us learn our age's needs   and meet those needs with caring,
your world and people see in all,   your love and gospel sharing.

3. Lord, let us never pass our days   indifferent to others;
or build up walls that hide from sight   our sisters and our brothers;
through windows barred and shuttered tight   how can your sunshine reach us?
O make us open to your truth,   your love and service teach us.

4. May all the darkness we have made   and sins that have controlled us
fade in the glory of your light,   and your strong love enfold us.
Bring us to new Jerusalem,   your Bride from heaven descending,
the City of the Father's peace   and joy that has no ending.

Music © 2013 Harry Hicks
Words: Richard Sturch (b. 1936)

392   Under an Eastern sky

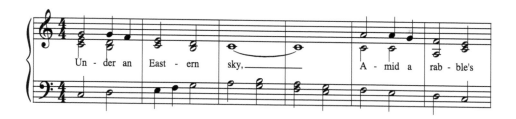

2. Thorn-crowned His blessed head,
Blood-stained His every tread;
Cross-laden, on He sped
       For me.

3. Pierced through His hands and feet
Three hours did o'er Him beat
Fierce rays of noontide heat,
       For me.

4. This wert Thou made all mine:
Lord, make me wholly Thine;
Grant grace and strength divine
       To me.

5. In thought and word and deed,
Thy will to do. Oh, lead
My soul, e'en though it bleed
       To Thee.

393 Up to the Lord

Isaac Watts

Up to the Lord that reigns on high, And views the na-tions from a-far,

Let ev-er-last-ing prai-ses fly, And tell how large his boun-ties are.

2. He that can shake the worlds he made,
Or with his word, or with his rod,
His goodness how amazing great!
And what a condescending God!

3. God that must stoop to view the skies,
And how to see what angels do,
Down to our earth he casts his eyes,
And bends his footsteps downward too.

4. He over-rules all mortal things,
And manages our mean affairs;
On humble souls the King of kings
Bestows his counsels and his cares.

5. Our sorrows and our tears we pour
Into the bosom of our God,
He hears them in the mournful hour,
And helps us bear the heavy load.

6. In vain might lofty princes try
Such condescension to perform;
For worms were never raised so high
Above their meanest fellow-worm.

7. O could our thankful hearts devise
A tribute equal to thy grace,
To the third heav'n our songs should rise,
And teach the golden harps thy praise.

Music © 2014 Harry Hicks

394   Upon the cross

Brenda Gallant

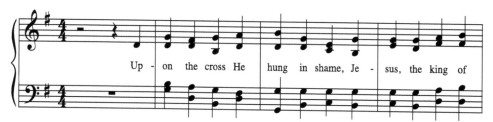

Up - on the cross He hung in shame, Je - sus, the king of

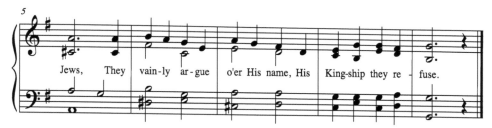

Jews, They vain-ly ar-gue o'er His name, His King-ship they re - fuse.

2. Then for His raiment soldiers played,
   That Scripture be fulfilled,
On earthly gain their minds were stayed,
   The Prince of Life they killed.

3. His mother, Mary, standing there,
   Watching His pain and woe,
Heard Him commit her to the care
   Of one who loved Him so.

4. God's Word was once again fulfilled,
   "I thirst" they heard Him cry,
A sponge with vinegar was filled,
   To give Him e'er He die.

5. Then "It is finished" Jesus said,
   And bowed His head and died.
He gave His life in sinners' stead
   When He was crucified.

6. None of His bones were broken, that
   More Scripture be fulfilled,
But when with spear they pierced His side,
   Water and blood was spilled.

7. This is the record and it's true,
   Giv'n that we might believe,
Salvation freely offered to
   All who His love receive.

8. Look on this pierced form and see
   His heart of selfless love,
Trust Him for all eternity,
   He, who now reigns above.

395   Vain are the hopes

Isaac Watts

Vain are the hopes the sons of men On their own works have built;

Their hearts by na - ture all un - clean, and all their ac - tions guilt.

2. Let Jew and Gentile stop their mouths
Without a murmuring word,
And the whole race of Adam stand
Guilty before the Lord.

3. In vain we ask God's righteous law
To justify us now,
Since to convince and to condemn
Is all the law can do.

4. Jesus, how glorious is thy grace,
When in thy name we trust,
Our faith receives a righteousness
That makes the sinner just.

396   Watching, waiting

Brenda Gallant

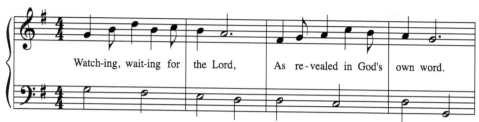

Watch-ing, wait-ing for the Lord, As re-vealed in God's own word.

Si - me-on was rea - dy, when God, in Christ, ap - peared to men.

2. When the parents brought the child,
Lowly infant, meek and mild.
He was recognised by one
Long prepared for God's dear Son.

3. Open arms received with joy
Mary's little baby boy,
God's own promise had come true,
Gospel light was shining through.

4. Anna, too, had waited long
For the One to right all wrong,
She gave thanks with grateful heart,
In His story shares a part.

5. Have you recognised God's Son
As the true and only One,
Who can take away your sin
If you will invite Him in.

6. Be like those who in the past
Both received Messiah at last.
Lifted hearts with praise above,
Thanking God for His great love.

397   We celebrate God's word to us

Jan Grimwood

We cel-e-brate God's word to us, our liv-ing in-spi-ra-tion, passed on and treas-ured for its truth through ev' ry gen-er-a-tion. Though val-ues change, God's word re-mains our source of hope that strength-ens us, and draws us clo-ser to him.

2. Deep woven through each Bible page
   in vibrant song and story,
   the ancient memories entwine
   that speak of God's great glory.
   Through prophecy and history,
   In sad lament and joyful praise,
   Runs faith that spans the ages.

3. God's love transcends the turning years,
   in glorious revelation;
through God in Christ, the Word made flesh,
   the promise of salvation.
   By day and night, by candlelight,
   By word of mouth and sweep of pen,
   These truths have been recorded.

398   We have found the Christ

We have found the Christ who's all in all, He is ev-'ry thing to us;
O how blest up-on His name to call, How di-vine, how glo-ri-ous! It is
joy un-speak-a-ble and full of glo-ry, full of glo-ry, full of glo-ry, It is
joy un-speak-a-ble and full of glo-ry, And the half has ne-ver yet been told!

2. We have found that Christ the Spirit is
Who within our spirit dwells;
How available, how near He is,
And His sweetness all excels.
It is joy unspeakable and full of glory,
Full of glory, full of glory;
It is joy unspeakable and full of glory,
And the half has never yet been told!

3. We have found the way to live by Christ,
Pray His Word and call His name!
This - the eating, drinking - has sufficed
And its worth we now proclaim.
It is joy......

4. We have found the local church, our home;
We are home and home indeed!
Nevermore in Babylon we roam;
In the church is all we need.
It is joy......

5. We have found that meeting with the saints
Is the greatest joy on earth;
'Tis by this our spirit never faints
And our lives are filled with worth.
It is joy unspeakable and full of glory,
Full of glory, full of glory;
It is joy unspeakable and full of glory,
And the half has never yet been told!

Music © 2016 Harry Hicks

399   We praise Thee, we bless Thee

F.J.Crosby

We praise, Thee, we bless Thee, Our Sav-iour di - vine, All
pow'r and do - min-ion for ev - er be Thine! We sing of Thy mer-cy with
joy-ful ac - claim, For Thou hast re - deemed us, all praise to Thy name!

2. All honour and praise to thine excellent name,
Thy love is unchanging for ever the same!
We bless and adore Thee, O Saviour and King;
With joy and thanksgiving Thy praises we sing!

3. The strength of the hills, and the depths of the sea,
The earth and its fulness belong unto Thee;
And yet to the lowly Thou bendest Thine ear,
So ready their humble petitions to hear!

4. Thine infinite goodness our tongues shall employ;
Thou givest us richly all things to enjoy;
We'll follow Thy footsteps, we'll rest in Thy love,
And soon shall we praise Thee in mansions above.

400   We saw Thee not

J.H. Gurney

2. We did not see Thee lifted high
Amid that wild and savage crew,
Nor heard Thy meek, imploring cry,
"Forgive, they know not what they do;"
Yet we believe the deed was done,
Which shook the earth and veiled the sun.

3. We stood not by the empty tomb
Where late Thy sacred body lay,
Nor sat within that upper room,
Nor met Thee in the open way;
But we believe that angels said,
"Why seek the living with the dead?"

4. We did not mark the chosen few,
When Thou didst through the clouds ascend,
First lift to heaven their wondering view,
Then to the earth all prostrate bend;
Yet we believe that mortal eyes
Beheld that journey to the skies.

5. And now that Thou dost reign on high,
And thence Thy waiting people bless.
No ray of glory form the sky
Doth shine upon our wilderness;
But we believe Thy faithful word,
And trust in our redeeming Lord.

401   We sing a loving Jesus

Sarah Doudney

We sing a lov-ing Je-sus Who left His throne a-bove, And came on earth to ran-som The child-ren of His love; It is an oft-told sto-ry, And yet we love to tell How Christ, the King of glo-ry Once deigned with man to dwell.

2. We sing a holy Jesus;
No taint of sin defiled
The babe of David's city,
The pure and spotless Child;
Oh, reach us, blessed Saviour,
Thy Heavenly grace to seek,
And let our whole behaviour,
Like Thine, be mild and meek.

3. We sing a lowly Jesus,
No kingly crown He had:
His heart was wrung with anguish,
His face was marred and sad;
In deep humiliation
He came, His work to do;
O Lord of our salvation,
Let us be humble too.

4. We sing a mighty Jesus,
Whose voice could raise the dead,
The sightless eyes he opened,
The famished crowds He fed.
Thou camest to deliver
Mankind from sin and shame;
Redeemer and Life-giver,
We praise Thy mighty Name!

5. We sing a coming Jesus;
The time is drawing near
When Christ with all His angels
In glory shall appear:
Lord, save us, we entreat Thee,
In this Thy day of grace,
That we may gladly meet Thee,
And see Thee face to face.

Music © 2016 Harry Hicks

402   We sing the glories

(The song of Moses)

Isaac Watts

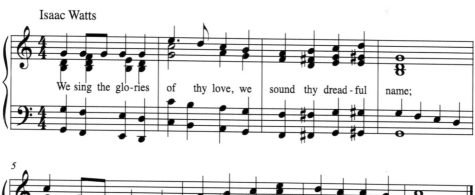

We sing the glo-ries of thy love, we sound thy dread-ful name;

The Christ-ian church u - nites the songs of Mo - ses and the Lamb.

2. Great God, how wondrous are thy works
Of vengeance and of grace!
The King of saints, Almighty Lord,
How just and true thy ways!

3. Who dares refuse to fear thy name,
Or worship at thy throne?
Thy judgements speak thine holiness
Through all the nations known.

4. Great Babylon, that rules the earth,
Drunk with the martyrs' blood,
Her crimes shall speedily awake
The fury of our God.

5. The cup of wrath is ready mixed,
And she must drink the dregs;
Strong is the Lord her sovereign Judge,
And shall fulfil the plagues.

403   We thank thee for Thy presence

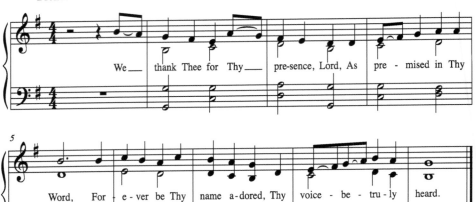

Brenda Gallant

We __ thank Thee for Thy __ pre-sence, Lord, As pre - mised in Thy

Word, For - e - ver be Thy name a-dored, Thy voice - be - tru - ly heard.

2. We thank Thee for Thy wondrous grace,
Thy love, immense and free,
Extended to our sinful race,
To draw us, Lord, to Thee.

3. We thank Thee, Lord, that Thou dost speak
And move from heart to heart,
The sinful, restless souls to seek,
Forgiveness to impart.

4. We pray Thee, Lord, Thy truth to take,
In Holy Spirit power,
And on our lives Thine imprint make,
As from this very hour.

4. We pray Thee that Thy still small voice
Will penetrate the soul,
That many here will make the choice,
By Thee to be made whole.

6. This prayer, we offer, Lord, to Thee,
Move in our midst we pray,
Cause seeking ones to be set free,
Oh, let them come today.

404   We thank Thee, Lord

G.E.L.Cotton

We - thank - thee Lord - for this - fair earth, The - glitt'r - ing sky - the sil - ver sea; For - all - their beau - ty all - their worth, Their - light - and beau - ty come - from Thee.

2. Thanks for the flowers that clothe the ground,
The trees that wave their arms above,
The hills that gird our dwellings round,
As Thou dost gird thine own with love.

3. Yet teach us still how far more fair
More glorious, Father, in thy sight,
Is one pure deed, one holy prayer,
One heart that owns thy Spirit's might.

4. So, while we gaze with thoughtful eye
On all the gifts thy love has giv'n,
Help us in Thee to live and die,
By Thee to rise from earth to heav'n.

Music © 2008 Harry Hicks

405   Welcome sweet day of rest

Isaac Watts

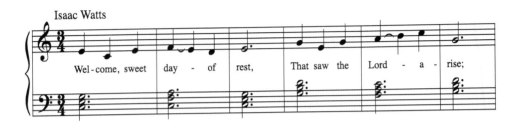

Wel - come, sweet day - of rest, That saw the Lord - a - rise;

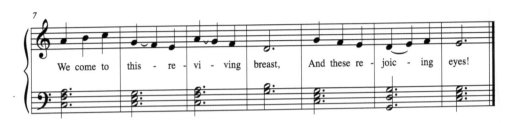

We come to this - re - vi - ving breast, And these re - joic - ing eyes!

2. The King himself comes near,
And feasts his saints today,
Here we may sit, and see him here,
And love, and praise, and pray.

3. One day amidst the place
Where my dear God hath been,
Is sweeter than ten thousand days
Of pleasurable sin.

4. My willing soul would stay
In such a frame as this,
And sit and sing herself away
To everlasting bliss.

406   What a wonderful salvation

Brenda Gallant

What___ a won-der-ful sal - va-tion! We - are priv'-leged to pro - claim,___ From - the heart of God the Fath-er, And___ His bles-sed Son who came. On___ the cru-el cross sus - pen-ded Christ___ Him-self bore all your sin, There___ that spot-less life was end-ed So___ that you might en-ter in.

2. What a wonderful salvation!
Purchased for you long ago,
By the death of Christ the Saviour,
That forgiveness you may know.
For your sin, though red like crimson,
Can be whiter than the snow,
You can flee to Him for refuge,
Peace and safety you can know.

3. What a wonderful salvation!
Freely by God's grace supplied,
Offered to you by the Saviour,
Who has suffered, bled, and died.
By His death and resurrection
You can full salvation know,
For His blood is your protection,
If you plunge beneath that flow.

4. What a wonderful salvation!
Have you made it all your own?
Are you trusting in God's mercy,
Which, in Christ, is fully shown!
God, Himself will be your refuge,
He's a strong and mighty tower,
He will shelter and protect you,
By His own almighty power.

407 What equal honours

Isaac Watts

What e-qual ho-nours shall we bring To thee, O Lord our God, the Lamb, When all the notes that an-gels sing Are far in-fer-ior to thy Name?

2. Worthy is he that once was slain,
The Prince of Peace that groaned and died,
Worthy to rise, and live, and reign
At his Almighty Father's side.

3. Power and dominion are his due,
Who stood condemned at Pilate's bar:
Wisdom belongs to Jesus too,
Though he was charged with madness here.

4. All riches are his native right,
Yet he sustained amazing loss:
To him ascribe eternal might,
Who left his weakness on the cross.

5. Honour immortal must be paid,
Instead of scandal and of scorn:
While glory shines around his head,
And a bright crown without a thorn.

6. Blessings for ever on the Lamb,
Who bore the curse for wretched men:
Let angels sound his sacred Name,
And every creature say, Amen.

408   When Christ was born

2. That star was there to be a guide,
   To shed abroad the light,
   A radiance spreading far and wide,
   Unveiled to human sight.

3. Jesus, Himself, is that true light,
   And all who follow Him,
   Will find their darkness turned to sight,
   A sight that grows not dim.

4. Come to the Light, and let Him shine
   Into your sinful heart,
   Yield to that radiance, all divine,
   Christ will Himself impart.

409 When from the East

J.H. Hopkins

When from the East the wise men came, Led by the Star of Beth le hem, The gifts they brought to Je sus were Of gold and fran kin cense and myrrh.

vv1-4

last verse only   Fin   alternative ending of vv 1-4

Sac ri fice.

2 Bright gold of Ophir,* passing fine,   Proclaims a King of royal line;
For David's son in David's town,   Is born the heir of David's crown.

3 The incense-clouds, with fragrance rare,   The presence of a God declare;
Lo! kings in adoration fall,   For Mary's Son is Lord of all.

4 The myrrh, with bitter taste, foreshows   A life of sorrows, wounds and woes;
The deadly cup, that overran   With anguish for the Son of Man.

5 Our gold upon Thine altar lies;   Our prayers to Thee, as incense, rise;
Accept as myrrh our tears and sighs: O King, O God, O Sacrifice!

Music © 2012 Harry Hicks   * Ophir: a region in Biblical times famous for its wealth.

410 When God the Spirit came

Timothy Dudley-Smith

When God the Spi rit came u pon his church out poured in sound of wind and flame, they spread his truth a broad, and filled with the Spi rit pro claimed that Christ is Lord.

2. What courage, power and grace that youthful church displayed!
to those of every tribe and race they witnessed unafraid,
and filled with the Spirit they broke their bread and prayed.

3. They saw God's word prevail, his kingdom still increase,
no part of his purpose fail, no promised blessing cease,
and filled with the Spirit knew love and joy and peace.

4. Their theme was Christ alone, the Lord who lived and died,
who rose to his eternal throne at God the Father's side;
and filled with the Spirit the church was multiplied.

5. So to this present hour our task is still the same,
in pentecostal love and power his gospel to proclaim,
and filled with the Spirit, rejoice in Jesus' Name.

Music © 2012 Harry Hicks   Words: 'When God the Spirit came' by Timothy Dudley-Smith (b. 1926)
© Timothy Dudley-Smith in Europe and Africa. © Hope Publishing Company in the United States of America and the rest of the world.

411 When He comes

Timothy Dudley-Smith

When he comes, when he comes, we shall see the Lord in glo-ry when he comes!

As I read the gos-pel sto-ry we shall see the Lord in glo-ry, we shall see the Lord in glo-ry when he comes!

With the Al - le - lu-ias ring-ing to the sky, with the Al - le - lu-ias ring-ing to the sky!

As I read the gos-pel sto-ry we shall see the Lord in glo-ry with the Al - le-lu - ias ring-ing to the sky!

2. When he comes, when he comes,
we shall hear the trumpet sounded when he comes!
We shall hear the trumpet sounded,
See the Lord with saints surrounded,
We shall hear the trumpets sounded when he comes!
With the Allelulias ringing to the sky,
with the Alleluias ringing to the sky!
We shall hear the trumpet sounded,
see the Lord with saints surrounded,
with the Alleluias ringing to the sky!

3. When he comes, when he comes,
we shall all rise up to greet him when he comes!
When he calls his own to greet him
we shall all rise up to greet him,
we shall all rise up to greet him when he comes!
With the Allelulias ringing to the sky,
with the Alleluias ringing to the sky!
we shall all rise up to greet him
when he calls his own to greet him
with the Alleluias ringing to the sky!

Music © 2011 Harry Hicks   Words: 'When he comes' by Timothy Dudley-Smith (b. 1926)
© Timothy Dudley-Smith in Europe and Africa. © Hope Publishing Company in the United States of America and the rest of the world.
Reproduced by permission of Oxford University Press. All rights reserved.

412　When I shall come

W.C. Poole

When I shall come to the end of my way, When I shall rest at the close of life's day, When "Wel-come home" I shall hear Je-sus say, That will be sun-rise for me. -

Chorus

Sun-rise to - mor-row, sun-rise to - mor-row, Sun-rise in glo-ry is wait-ing for me; Sun-rise to - mor-row, sun-rise to - mor-row, Sun-rise with Je-sus for e - ter-ni - ty!

2. When in his beauty I see the great King, Join with the ransomed His praises to sing,
When I shall join them my tributes to bring, That will be sunrise for me.
Sunrise tomorrow, sunrise tomorrow, Sunrise in glory is waiting for me;
Sunrise tomorrow, sunrise tomorrow, Sunrise with Jesus for eternity.

3. When life is over and daylight is passed, In heaven's harbour my anchor is cast,
When I see Jesus my saviour at last, That will be sunrise for me.
Sunrise tomorrow, sunrise tomorrow, Sunrise in glory is waiting for me;
Sunrise tomorrow, sunrise tomorrow, Sunrise with Jesus for eternity.

413   When I survey (1st tune)

When I sur-vey the won-drous cross on which the Prince of Glo-ry died, My rich-est gain I count but loss and pour con-tempt on all my pride.

2. Forbid it. Lord, that I should boast,
save in the death of Christ my God:
all the vain things that charm me most,
I sacrifice them to His blood.

3. See from His head, His hands, His feet,
sorrow and love flow mingled down:
did e'er such love and sorrow meet,
or thorns compose so rich a crown?

4. Were the whole realm of nature mine
that were an offering far too small,
love so amazing, so divine,
demands my soul, my life, my all.

413   When I survey (2nd tune)

Isaac Watts

When I sur-vey the won-drous cross, On which the Prince of glo-ry died, My rich-est gain I count but loss, And pour con-tempt on all my pride.

2. Forbid it, Lord, that I should boast
Save in the cross of Christ my God,
All the vain things that charm me most
I sacrifice them to His blood.

3. See from His head, His hands, His feet,
Sorrow and love flow mingled down;
Did e'er such love and sorrow meet,
Or thorns compose so rich a crown?

4. Were the whole realm of nature mine,
That were an offering far too small;
Love so amazing, so divine,
Demands, my soul, my life, my all.

414   When in the light

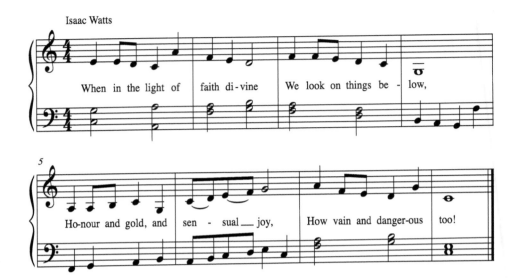

Isaac Watts

When in the light of faith di-vine We look on things be-low,
Ho-nour and gold, and sen - sual joy, How vain and danger-ous too!

2. Honour's puff of noisy breath:
   Yet men expose their blood,
   And venture everlasting death
   To gain that airy good.

3. Whilst others feed on nobler mind,
   And feed on shining dust,
   They rob the serpent of his food
   T'indulge a sordid lust.

4. The pleasures that allure our sense
   And dangerous snares to souls;
   There's but a drop of flattering sweet,
   And dashed with bitter bowls.

5. God is my all-sufficient good,
   My portion and my choice;
   In him my vast desires are filled,
   And all my powers rejoice.

6. In vain the world accosts my ear,
   And tempts my heart anew;
   I cannot buy your bliss so dear,
   Nor part with heaven for you.

415   When law and trust break down

Jan Berry

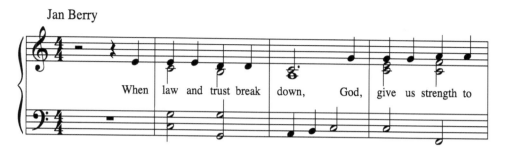

When law and trust break down, God, give us strength to

cope; and in the heart-ache of our loss show us a sign of hope.

2. When all around is hate,
and voices cry in fear,
God of our streets and urban life,
come, dwell amongst us here.

3. When beauty is destroyed
and pride gives way to shame,
in our bewilderment and pain
we call your holy name.

4. When empty streets are dead,
and smoke pervades the night,
God, reach in to our troubled hearts
and bring us safe to light.

5. When morning brings new calm,
the debris washed with rain,
as people clear the shattered shards,
God, help us build again.

416 When music and our hearts combine

Steve Parish

When mu-sic and our hearts com-bine To raise the song of ho-ly praise

Then shall our voi-ces and our lives Pro-claim God's good-ness all our days.

Optional twiddly bit between verses!

2. Christ is God's instrument of love,
restoring peace for all he made,
and in a world of discord now
that melody need never fade.

3. God's spirit tunes our will to his,
and hope springs up in every breath
until in heavenly symphony
our chorus triumphs over death.

4. So players, singers, join in one,
create an anthem to our King
of service, love and worship here,
that all may hear of whom we sing.

417   When the great Builder

Isaac Watts

When the great Build-er arched the skies, And formed all na-ture with a word, The joy - ful che-rubs tuned his praise, And ev - 'ry bend - ing throne a-dored.

2. High in the midst of all the throng,
Satan, a tall archangel, sat,
Amongst the morning stars he sung
Till sin destroyed his heav'nly state.

3. 'Twas sin that hurled him from his throne,
Grov'ling in the fire the rebel lies:
"How art thou sunk in darkness down,
Son of the Morning, from the skies!"

4. And thus our first two parents stood
Till sin defiled their happy place
They lost their garden and their God,
And ruined all their unborn race.

5. So sprang the plague from Adam's bower,
And spread destruction all abroad;
Sin, the cursed name, that in one hour
Spoiled six days labour of our God.

6. Tremble, my soul, and mourn for grief,
That such a foe should seize thy breast;
Fly to the Lord for quick relief;
O! may he slay this treacherous guest.

7. Then to thy throne, victorious King,
Then to thy throne our shouts shall rise,
Thine everlasting arm we sing,
For sin the monster bleeds and dies.

418   When the Lord in glory comes

Timothy Dudley-Smith

2. When the Lord is seen again
Not the glories of his reign,
Not the lightnings through the storm,
Not the radiance of the form,
Not his pomp and power alone,
Not the splendours of his throne,
Not his robe and diadems,
Not the gold and not the gems,
But his face upon my sight
Shall be darkness into light -
But his face upon my sight
Shall be darkness into light.

3. When the Lord to human eyes
Shall bestride our narrow skies,
Not the child of humble birth,
Not the carpenter of earth,
Not the man by all denied,
Not the victim crucified,
But the God who died to save,
But the victor of the grave,
He it is to whom I fall,
Jesus Christ, my All in all -
He it is to whom I fall,
Jesus Christ my All in all.

419   When the Lord shall come

Brenda Gallant

8ves in the bass

When__ the Lord shall come in pow'r, In__ that bles-sed un-known hour,

Will__ you be 'caught up' with Him, Where__ the light will not grow dim?

Are__ you look-ing day by day, When__ He comes with-out de - lay?__

Trump shall sound, arch-an-gel voice, Sin__ ner, have you made your choice?

2. Living in this day of grace,
You can humbly seek His face,
Turn from sin and trust His love,
He will then all guilt remove.
He will wash your sins away,
Heed what Holy Scriptures say,
Jesus calls - "Come unto Me,
Find salvation full and free."

Music © 2013 Harry Hicks
Words © 2013 Brenda Gallant

420   When to our world

Timothy Dudley-Smith

When to our world the Sav - iour came the sick and
help - less heard - his Name, and in their weak - ness
longed to see the heal-ing Christ of Ga - li lee.

2. That good physician! Night and day   the people thronged about his way;
and wonder ran from soul to soul-   'The touch of Christ has made us whole!'

3. His praises then were heard and sung   by opened ears and loosened tongue,
while lightened eyes could see and know   the healing Christ of long ago.

4. Of long ago - yet living still,   who died for us on Calvary's hill;
who triumphed over cross and grave,   his healing hands stretched forth to save.

5. Those wounded hands are still the same,   and all who serve that saving Name
may share today in Jesus' plan -   the healing Christ of everyman.

6. Then grant us, Lord, in this our day,   to hear the prayers the helpless pray;
give to us hearts their pain to share,   make of us hands to tend and care.

7. Make us your hands! For Christ to live,   in prayer and service, swift to give;
till all the world rejoice to find   the healing Christ of all mankind.

421   When we are raised

Isaac Watts

When we are raised from deep distress, our God deserves a song; We take the pattern of our praise from Hezekiah's song.

2. The gates of the devouring grave
Are opened wide in vain,
If he that holds the keys of death
Commands them fast again.

3. Pains of the flesh are want t'abuse
Our minds with slavish fears,
"Our days are past, and we shall lose
The remnant of our years."

4. We chatter like a swallow's voice,
O like a dove we mourn,
With bitterness instead of joys,
Afflicted and forlorn.

5. Jehovah speaks the healing word,
And no disease withstands;
Fevers and plagues obey the Lord,
And fly at his commands.

6. If half the strings of life should break,
He can our frame restore;
He casts our sins behind his back,
And they are found no more.

422 When Zaccheus came

Kaye Lee

Music © 2013 Harry Hicks
Words © Kaye Lee

423 Where is He?

Brenda Gallant

Where is He, the new-born King, Lately come from heaven to earth,
Is He in a pal-ace fair, As be-fits his no-ble birth?
Nay, but in a sta-ble He, Cast up-on man's cha-ri-ty.

2. Where is he, the infant Lord,
Maker of the earth and skies,
Is He in a downy bed,
God come down in human guise?
No, but in a manger bare
With the cattle thus to share.

3. Where is he, the Saviour King,
Heralded by angels bright?
Hurriedly the shepherds go
To see the amazing sight.
Kingly robes are laid aside,
Human form now dignified.

4. Where is he, born King of Jews?
Wise men from the east inquired,
Travelled to Jerusalem
To give homage they desired.
Found Him in a humble town,
At his feet they bowed them down.

5. Where is he? The Son of Man
As he heals the sick and sad,
Cheering sin benighted lives,
Bringing joy and making glad.
He is lost among the crowd
As they clamour long and loud.

6. Where is he? In Pilate's hall,
Lone, despised and cast aside,
Buffeted and spat upon
"Crucify Him," they have cried,
Now He hangs upon a cross,
Bearing all our sin and loss.

7. Where is he? Cold in the tomb,
Carried there by caring friends,
Gently laid at last to rest,
Thus his earthly life he ends.
Soldiers seal and guard the grave,
Christ, who died our souls to save.

8. Where is he? The tomb is bare,
Death is vanquished once for all!
Christ has triumphed over death,
He will save all those who call.
Now he reigns once more above,
Object of His Father's love.

9. Where is he? This Christmas time,
As we celebrate His birth,
Is he present in your home,
Have you recognised His worth?
Or is He still left outside,
Spurned by those for whom He died.

10. Where is he? Enthroned on high,
Worshipped by the hosts above,
He who stooped to bring us nigh,
Now desires our lives, our love,
He will come to earth again;
Crown Him King, and let Him reign!

Music © 2013 Harry Hicks
Words © 2013 Brenda Gallant

424   Where oh where

Brenda Gallant

Where oh where may I be-hold Him, Where can he be found?

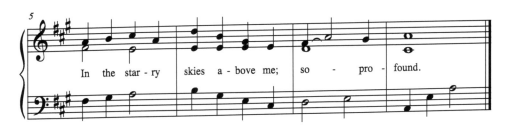

In the star-ry skies a-bove me; so - pro - found.

2. Where oh where may I behold Him,
   In the ocean deep?
   All it's waves and all it's billows
   Bounds must keep.

3. Where oh where may I behold Him
   In the forest green?
   All the waving branches witness
   Pow'r unseen.

4. Where oh where may I behold Him?
   On a lonely hill,
   Hanging on a cross suspended,
   Cold and still.

5. Where oh where may I behold Him?
   In a borrowed grave,
   He who came to earth from heaven
   Just to save.

6. Where oh where may I behold Him?
   Risen from the tomb,
   By His rising He has banished
   Fear and gloom.

7. Where oh where may I behold Him?
   In the glory now,
   Unto Him who died to save us
   We must bow.

8. If you truly want to find Him,
   You must seek His face,
   He will save and keep you always
   By His grace.

425 While the earth remains

Brenda Gallant

While the earth re - main-eth, We have God's prom - ise true. As the bow pro - claim - eth In ev - 'ry flash - ing hue. In the heav'ns re - splen-dant, And reach-ing down to earth, Won - der-ful, trans - cen - dent A sign of it's true worth.

2. This promise is God's word,
No flood will e'er again
As long ago occurred
Obliterate with rain.
The earth, that He had made,
And ev'ry living thing,
His judgement thus displayed,
On feather, fur and wing.

3. Mankind were all destroyed,
Only eight were saved -
These, then, to be deployed
To use what God had made.
Now many years have rolled,
God's promise is secure,
And all that we've been told
Has proven to be sure.

4. So, let's all thank the Lord,
For all He does provide,
But mostly for His Word
Which will for aye abide.
For food, which makes us strong,
And for the living Bread
That we to Christ belong,
Our Saviour and our Head.

5. We thank Him for His grace
To us so freely giv'n,
That we might see his face;
Ransomed, redeemed, forgiv'n.
Lord of the harvest, we
Would give ourselves to You
In service glad and free,
The show us what to do,

6. To reap a harvest here
Of precious souls in need,
This is our humble prayer,
While sowing gospel seed.
Oh may we never cease
To spread abroad your Word,
The gospel of Your peace
Which has so long endured.

(From bar 9)
7. The labourers are few,
But we would labour on
In service glad and true,
Until our work is done.

Music © 2016 Harry Hicks
Words © 2015 Brenda Gallant

426 Who came down

El Nathan

Who came down from heav'n to earth? Je - sus Christ our Sav - iour!

Came a child of low - ly birth? Je - sus Christ our Sav - iour!

Chorus

Sound the cho - rus loud and clear; he hath brought sal - va - tion near;

none so prec - ious, none so dear, Je - sus Christ our Sav - iour!

2. Who was lifted on the tree? Jesus Christ our Saviour!
There to ransom you and me? Jesus Christ our Saviour!
Sound the chorus loud and clear, He has brought salvation near;
None so precious, none so dear, Jesus Christ our Saviour!

3. Who has promised to forgive? Jesus Christ our Saviour!
Who has said "Believe and live"? Jesus Christ our Saviour!
Sound the chorus ....

4. Who is now enshrined above? Jesus Christ our Saviour!
Who should we obey and love? Jesus Christ our Saviour!
Sound the chorus ....

5. Who again from heav'n shall come? Jesus Christ our Saviour!
Take the glory all his own? Jesus Christ our Saviour!
Sound the chorus ....

427 Who is this so weak and helpless (1st tune)

W.W.How

Who is this so weak and help-less, Child of lowly He brew maid,
Rude-ly in a sta-ble shel-tered, Cold-ly in a man-ger laid?
'Tis the Lord of all cre-a-tion, Who this won-drous path hath trod;
He is God from e-ver-last-ting, and the e-ver-last-ing God.

2. Who is this - a Man of Sorrows,
Walking sadly life's hard way,
Homeless, weary, sighing, weeping
Over sin and Satan's sway?
'Tis our God, our glorious Saviour,
Who above the starry sky
Now for us a place prepareth,
Where no tear can dim the eye.

3. Who is this - behold Him shedding
Drops of blood upon the ground?
Who is this - despised, rejected,
Mocked, insulted, beaten, bound?
'Tis our God, who gifts and graces
On His Church now poureth down;
Who shall smite in righteous judgment
All His foes beneath His throne.

4. Who is this that hangeth dying,
While the rude world scoffs and scorns;
Numbered with the malefactors,
Torn with nails, and crowned with thorns?
'Tis the God who ever liveth
'Mid the shining ones on high,
In the glorious golden city
Reigning everlastingly.

Music © 2016 Harry Hicks

427　Who is this so weak and helpless (2nd tune)

W.W.How

Who is this, so weak and help-less, Child of low-ly He-brew maid, Rude-ly in a sta-ble shel-tered, Cold-ly in a man-ger laid? 'Tis the Lord of all cre-a-tion, Who this won-drous path hath trod, He is God from ev-er-last-ing, And the ev-er-last-ing God.

2. Who is this - a Man of Sorrows,
Walking sadly life's hard way,
Homeless, weary, sighing, weeping
Over sin and Satan's sway?
'Tis our God, our glorious Saviour,
Who above the starry sky
Now for us a place prepareth,
Where no tear can dim the eye.

3. Who is this - behold Him shedding
Drops of blood upon the ground?
Who is this - despised, rejected,
Mocked, insulted, beaten, bound?
'Tis our God, who gifts and graces
On His Church now poureth down;
Who shall smite in righteous judgment
All His foes beneath His throne.

4. Who is this that hangeth dying,
While the rude world scoffs and scorns;
Numbered with the malefactors,
Torn with nails, and crowned with thorns?
'Tis the God who ever liveth
'Mid the shining ones on high,
In the glorious golden city
Reigning everlastingly.

Music © 2016 Harry Hicks

427 Who is this so weak and helpless (3rd tune)

W.W.How

Who is this so weak and help-less, Child of low-ly Heb-rew maid,

Rude-ly in a sta-ble shel-tered, Cold-ly on a mang-er laid?

'Tis the Lord of all cre-a-tion, Who this won-drous path hath trod,

He is God from e-ver-last-ing, And the e-ver-last-ing God.

2. Who is this - a Man of sorrows,
Walking sadly life's hard way,
Homeless, weary, sighing, weeping
Over sin and Satan's way?
'Tis our God, our glorious Saviour,
Who above the starry sky,
Now for us a place prepareth,
Where no tear can dim the eye.

3. Who is this - behold Him shedding
Drops of blood upon the ground?
Who is this - despised, rejected,
Mocked, insulted, beaten, bound?
'Tis our God, who gifts and graces
On His church now poureth down;
Who shall smite in holy vengeance
All His foes beneath His throne.

4. Who is this that hangeth dying,
While the rude world scoffs and scorns,
Numbered with the malefactors,
Torn with nails and crowned with thorns?
'Tis the God who ever liveth,
'Mid the shining ones on high,
In the glorious golden city
Reigning everlastingly.

428 Who shall the Lord's elect condemn

Isaac Watts

Who shall the Lord's e - lect __ con-demn? 'tis God that jus-ti - fies their souls,

And mer-cy like a migh-ty __ stream O'er all their sins di - vine-ly rolls.

2. Who shall adjudge the saints to hell?
'tis Christ that suffered in their stead,
And the salvation to fulfil,
Behold him rising from the dead.

3. He lives, he lives, and sits above,
For ever interceding there:
Who shall divide us from his love?
Or what should tempt us to despair?

4. Shall persecutions, or distress,
Famine, or sword, or nakedness?
He that hath loved us bears us through,
And makes us more than conquerors too.

5. Faith hath an overcoming power,
It triumphs in the dying hour;
Christ is our life, our joy, our hope,
Nor can we sink with such a prop.

6. Not all that men on earth can do,
Nor powers on high nor powers below,
Shall cause his mercy to remove,
Or wean our hearts from Christ our love.

429   Wholly Thine

Mrs. A.S.Hawks

Thine, most gra - cious Lord, Oh, make me whol - ly Thine,

Thine in thought, in word and deed, For Thou, O Christ, ___ art mine.

Refrain A little faster

Whol - ly

Thine! whol - ly Thine! Thou hast bought me I am Thine;

Bles - sed Sav - iour, Thou art mine; make me whol - ly Thine.

2. Wholly Thine, my Lord, To go when Thou dost call;
This to yield my very self in all things great and small.
Wholly Thine! Wholly Thine! Thou hast bought me, I am Thine;
Blessed Saviour, Thou art mine; make me wholly Thine.

3. Wholly Thine, O Lord, in ev'ry passing hour;
Thine in silence, Thine to speak, as Thou dost grant the power.
Wholly Thine.........

4. Wholly Thine, O Lord, to fashion as Thou wilt;
Strengthen, bless, and keep the soul which Thou hast saved from guilt.
Wholly Thine.........

5. Thine, Lord, wholly Thine, for ever one with Thee -
Rooted, grounded in Thy love abiding, sure and free.
Wholly Thine.........

430   Why seek the living

Brenda Gallant

Why seek the li-ving with the dead, Thus did the an-gel say

To wo-men, as sad tears they shed On re-sur-rec-tion day.

2. The tomb is bare, the body gone,
The Saviour lives to save,
Into the hearts the glory shone,
And sweet assurance gave.

3. They then remembered His own word,
That he would rise again,
The glorious news their sad hearts stirred,
Erasing all the pain.

4. They went with joy, the news to spread
That their beloved Lord
Had ris'n triumphant from the dead;
The ever-living Word.

5. Oh, have you viewed the empty grave,
And seen the empty cross?
For Jesus died your soul to save
From death and certain loss.

6. Now at the dawn of this new year,
Be sure you seek and find
The One who casteth out all fear;
So loving, good and kind.

7. He will forgive and cleanse from sin,
And live within your heart,
If you will only ask Him in:
Now is the time to start.

431   With cheerful voice

With cheer-ful voice I sing the tit-les of my Lord,— And bor-row all the names of ho-nour from his word: Na-ture and art can ne'er sup-ply suf-fic-ient forms of ma-jes-ty.

Isaac Watts

2. In Jesus we behold his Father's glorious face,
Shining for ever bright with mild and lovely rays:
Th'eternal God's eternal Son   inherits and partakes the throne.

3. The Sov'reign King of kings, the Lord of lords most high,
Writes his own name upon his garment and his thigh:
His name is called "The Word of God;"   he rules the earth with iron rod.

4. Where promises and grace can neither melt nor move,
The angry Lamb resents the injuries of his love;
Awakes his wrath without delay,   as lions roar and tear their prey.

5. But when works of peace the great Redeemer comes,
What gentle characters, what titles he assumes!
"Light of the world, and Life of men"   nor will he bear those names in vain.

6. Immense compassion reigns in our Immanuel's heart,
When he descends to act a Mediator's part:
He is a friend and brother too;   divinely kind, divinely true.

7. At length the Lord the Judge his awful throne ascends,
And drives the rebels far from favourites and friends:
Then shall the saints completely prove   the heights and depths of all his love.

Music © 2013 Harry Hicks

432   With hope   (Rev. 14:3)

Rev. A.T. Pierson

P.P. Bliss

With— hope and with— vi - als there - stands a great throng, In the

pre-sence of Je - sus and sing this new song: Un-to Him who has - loved us and

washed us from sin, Un-to Him be the glo-ry for ev - er, A - men!

2. All these were once sinners, defiled in His sight,
Now arrayed in pure garments in praise they unite:
Unto Him who has loved us and washed us from sin,
Unto Him be the glory for ever, Amen!

3. He maketh the rebel a priest and a king,
He hath brought us and taught us this new song to sing:
Unto Him who has loved us and washed us from sin,
Unto Him be the glory for ever, Amen!

4. How helpless and hopeless we sinners have been,
If He never had loved us till cleansed from our sin.
Unto Him who has loved us and washed us from sin,
Unto Him be the glory for ever, Amen!

5. Aloud in His praises our voices shall ring,
So that others believing this new song shall sing:
Unto Him who has loved us and washed us from sin,
Unto Him be the glory for ever, Amen!

433   With songs and honours

With songs and hon-ours sound-ing loud, ad-dress the Lord on high;
Ov-er the heav'ns he spreads his cloud, and wa-ters veil the sky.
He sends his showers of bles-sings down, to cheer the plains be-low;
He makes the grass the moun-tains crown, and corn in val-leys grow.

2. His steady counsels change the face of the declining year;
He bids the sun cut short his race, and wintry days appear.
His hoary frost, his fleecy snow, descend and clothe the ground;
The liquid streams forbear to flow, in icy fetters bound.

3. He sends his word and melts the snow, the fields no longer mourn;
He calls the warmer gales to blow, and bids the spring return.
The changing wind, the flying cloud, obey his mighty word;
With songs and honours sounding loud, praise ye the sovereign Lord!

434   Wounded for me

Wound-ed for me! wound-ed for me, There on the cross He was wound-ed for me: Gone my trans-gres-sions, and now I am free, All be-cause Je-sus was wound-ed for me.

2. Dying for me! dying for me,
There on the cross He was dying for me,
Now in His death my redemption I see,
All because Jesus was dying for me.

3. Risen for me! risen for me,
Up from the grave He has risen for me,
Now evermore from death's sting I am free,
All because Jesus has risen for me.

4. Living for me! living for me,
Up in the skies He is living for me,
Daily He's pleading and praying for me
All because Jesus is living for me.

5. Coming for me! coming for me,
Soon to appear He is coming for me,
O what a joy when His face I shall see,
All because Jesus is coming for me.

Music © 2016 Harry Hicks

435   Ye thirsty for God

C. Wesley

Ye thirs-ty for God, To Je-sus give ear, And take, through his blood, A power to draw near; His kind in-vi-ta-tion, Ye sin-ners, em-brace, Ac-cept-ing sal-va-tion, Sal-va-tion by grace.

2. Sent down from above, Who governs the skies,
In vehement love, To sinners he cries,
"Drink into my Spirit, Who happy would be,
And all things inherit, By coming to me."

3. O Saviour of all, Thy word we believe,
And come at thy call, Thy grace to receive;
The blessing is given Wherever thou art,
The earnest of heaven Is love in the heart.

4. To us, at thy feet, The Comforter give,
Who gasp to admit Thy Spirit, and live;
The weakest believers Acknowledge for thine,
And fill us with rivers Of water divine!

436   Yes, God is good

J.H. Gurney

Yes, God is good: in earth and sky, From o - cean

depths and spread-ing wood, Ten thou-sand voi - ces

seem __ to cry, God made us all, and God is good.

2. The sun that keeps his trackless way,
And downward pours his golden flood,
Night's sparkling hosts, all seem to say,
In accents clear, that God is good.

3. The merry birds prolong the strain,
Their song with every spring renewed;
And balmy air and falling rain,
Each softly whispers, God is good.

4. I hear it in the rushing breeze;
The hills that have for ages stood,
The echoing sky and roaring seas,
All swell the chorus, God is good.

5. Yes, God is good, all nature says,
By God's own hand with speech endued;
And man, in louder notes of praise,
Should sing for joy, that God is good.

6. For all thy gifts we bless Thee, Lord,
But chiefly for our heavenly food;
Thy pardoning grace, Thy quickening word,
These prompt our song, that God is good.

Music © 2016 Harry Hicks

437   Yes, the Redeemer rose (1)

Philip Doddridge

Yes, the Re-deem-er rose; The Sa-viour left the dead And o'er our hell-ish foes High raised his con-quering head: In wild dis-may The guards a-round Fall to the ground, And sink a-way. Yes, the Re-deem-er rose: The Sav-iour left the dead!

2. Lo! the angelic bands
In full assembly meet,
To wait his high commands,
And worship at his feet:
Joyful they come,
And wing their way
From realms of day
To Jesus' tomb.
Lo! the angelic bands
In full assembly meet!

3. Then back to Heaven they fly,
The joyful news to bear:
Hark! as they soar on high,
What music fills the air!
Their anthem say.
"Jesus who bled
Hath left the dead:
He rose today."
Then back to Heaven they fly,
The joyful news to bear!

4. Ye mortals, catch the sound,
Redeemed by Him from hell;
And send the echo round
The globe on which you dwell:
Transported, cry:
'Jesus, who bled,
Hath left the dead,
No more to die.'
Ye mortals, catch the sound,
Redeemed by Him from hell!

5. All hail! triumphant Lord,
Who sav'st us by Thy blood;
Wide be Thy name adored,
Thou rising, reigning God!
With Thee we rise,
With thee we reign,
And empires gain
Beyond the skies.
All hail! triumphant Lord,
Who sav'st us by Thy blood!

438   Yes, the Redeemer rose (2)

P. Doddridge

Yes, the Re-deem-er rose; The sa-viuour left the dead, And o'er our hell-ish foes High raised His con - quering head. In wild dis-may The guards a-round Fell to the ground And sank a - way.

2. Lo! the angelic bands,
In full aseembly meet,
To wait His high commands,
And worship at His feet;
Joyful they come,
And wing their way
From realms of day
To see His tomb.

3. Then back to heaven they fly,
And the glad tidings bear.
Hark! as they soar on high
What music fills the air!
Their anthems say:
'Jesus, who bled,
Hath left the dead,
He rose today.'

4. Ye mortals, catch the sound,
Redeemed by Him from hell;
And send the echo round
The globe on which you dwell:
Transported, cry:
'Jesus, who bled,
Hath left the dead,
No more to die.'

5. All hail! triumphant Lord,
Who sav'st us by Thy blood;
Wide be Thy name adored,
Thou rising, reigning God!
With Thee we rise,
With thee we reign,
And empires gain
Beyond the skies.

Note: This second tune does not repeat the first two lines of each verse at the end of that verse (as does the first tune).

Music © 2016 Harry Hicks

439   You came in peace to broken men

Andrew Pratt

You came in peace to broken men,
To women who would hear your call
To build, renew, and reconcile
And now we come to give our all.

2. We do not know where this will lead,
we only know that love remains,
that Christ has given us his peace,
the Holy Spirit still sustains.

3. We set our faces to the world
and trusting one who brought us birth,
we take again your hand, O God,
to dance upon this shaking earth.

4. To go to where your rhythm leads,
to bring your kingdom values near,
to trace, in faltering steps, your love,
to face the future, counter fear.

440   You shall go out with joy

N.T.Wright

You shall go out with joy and come a-gain in peace; the moun-tains and the hills shall sing and ne-ver cease; the Son of God is ris'n a-gain, his love has con-quered death's do-main.

2. The trees in ev'ry field
shall clap their hands, and say
'Come shout aloud, and help
us celebrate this day!'
Jesus, the King, has burst the grave,
And lives once more to heal and save.

3. The Word, like rain or snow,
has come down from above,
and now reveals to all
God's purposes of love;
The Word made flesh, once dead, now lives,
New life to all he freely gives.

4. The myrtle for the briar,
the cypress for the thorn,
shall rise to tell the world
of its awakening dawn.
Jesus, the Life, the Truth, the Way,
Has ushered in God's great new day.

Music © 2011 Harry Hicks
Words © The Right Reverend N.T.Wright

441   Your God is here

Brenda Gallant

Your God is here, the an-gel___ said To shep-herds long a-

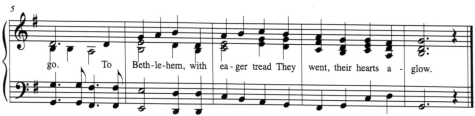

go. To Beth-le-hem, with ea-ger tread They went, their hearts a-glow.

2. Your God is here, in manger bare
Where cattle once were fed,
His mother laid Him gently there,
To rest His infant head.

3. Your God is here, in humble home,
The wise men find the child,
With gold, myrrh, frankincense they come
To Him, the undefiled.

4. Your God is here, in honest toil,
A carpenter by trade,
No imperfection there to spoil
His deity displayed.

5. Your God is Love, beside the sea
In city and in mart,
To teach and heal and set men free,
And soothe the broken heart.

6. Your God is here, upon the tree,
Unwanted, bruised and torn,
The Scripture says it was for thee
This cruelty was borne.

7. Your God is here, in garden tomb,
To bear your sin He died,
But now He breaks from that dark womb,
Raised up and glorified.

8. Your God is here this Christmas morn,
Don't lose Him in the throng,
It was for you that He was born,
Come praise him in this song:

9. At His first Advent we rejoice,
Then look with eager eye,
Proclaiming Him with heart and voice
Whose coming draweth nigh.

10. The second Advent soon will come,
May we for Him prepare,
For He will take His people home;
His glory we will share.

11. All glory be to God on high
And praise to Christ the Son,
The Holy Spirit brings us nigh,
Praise God, the Three in One.

442   Your life is borrowed

Brenda Gallant

Your life is bor-rowed from the Lord, He made you for His own, So why not heed His Ho-ly Word, And make your Heart His throne?

2. The human heart is dead in sin
'Til quickened from above,
Then His new life will reign within;
The outcome of His love.

3. Until that time the soul is lost,
And wandering on alone,
But, oh, at what an awesome cost,
The soul is sought and won.

4. He came right down to where we are,
Leaving His throne on high,
And even though we wandered far,
He sought to bring us nigh.

5. Will you respond to His dear voice?
Now is the time choose.
If you make the Lord your choice,
Your life He'll surely use.

6. It won't be long 'til His return
To snatch His own away,
Do not His invitation spurn,
Be ready for that day!

Music © 2013 Harry Hicks
Words © 2013 Brenda Gallant

443 Your Word, O God

Albert Bayly

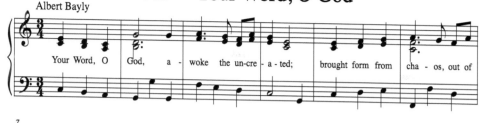

Your Word, O God, a - woke the un-cre - a - ted; brought form from cha - os, out of

dark - ness, light: till life, by si - lent a - ges long a - wait-ed, dis-played its

grow - ing beau - ty in your sight. In field and fo - rest, o - cean, air and ri - ver,

your eyes be - held your crea - tures ve-ry good; and quick-ened by your

breath, Al-migh-ty Gi - ver; your hu - man i - mage in your pre-sence stood.

2. Your Word, O God, awoke prophetic voices
on Carmel's height, and Judah's rocky hills;
the great Isaiah's ardent soul rejoices,
and Jeremiah's tortured bosom thrills.
To sage and psalmist comes your inspiration,
in song sublime and wisdom's subtle page;
and in the law and records of a nation,
your word, O God, speaks on from age to age.

3. Your Word, O God, took flesh for our salvation,
and we beheld this glory, truth and grace;
he brings the Gospel of our liberation,
the tidings of your mercy light his face.
In healing deeds of love and holy story
we hear the music of your gracious Name;
still more, his Cross and resurrection glory
the sovereign triumphs of your love proclaim.

4. Now speak again your Word unto the nations,
in all the fullness of your Spirit's power;
and as your voice woke former generations,
declare your purpose for this present hour.
O speak to smite, to cleanse and to renew us,
your church awaits the judgement of your sword;
until with power your Spirit shall endue us
to give the world the Gospel of our Lord.

Music © 2012 Harry Hicks
Words: 'Thy/Your word, O God, awoke
the uncreated' by Albert Bayly (1901-84)
© 1988 Oxford University Press.
Reproduced by permission. All rights reserved.

444   Zion rejoice

Isaac Watts

Zi - on re-joice, and Ju - dah sing: The Lord as-sumes his throne, Let

Bri - tain own the heav'n - ly King, And make his glo - ries known.

2. The great, the wicked and the proud,
   From their high seats are hurled;
   Jehovah rides upon the cloud,
   And thunders through the world.

3. He reigns upon th'eternal hills,
   Distributes mortal crowns,
   Empires are fixed beneath his smiles,
   And totter at His frowns.

4. Navies that rule the ocean wide,
   Are vanquished by his breath;
   And legions armed with pow'r and pride
   Second to watery death.

5. Let tyrants make no more pretence
   To vex our happy land;
   Jehovah's Name is our defence,
   Our buckler in his hand.

6. Long may our King our Sovereign live
   To rule us by his word;
   And all the honours he can give
   be offered to the Lord.

Music © 2013 Harry Hicks

445 God's Spirit is in my heart

Hubert J. Richards

1.God's Spi-rit is in my heart. He has called me and set me a - part. This is what I have to do.

Refrain

He sent me to give the Good news to the poor, tell pris-'ners that they are pris-'ners no more, tell blind peo-ple that they can see, and set the down-trod-den free, and go tell ev-'ry-one the news that the king-dom of God has come, and go tell ev-'ry-one the news that God's king-dom has come.

2. Just as the Father sent me
so I'm sending you out to be
my witnesses throughout the world.
He sent me to give the Good News to the poor,
till pris'ner that they are pris'ners no more,
tell blind people that they can see,
and set the down-trodden free,
and go tell ev'ryone
the news that the kingdom of God has come,
and go tell ev'ryone
the news that God's kingdom is come.

3. Don't carry a load in your pack,
you don't need two shirts on your back.
A workman can earn his own keep.
He sent me......

4. Don't worry what you have to say,
don't worry because on that day
God's Spirit will speak in your heart.
He sent me......

Music © 2016 Harry Hicks
Words: Hubert J Richards (b. 1921)

Index

A mighty fortress	1
A special day	2
A wonderful Saviour	3
Above me hangs	4
Alas! and did my Sav..	5
All day log	6
All for Jesus	7
All glory to Jesus	8
All our lives	9
All the way	10
Alleluia! Sing to Jesus	11
And is this life	12
And must this body die	13
Angels holy	14
Angels sang in celeb…	15
Approach, my soul	16
Arise my soul	17
Arm, soldiers of the L..	18
As the light upon the r..	19
As you travel	20
At Christmas time	21
Author of faith	22
Awake, my heart	23
Awake my soul	24
Be present, Spirit	25
Beautiful Saviour	26
Behold the glories	27
Behold the Saviour	28
Beneath the cross of J..	29
Beyond all mortal p…	30
Birth brings a promise	31
Bless the Lord, creation	32
Bless the Lord	33
Blessed are the humble	34
Blessed be	35
Bright is the path	36
Bright King of Glory	37
Builder of the starry fr…	38

By angel's word	39
Called to be saints	40
Chill of the nightfall	41
Christ be my leader	42
Christ call us to be d…	43
Christ high-ascended	44
Christ is coming	45
Christ is our light!	46
Christ is risen	47
Christ is the only ans…	48
Christ is the world's tr..	49
Christ the Lord	50
Christ the Lord is risen	51
Christ's pastures	52
Christian people every..	53
Christians! Join in cel..	54
Come and see where J	55
Come let us join a ch…	56
Come with gladness	57
Come all harmonious	58
Come, gracious Spirit	59
Come, happy souls	60
Come, Holy Ghost, in l.	61
Come, Holy Ghost	62
Come, Holy Spirit, c…	63
Come, Holy Spirit	64
Come let us lift our joy..	65
Come, sound His pr….	66
Come, Thou almighty…	67
Come Thou Saviour	68
Comfort all your people	69
Creation & Redemption	70
Cross of Jesus	71
Crown Him!	72
Day by day	73
Dear Christians	74
Dear Jesus	75
Depth of mercy	76

Descend from heaven	77
Do I believe	78
Emmanuel, the true	79
Enthroned is Jesus	80
Eye has not seen	81
Faith looks to Jesus	82
Father let me dedicate	83
Fear not the future	84
Fear not! God is thy	85
Finished	86
Firm as the earth	87
For Mary	88
For those disciples	89
From the night of ages	90
From Thee, my God	91
Full of glory, full of w…	92
Full of glory	93
Fully trusting	94
Give us the wings	95
Gloria, Gloria	96
Glorious Saviour	97
Glory be to God on h…	98
Glory be to God	99
Glory be to Jesus	100
Glory in highest heaven	101
Glory, glory everlasting	102
Go forth	103
Go into all the world	104
God be with you	105
God in his wisdom	106
God loved the world	107
God of the seas	108
God of the star-fields	109
God show his love	110
God speaks to us today	111
God who didst so d….	112
God will tale care of y..	113
God, who made the	114

God's promise	115
God's Spirit	116
God's Spirit is in my h..	445
Grant me Lord, serenity	117
Great god, how infinite	118
Hail Father, Son and H.	119
Hallalujah, He is risen	120
Happy the heart	121
Hark! the voice of love	122
Hark! What mean these	123
Have you love in your	124
He gave His life	125
He is risen, He is risen	126
He lay in a manger	127
He will take care of you	128
Healer of the sick	129
Hear how the bells	130
Heavenly Father	131
Hence from my soul	132
Here at the cross	133
High on a hill	134
Holy Father, in thy m…	135
Holy Jesus, by thy p….	136
Holy Spirit, hear us	137
Holy Spirit, truth divine	138
Holy, holy, holy is the L	139
Holy, holy, holy Lord	140
Home at last	141
Hosanna to our conqu..	142
Hosanna to the living L.	143
Hosanna to the Prince	144
Hosanna to the royal S.	145
Hosanna, with a cheer..	146
How can I	147
How fearsome and far	148
How shall I sing that m.	149
How shall we sing	150
How strong thine arm	151

How vast a fortune	152	Jeus. grant me this	190
How wondrous great	153	Jesus my strength	191
Hush my dear	154	Jesus, name above all	192
Hush you, my baby	155	Jesus, stand among us	193
I adore Thee	156	Jesus, tender shepherd	194
I came a wander	157	Jesus, the crucified	195
I come with joy	158	Jesus, those eyes	196
I know He cares for me	159	Jeus, thou soul	197
I know I'll see Jesus	160	Jesus, I will trust Thee	198
I know that my Redee..	161	Jesus. meek and gen..	199
I know that my Rede..	162	Join all the glorious	200
I lay my sins of Jesus	163	Join all the names	201
I lift my heart to Thee	164	Lead me to the rock	202
I need Thee	165	Let all creation dance	203
I stand all amazed	166	Let all mortal flesh	204
I stand amazed	167	Let earth and heaven	205
I will sing of my Redee.	168	Let me – Wonderful pl..	206
I will sing	169	Let saints on earth	207
I'm not ashamed	170	Let the seventh angel	208
If Christ were born in	171	Let the song go round	209
If I live for the Saviour	172	Let the whole creation	210
In death's strong grasp	173	Let them neglect	211
In faith we come	174	Let us join	212
In stillness, God	175	Life is the time	213
In the beginning	176	Light of gladness	214
In the fullness	177	Listen sweet dove	215
In the hollow of His h...	178	Live out thy life	216
Is it well with thy soul?	179	Long before the world	217
It is well with my soul	180	Long, long ago	218
It's about the cross	181	Look, ye saints!	219
Jesu. if still the same	182	Lord in your love	220
Jesus alone	183	Lord Jesus Christ	221
Jesus Christ, the same	184	Lord Jesus	222
Jesus died for me	185	Lord of mercy	223
Jesus for me	186	Lord of the brave	224
Jesus the Saviour	187	Lord of the restless o..	225
Jesus will walk with me	188	Lord of the Twelve	226
Jesus, God's son	189	Lord, as the day begins	227

Lord, dismiss us	228
Lord, that I may learn	229
Lord, whose Son arose	230
Low in thine agony	231
Make me a captive	232
Mary and Joseph	233
May the grace of Christ	234
May the words	235
Meet and right	236
Mine eyes have seen	237
Most high and holy L..	238
My faith looks up to Th.	239
My God, accept my h..	240
My God, my King	241
My God, my life, my l..	242
My God, the spring of	243
My God, what endless	244
My heavenly home	245
My latest sun is sink..	246
My Shepherd leads	247
My song shall be of J..	248
My spirit longs for Thee	249
My whole world was l...	250
Nature with all her p....	251
Near the cross	252
Nearer, still nearer	253
No other way	254
No tramp of soldiers' m	255
Nor eye has seen	226
Not to condemn	257
Not to us be glory	258
Nothing but the blood	259
Nothing to pay	260
Now be the God	261
Now for a tune	262
Now I belong to Jesus	263
Now the green blade	264
Now to the Lord	265

Now to the Lord we b..	266
Now to the power	267
O day of rest and glad..	268
O for a closer walk	289
O for a heart	270
O give thanks	271
O God of truth	272
O happy day	273
O Jesus, Jesus	274
O Lamb of God	275
O love divine	276
O love how deep	277
O love of God	278
O love that will not let	279
O Prince of Peace	280
O the almighty Lord	281
O Thou from whom	282
Oh flee as a bird	283
Oh who is this	284
Of safe to the rock	285
Once more my soul	286
Only trust Him	287
Our father in heaven	288
Our Lord is risen	289
Our Saviour	290
Our sins, alas	291
Our souls shall magnify	292
Peace, peace is mine	293
Poor and needy	294
Praise Him! Praise Him	295
Praise the God of truth	296
Praise the Lord and b..	297
Praise the Lord of h...	298
Praise the Lord!	299
Praise ye the Lord	300
Praise, everlasting p...	301
Precious, precious bl..	302
Precious, precious	303

Present in creation	304	The glories of my M....	342
Put thou thy tryst	305	The heavens are sing..	343
Praise your triumphant	306	The heavens declare	344
Rise, rise, my soul	307	The Holy Trinity	345
Save me at the cross	308	The king of love	346
Saved through Jesus'	309	The Lamb of God	347
Saviour Christ	310	The lands that long in	348
Saviour, again	311	Th Lord bless you	349
Saviour, blessed Sav...	312	The Lord is here	350
Saviour, thy dying love	313	The Lord is King!	351
See the Conqueror	314	The Lord is King	352
See, to us a boy is born	315	The Lord Jehovah	353
Seek, oh seek the Lord	316	The Lord my shepherd	354
Seeking for me	317	The Lord of Heaven	355
Shall we go	318	The Lord on high	356
Shout to the Lord	319	The old account	357
Simply trusting	320	The Saviour Christ	358
Sing to the Lord	321	The sea	359
Sing unto the Lord	322	The solid rock	360
Singing for Jesus	323	The strife is o'er	361
Slumbering in a man...	324	The sun is sinking fast	362
Some day	325	The true Messiah	363
Some happy day	326	The will of God	364
Songs of praise the a..	327	Thee will I love	365
Sound the angel's	328	There is a house	366
Spirit of faith	329	There is a land	367
Spirit of God within me	330	There's a spirit in the	368
Stand up, my soul	331	These glorious minds	369
Stand up!	332	They bound the hands	370
Stars of heaven, clear	333	This awesome world	371
Summer suns are gl...	334	This cherished child	372
Sun of my soul	335	This day above all days	373
Tell me the story of J...	336	This happy Christmas	374
Tell the world	337	This is the day of I...	375
Ten thousand thanks	338	This is the day	376
Tenderly the shepherd	339	This is the threefold	377
The billows swell	340	Thou art the Way	378
The blessed Saviour	341	Thou hidden source	379

Thou whom my soul	380
Throned upon the awful	381
Through good report	382
Through the love of G..	383
Thus far the Lord	384
Thy way, not mine	385
To God be glory	386
To God the only wise	387
To Him that chose us	388
To us a child	389
To us in Bethlem city	390
To you, o Christ	391
Under an Eastern sky	392
Up to the lord	393
Upon the cross	394
Vain are the hopes	395
Watching, waiting	396
We celebrate God's w..	397
We have found the Ch.	398
We praise Thee, we	399
We saw Thee not	400
We sing a loving Jesus	401
We sing the glories	402
We thank Thee for Thy	403
We thank The, Lord	404
Welcome sweet day	405
What a wonderful sal..	406
What equal honours	407
When Christ was born	408
When from the East	409
When God the Spirit	410
When he comes	411
When I shall come	412
When I survey	413
When in the light	414
When law and trust	415
When music and our h.	416
When the great	417

When the Lord in glory	418
When the Lord shall	419
When to our world	420
When we are raised	421
When Zaccheus came	422
Where is he?	423
Where oh where	424
While the earth rem…	425
Who came down	426
Who is this so weak	427
Who shall the Lord's	428
Wholly Thine	429
Why seek the living	430
With cheerful voice	431
With hope	432
With songs and hon…	433
Wounded for me	434
Ye thirsty for God	435
Yes, God is good	436
Yes, the Redeemer r..	437
Yes, the Redeemer r..	438
You came in peace	439
You shall go out with j..	440
Your God is here	441
Your life is borrowed	442
Your Word, O God	443
Zion, rejoice	444

89 For those disciples
120 Hallelujah, He is risen
126 He is risen, He is risen
142 Hossanna to our Conquering
164 I lift my heart to Thee
173 In death's strong grasp
174 In faith we come
219 Look, ye saints!
284 Oh who is this
289 Our Lord is risen
328 Sound the angel's
361 The strife is o'er
373 This day above all days
377 This is the threefold truth
430 Why seek the living
437 Yes, the Redeemer rose
439 You came in peace

Subject suggestions

Good Friday
5 Alas! And did my Saviour die
21 At Christmas time
71 Cross of Jesus
86 Finished
99 Glory be to God
100 Glory be to Jesus
122 Hark! The voice of love
133 Here at the cross
136 Holy Jesus, by thy passion
147 How can I
186 Jesus for me
195 Jesus, the crucified
231 Low in thine agony
252 Near the cross
276 O love divine
284 Oh who is this
290 Our Saviour
308 Save me at the cross
310 Saviour Christ
313 Saviour, thy dying love
363 The true Messiah
370 They bound the hands
381 Throned upon the awful tree
392 Under an Eastern sky
394 Upon the cross

Easter
47 Christ is risen
51 Christ the Lord is risen
55 Come and see where Jesus
72 Crown Him!
80 Enthroned is Jesus now
86 Finished

Jesus
46 Christ is our light
47 Christ is risen
48 Christ is the only answer
49 Christ is the world's true
57 Come with gladness
68 Come Thou Saviour
74 Dear Christians
90 From the night of ages
91 From Thee, my God
99 Glory be to god
109 God of the star-fields
125 He gave his life
134 High on a hill
144 Hosanna to the Prince
145 Hosanna to the royal
161 I know that my Redeemer
162 I know that my Redeemer
184 Jesus Christ, the same
186 Jesus for me
189 Jesus, God's Son
192 Jesus, name above all
196 Jesus, those eyes
197 Jesus, thou soul
205 Let earth and heaven
217 Long before the world
218 Long, long ago
221 Lord Jesus Christ
222 Lord Jesus
223 Lord of mercy
233 Mary and Joseph
248 My song shall be of Jesus
250 My whole world
274 O Jesus, Jesus
289 Our Lord is risen

296 Praise the God of truth
301 Praise, everlasting praise
323 Singing for Jesus
336 Tell me the story of Jesus
360 The solid rock
378 Thou art the way
396 Watching, waiting
400 We saw Thee not
408 When Christ was born
423 Where is He?
424 Where oh where
426 Who came down

Living the Christian life

6 All day long
18 Arm, soldiers of the Lord
20 As you travel
36 Bright is the path
40 Called to be saints
43 Christ calls us
44 Christ high-ascended
112 God who didst so
124 Have you love in your life
128 He will take care of you
135 Holy Father, in thy
149 How shall I sing that
152 How vast a fortune
158 I come with joy
160 I know I'll see Jesus
165 I need Thee
172 If I live for the Saviour
201 Join all the names
212 Let us join
213 Life is the time
214 Light of gladness
252 Near the cross
258 Not to us be glory
269 O for a closer walk
288 Our Father in heaven
291 Our sins, alas
293 Peace, peace is mine
294 Poor and needy
313 Saviour, Thy dying love
318 Shall we go
319 Shout to the Lord
326 Some happy day
331 Stand up, my soul
332 Stand up!
335 Sun of my soul
341 The blessed Saviour
358 The Saviour Christ
382 Through good report
383 Through the love of God

384 Thus far the Lord
391 To you, O Christ
400 We saw Thee not
401 We sing a loving Jesus
402 We sing the glories
403 We thank Thee for Thy
414 When in the light
415 When law and trust break
422 When Zaccheus came
429 Wholly Thine
431 With cheerful voice
435 Ye thirsty for God
440 You shall go out with joy

The life of Jesus

47 Christ is risen
51 Christ the Lord is risen
55 Come and see where Jesus
72 Crown Him!
80 Enthroned is Jesus now
86 Finished
89 For those disciples
120 Hallelujah, He is risen
126 He is risen he is risen
142 Hosanna to our conquering
144 Hosanna to the Prince
174 In faith we come
219 Look, ye saints!
284 Oh who is this
289 Our Lord is risen
361 The strife is o'er
373 This day above all days
377 This is the threefold truth
430 Why seek the living
437 Yes, the redeemer lives
439 You came in peace

At sea

4 Above me hangs the silent sky
20 As you travel

Worship

2 A special day
23 Awake, my heart
83 Father, let me dedicate
162 I know that my Redeemer
200 Join all the glorious
201 Join all the names
209 Let the song go round

210 Let the whole creation
211 Let them neglect
214 Light of gladness
319 Shout to the Lord
416 When music and our hearts

Christ's return
45 Christ is coming
411 When He comes

Christmas
2 A special day
15 Angels sang in celebration
41 Chill of the nightfall
57 Come with gladness
68 Come Thou Saviour
109 God of the star-fields
115 God's promise
123 Hark! What mean those
127 He lay in a manger
130 Hear how the bells
155 Hush you, my baby
171 If Christ were born in
176 In the beginning
177 In the fullness
181 It's about the cross
204 Let all mortal flesh
221 Lord Jesus Christ
264 Now the green blade
280 O Prince of peace
315 See, to us a boy is born
324 Slumbering in a manger
327 Songs of praise the angels
333 Stars of heaven
355 The Lord of heaven
389 To us a child
390 To us in Bethlem city
408 When Christ was born
409 When from the East
423 Where is he?
441 Your God is here

New life
31 Birth brings a promise
154 Hush my dear
166 I stand all amazed
167 I stand amazed
272 O God of truth

361 The strife is o'er

Praise
14 Angels holy
30 Beyond all mortal praise
32 Bless the Lord, creation
33 Bless the Lord
35 Blessed be
37 Bright King of Glory
56 Come let us join
58 Come all harmonious
60 Come, happy souls
66 Come, sound His praises
67 Come, Thou Almighty
91 From Thee, my God
98 Glory be to God on high
101 Glory on highest heaven
102 Glory, glory everlasting
118 Great God, how infinite
131 Heavenly Father
132 Hence from my soul
139 Holy, holy, holy is the Lord
142 Hosanna to our conquering
143 Hosanna to the living Lord
149 How shall I sing that majesty
151 How strong Thine arm
166 I stand all amazed
167 I stand amazed
168 I will sing of my Redeemer
207 Let saints on earth
208 Let the seventh angel
224 Lord of the brave
225 Lord of the restless ocean
238 Most high and holy Lord
241 My God, My King
242 My God, my life
251 Nature with all her
261 Now be the God
262 Now for a tune
265 Now to the Lord
267 Now to the power
281 O the almighty Lord
294 Poor and needy
295 Praise Him! Praise Him
296 Praise the God of truth
297 Praise the Lord and
298 Praise the Lord of heaven
306 Praise your triumphant
312 Saviour, blessed Saviour
314 See the Conqueror

321 Sing to the Lord
322 Sing unto the Lord
323 Singing for Jesus
343 The heavens are singing
352 The Lord is King
353 The Lord Jehovah
365 Thee will I love
377 This is the threefold truth
386 To God be glory
388 To Hiom that chose us
390 To us in Bethlem city
399 We praise Thee
407 What equal honours
416 When music and our hearts
431 With cheerful voice
432 With hope
436 Yes, God is good

Morning
24 Awake, my soul
227 Lord, as the day begins
286 Once more my soul

Strength in God
18 Arm, soldiers of the Lord
29 Beneath the cross of Jesus
128 He will take care of you
159 I know He cares for me
161 I know that my Redeemer
169 I will sing
220 Lord in your love
232 Make me a captive
346 The King of love
364 The will of God
429 Wholly Thine

The Holy Spirit
59 Come, gracious Spirit
61 Come, Holy Ghost, in love
62 Come, Holy Ghost
63 Come, Holy Spirit
64 Come, Holy Spirit
77 Descend from heaven
112 God who didst so
137 Holy Spirit, hear us
138 Holy Spirit, truth divine
193 Jesus, stand among us
215 Listen sweet dove
329 Spirit of faith
330 Spirit of God within me

Creation
26 Beautiful Saviour
38 Builder of the starry
140 Holy, holy, holy Lord
148 How fearsome and far
203 Let all creation dance
210 Let the whole creation
304 Present on creation
327 Song of praise the angels
371 This awesome world

Our future
27 Behold the glories
309 Saved through Jesus'

Baptism
31 Birth brings a promise
266 Now to the lord we bring
349 The Lord bless you
372 This cherished child

God's mercy
76 Depth of mercy
223 Lord of mercy
316 Seek, oh seek the Lord

The wonder of God
77 Descend from heaven
79 Emmanuel, the true
81 Eye has not seen
93 Full of glory
109 God of the star-fields
140 Holy, holy, holy Lord
149 How shall I sing that majesty
404 We thank Thee, Lord

Parting
84 Fear not the future
311 Saviour, again
349 The Lord bless you

Mary, Jesus' mother
88 For Mary
292 Our souls shall magnify

Mission
103 Go forth
104 Go into all the world
337 Tell the world

God's word
106 God in His wisdom
140 Holy, holy, holy Lord
176 In the beginning
214 Light of gladness
218 Long, long ago
220 Lord in your love
344 The heavens declare
397 We celebrate God's word
443 Your Word, O God

God's love
107 God loved the world
113 God will take care of you
114 God, who made
116 God's Spirit
128 He will take care of you
166 I stand all amazed
167 I stand amazed
218 Long, long ago
277 O love how deep
279 O love that will not let

The Trinity
119 Hail, Father, Son and
131 Heavenly Father
345 The Holy Trinity

The grace of God
121 Happy the heart
147 How can I
168 I will sing of my Redeemer
183 Jesus alone
404 We thank Thee, Lord
406 What a wonderful salvation

Lent
175 In stillness, God

Palm Sunday
255 No tramp of soldier's

Pentecost
410 When God the Spirit

Supplication
129 Healer of the sick
156 I adore Thee
193 Jesus, stand among us
224 Lord of the brave
229 Lord that I may learn
234 May the grace of Christ
240 My God, accept my heart
249 My spirit longs for Thee
270 O for a heart
272 O God of truth
340 The billows swell

Nearing home
141 Home at last
244 My God, what endless
245 My heavenly home
246 My latest sun is sinking
318 Shall we go
366 There is a house
412 When I shall come

Finding Jesus
157 I came a wanderer
218 Long, long ago
287 Only trust Him
293 Peace, peace is mine

Looking forward
160 I know I'll see Jesus
170 I'm not ashamed
180 It is well with my soul
244 My God, what endless
247 My Shepherds leads
256 Nor eye has seen
275 Not to condemn
305 Put thou thy trust
325 Some day
326 Some happy day
366 There is a house
367 There is a land
419 When the Lord

Submission

164 I lift my heart to Thee
165 I need Thee
197 Jesus, Thou soul
216 Live out thy life
223 Lord of mercy
229 Lord, that I may learn
241 My God, my King
315 See, to us a boy is born
320 Simply trusting
340 The billows swell
391 to you, O Christ

Personal Testimony
179 Is it well with thy soul?
180 It is well with my soul
186 Jesus for me

Evening
194 Jesus, tender shepherd
234 May the grace of Christ
311 Saviour, again
362 The sun is sinking fast

Security
202 Lead me to the rock
253 Nearer, still nearer
283 Oh flee as a bird
285 O safe to the rock
287 Only trust Him
293 Peace, peace is mine
309 Saved through Jesus'
318 Shall we go
346 The King of Love
377 This is the threefold truth
383 Through the love of God

Hope
239 My faith looks us to Thee
346 The King of love
383 Through the love of God

Journeying on
247 My Shepherd leads
248 My song shall be of Jesus

The Lord's day
286 Once more my soul
375 This is the day of light
405 Welcome, sweet day

Thanksgiving

183 Jesus alone
271 O give thanks
404 We thank Thee, Lord
406 What a wonderful salvation

Turning to Christ
316 Seek, oh, seek the Lord
349 The Lord bless you
378 Thou art the Way

Communion
377 This is the threefold

Harvest
404 We thank Thee, Lord
433 With songs and honours
443 Your Word, O God

Faith in God
1 A mighty fortress
11 Alleluia! Sing to Jesus
13 And must this body die
16 Approach, my soul
22 Author of faith
34 Blessed re the humble
78 Do I believe
82 Faith looks to Jesus
87 Firm as the earth
94 Fully trusting
95 Give us the wings
170 I'm not ashamed
178 In the hollow of His hand
179 Is it well with thy soul?
213 Life is the time
220 Lord in your love
243 My God, the spring
245 My heavenly home
301 Praise, everlasting praise
305 Put thou thy trust
320 Simply trusting
325 Some day
340 The billows swell
346 The King of love
383 Through the love of God
385 Thy way, not mine

Others
135 Holy Father, in thy

The penalty of rejection
257 Not to condemn